Abravanel !

Abravanel!

Lowell Durham

University of Utah Press
Salt Lake City
1989

To my wife Betty

Copyright © 1989 the University of Utah Press
All rights reserved
Manufactured in the United States of America

ISBN 0-87480-333-0

Front dust jacket photograph courtesy of Maurice Abravanel Photograph Collection in
    the Special Collections at the University of Utah Library (MAP).
Back dust jacket photograph by W. Claudell Johnson for the *Deseret News* in MAP.
Frontispiece photograph by Lynn Johnson.

Library of Congress Cataloging-in-Publication Data

Durham, Lowell M.
    Abravanel! / by Lowell M. Durham.
        p.   cm.
    ISBN 0-87480-333-0
    1. Abravanel, Maurice, 1903–   . 2. Conductors (Music)–
Biography. I. Title.
ML422.A24D9 1989
784.2′092–dc20
    [B]   89–37172
                                                                            CIP
                                                                            MN

Contents

Preface

During a visit to Salt Lake City in 1976, Aaron Copland autographed Maestro Abravanel's well-worn score of his own *Appalachian Spring* with these words: "For my dear friend Maurice – an exemplary model for us all to follow – with affection."

Long before he arrived in Utah at the age of forty-four, Abravanel had distinguished himself on three continents, with eleven years in Germany, one in Paris with conducting in Rome, three in Australia, two as conductor of the Metropolitan Opera, and eight on Broadway. This versatility was custom-made for Utah's Centennial, the year of his arrival.

In April of 1966 I delivered a paper at the annual spring meeting of the Utah Academy of Arts and Sciences at Weber College. "The Abravanel Years" was a summary of the Maestro's contributions from 1947 to 1966, and it was published in the Academy's *Proceedings*. Although I did nothing more at the time, the idea of an eventual Abravanel book did cross my mind. The idea received impetus in 1972, during Abravanel's Silver Anniversary with the Utah Symphony. At a dinner in the University of Utah Panorama Room, I cornered Symphony President Wendell J. Ashton. He encouraged me to go ahead.

A preliminary version of the first five chapters subsequently appeared in Utah Symphony programs. I soon reached a juncture where I needed authoritative information on some important points, however, and sent some questions to Abravanel. His response was cautious. "These questions are 'hot' politically. There is a million dollars at stake in one of them, and I don't want to rock the boat now. Can you delay the book?" I agreed to.

When Abravanel resigned as Music Director of the Symphony on April 6, 1979, I opened my files and decided to go ahead full speed. Several months later, in January of 1980, I arranged for Abravanel to give a series of weekly lectures on subjects of his choosing in the University of Utah Art and Architecture auditorium. The lectures were spontaneous, dynamic, candid, and fascinating.

The "Conversations with Abravanel" were recorded courtesy of Gene Pack of KUER-FM, the University's radio station, who later broadcast them. Several people, Sterling M. McMurrin and Boyer Jarvis among them, thought the "Conversations" should be published. When a succession of campus typists had trouble transcribing the tapes because of Abravanel's French accent, musical terminology, and idiomatic expressions, Betty D. Durham took over. She had known Abravanel for thirty-three years and had no problems finishing the job.

When I sent a roughly edited copy of the transcription to Abravanel in Santa Barbara, he was taken aback by the informality of the spoken word and asked that the lectures not be published in that form. Discouraged, I shelved the project for a year.

In June of 1981 I received a phone call that encouraged me to begin again. "This is your book, Lowell. I won't be looking over your shoulder!" As anyone knows who has tried, it is as much a challenge as a pleasure to write the biography of a living person. Now, freed by his call from any taint of "authorization," I was in motion again. Abravanel kept his promise.

Due to a combination of circumstances, the book, now much larger and close to completion, was in limbo again in the summer of 1986, when Sterling McMurrin nudged University officials during their reorganization of the University Press. McMurrin's persuasiveness and the added interest of Brigham D. Madsen got the project off dead center. A few days later Stephen Hess, Executive Director of Media Services, called at my office with David Catron, the Press's newly-appointed Director. They were there to express interest in the manuscript.

They also indicated that Trudy McMurrin had recently returned after three years as Director of Southern Methodist University Press in Dallas and was available as a freelance editor. This was good news, because Trudy had been the first to encourage me to complete the book, just before her departure for Texas. Steve Hess was very supportive in the months that followed. As soon as David Catron was well settled in, he took personal charge of the project in a dramatic turn of events. Not only was he anxious for the Press to publish, he insisted on an elite production with special design and materials and a wealth of photographs to enhance the story! The tempo accelerated and never slackened.

As editor, Trudy brought an unusual array of talents and disciplines to her task. As a fastidious technician she eliminated ambiguities and redundancies and fine-tuned chronology. Her mind is alert, quick yet probing. This combination was topped by her knowledge of and experience in the performing arts, including ongoing personal relationships with Abravanel and other key figures of the period. She gave a unified direction to the manuscript, raised the crucial questions, and at one point streamlined three chapters into one to make a tighter narrative. In general, she was a creative artist as well as a traffic cop.

Richard Firmage has brought years of broad experience and sensitivity toward the subject to his task as designer. Through the years of work I had always hoped that when it was finally published the book would have this kind of "class." Peter Schmid of the University of Utah Marriott Library's Special Collections made available the complete Abravanel collection, from which many of the photographs were drawn. Peter anticipated our needs and was pleasant and helpful. Martin Zwick's photographs, which are now also housed in Special Collections, show him to be an artist with the camera as well as the clarinet. They are works of art from "inside" the orchestra.

Gayle Gittins authorized the use of photographs of the late Alvin Gittins' fine portraits of key personalities. Elna Watts furnished photographs of her husband Ardean that were otherwise unavailable. Lynn Johnson gave permission for use of the frontispiece photograph, a favorite of the Maestro and his friends. *Deseret News* publisher James Mortimer granted permission for us to publish a number of photographs from the Abravanel collection and opened the *News* library, from which music staffer Dorothy Stowe made some much-needed photographs available.

We have tried diligently to properly credit all the photographs, and the Press staff and I greatly appreciate the generosity of all concerned.

University Music Department secretary Colleen Norman typed six to seven versions of the scribbled-and-corrected manuscript without skipping a beat. Janice Crellin labored through later edited versions, putting them on computer disks. Lavina Fielding Anderson, Lowell Durham, Jr., and Val D. MacMurray each read opening chapters early on, with encouraging nods. Lavina also did a helpful preliminary editing of several chapters in what now seem to have been prehistoric times.

The sources for this volume are extensive and varied. Abravanel generously devoted many afternoons recalling his years in Europe, Australia, and New York and clarifying the activities of his forty-two Utah years. He and Lucy made valuable news clippings and photographs available before they were donated to the University Library.

The Utah years are well documented in seventeen king-sized looseleaf volumes in my library which contain all the reviews and columns I wrote for the *Salt Lake Tribune* from 1946 to 1964. Forty-two bound volumes of Utah Symphony programs with my "Notes," from 1946 to 1987, chronicle Abravanel's thirty-two subscription concert seasons.

Huck Gregory, Executive Director of the Symphony from 1958 to 1966, worked hand-in-glove with Abravanel during the orchestra's crucial years. His detailed, witty accounts of the 1966 and 1971 tours abroad, plus his first-hand description of the drawn-out Symphony Hall story were major sources. Obert C. Tanner's *Bicentennial Center for the Arts* was also an invaluable resource, and Wendell J. Ashton's account of his Symphony stewardship for two decades as Board President is quoted from profusely. Carleen Landes always had immediate answers to the most minute questions, having been—as office manager, secretary to the Music Director, and finally as Artistic Manager—the longest-term Symphony staff member.

The most personal source is the "Conversations with Abravanel," and most first-person quotes are from these 1980 lectures. KUED released a fine filmed valedictory interview with Abravanel on September 22, 1986. Ricklen Nobis was the interviewer, and Ken Verdoia directed the show and made the tapes available.

The usual newspaper and magazine sources from the U.S., Latin America, and Europe are acknowledged and appear throughout.

Above all, I treasure my continual association with Maurice Abravanel from his first press conference in 1947 to the present—as liaison between the Symphony and the University from 1948, when the orchestra first made its home on the campus; as middleman for the Summer Festivals from 1948 to 1965; and as catalyst for the establishment of the Contemporary Music Festival by Abravanel and President Olpin in 1958, a series that ran until 1983. In short, I am an enthusiastic Abravanel-watcher.

This volume contains reminiscences, recollections, memories, and warm feelings about the most distinguished musical figure in Utah history—an adopted rather than a native son.

"Somewhere West of Denver"

"What do you know about Maurice Abravanel?"

The voice was that of Fred E. Smith, president of the Utah Symphony. It was early June of 1947, the centennial year of the settlement of Utah.

"Never heard of him!" I replied. And one *would* remember a moniker like that! The Utah Symphony Board had been months searching for a successor to Werner Janssen, who had come in from Hollywood like a lion in the autumn of 1946 and gone out like a lamb the following spring—a one-season conductor.

"Abravanel comes highly recommended by Bruno Walter," continued Smith.

"Sign him up!" I interrupted. No other twentieth-century conductor compared with Bruno Walter in my book.

When Abravanel asked where Salt Lake City was, Walter reportedly had said, "Somewhere west of Denver."

A few days later Smith was on the phone again: "Abravanel is coming out from New York for a series of interviews this week. Can you attend a luncheon meeting?"

At the appointed hour the Utah Symphony Board, civic, educational, and religious leaders, plus the media, gathered in the Hotel Utah's Empire Room. After lunch Mr. Smith introduced forty-four-year-old Abravanel, naturalized American citizen of Spanish-Jewish descent.

The guest of honor made a great first impression, particularly when one Board member asked, "Mr. Abravanel, will you conduct without a score?"

That particular Board member had been dazzled by Werner Janssen's conducting without score—something he should not have done at his final concert. At the program's climax, just as the "Liebestod" from Wagner's *Tristan und Isolde* was about to peak, Janssen had forgotten the score and arrived at the great moment two bars ahead of the orchestra.

Abravanel's reply was immediate, straightforward, and eye-twinkly: "Yes—if I *know* the score. Of course not, if I don't!"

The fledgling conductor at the age of twenty-two or twenty-three. MAP.

CHAPTER 1

Europe

Salonika seems an unlikely birthplace for an American conductor, but Maurice Abravanel relishes its international character: "I was born in a place that now belongs to Greece but was Turkish at that time and where we spoke Spanish at home!" He is neither Greek nor Turkish, but part of an old Spanish Sephardic Jewish family.

"One of my ancestors was Don Isaac de Abravanel," he told *Stereo Review*'s Roy Hemming in the October 1975 issue. "He was quite a man in his time—the fifteenth century—a minister to Portugal at the age of twenty-one and, later, chancellor to King Ferdinand and Queen Isabella. He left Spain in 1492 at the time of the Inquisition, although the king had asked him to remain. In 1517 one of his sons was invited by the Sultan Suleiman to settle in Turkey to help lure trade from Spain and Portugal, which he did very successfully."

The Abravanel family settled permanently in Salonika, which in 1517 was part of the Turkish empire. But through the centuries, "our family traditions remained Spanish. I remember my mother singing Spanish folksongs to me as a child," Abravanel recalls, "and she cooked Spanish too."

Edouard de Abravanel and Rachel Bitty were both born in Salonika in 1870. Edouard was a successful pharmacist who was able to retire at thirty-nine. He and Rachel had four children, Inez, Gaston, Ernest, and Maurice, the youngest, born January 6, 1903.

The de Abravanels moved their family to Lausanne, in French-speaking Switzerland, as Maurice neared six years of age. His memories of the Lausanne years have a musical tinge: "Busoni, Ansermet, Stravinsky—all were there!" For several years the de Abravanels lived in the same house as Ernest Ansermet, who would become the founder of the Orchestre de la Suisse Romande, and who even at that time was chief conductor for Diaghilev's Ballets Russes.

"Ansermet took me for my first sleigh ride," Abravanel affectionately recalls:

> And we used to play piano four-hands. He was an even worse pianist than I was! I also remember piano runthroughs at the house with Darius Milhaud for *Le Boeuf sur le Toit* and with Stravinsky for *L'Histoire du Soldat*. Igor Stravinsky came there often, as he lived only about a five-minute train ride from Lausanne. The first staged performance of his *Le Soldat*, in fact, was given almost entirely with students from my school. I was present at its premiere.

This musical excitement was tempered with everyday problems for young Abravanel, however. Schoolmates linked him with the hated Turks, then persecuting the Armenians. His Salonikan origins and naturally dark complexion, abetted by the tanning of his early years in the Mediterranean, made him a natural scapegoat for childish cruelty.

Partly to dispel his loneliness, Maurice turned to music at the age of nine. "My sister had started piano lessons, as did all dutiful daughters of middle-class families then. I think

Abravanel and his fraternity brothers at the University of Lausanne in 1919. Maurice is seated in the first row, second from the right. His brother Ernest stands third from the left in the third row. The sixteen-year-old Maurice arranged for a concert of works by Stravinsky, with the composer conducting. The enterprising Abravanel introduced chamber music into the group, orchestrating for whatever instruments were played by the members and conducting. MAP.

I enjoyed her practicing more than she did. I was in love with the minor scale especially. I thought it was too beautiful for words. The piano teacher was our governess." He adds slyly, "She was a very good-looking blond from Munich, which may also have had something to do with my eagerness to take piano lessons."

By the time he was twelve, Maurice was playing the piano well and doing some composing. He felt passionately about music. "I went to all the concerts I could as a teenager. I remember once riding on the back seat of a motorcycle all the way to Geneva—in the dead cold of winter—to hear *Lohengrin*. I think I also realized I lacked the talent to do anything else. I had to be a musician."

During his teens, Abravanel got at least two jobs through his music. He was hired as both performer and arranger of incidental music for shows at Lausanne's Municipal Theater. While leafing through miniature orchestra study scores he discovered that he could "read" a score and commit much of it to memory.

At sixteen he was music critic for a daily newspaper in Lausanne. "I remember rushing from a concert to the newspaper, writing my fifty lines, or whatever they wanted, at top speed, without ever stopping for one second and finishing it with a flourish—and going home to bed. Otherwise, my father would never have allowed it. And so, later on when I did not always totally enjoy the reviews of my own Utah Symphony concerts, I always thought 'Well, what did *I* do at age sixteen?' Mine were probably much worse than any reviews I have to read now. This has made me very patient with the critics!"

Music was now his first love, but his father insisted on a career in medicine. Edouard de Abravanel genuinely felt that a musical life would spell poverty for his son, whose brothers Gaston and Ernest became a lawyer-journalist and a chemist, respectively. As a last resort, Papa had sent his youngest child to study medicine at the university in Zurich, hoping the change would dissuade him. It did not.

Many years later (as University of Utah Commencement speaker in June of 1980) Abravanel recalled his pre-med studies: "I worked on corpses all winter. It was not pleasant. And I decided it would be even worse for a man of my sensibility to work on live people. I realized I would be a terrible doctor. I felt that being a terrible conductor might possibly be less dangerous to mankind!"

Eventually, Maurice ceased to attend his university classes and finally wrote his father: "I have come to the conclusion that I cannot live without music. I don't know now which way this will lead. But I shall be content even to be an assistant second percussionist in an orchestra if only I can hear and make music."

Abravanel's father, Edouard, in the 1950s at the age of about 85. He lived to be 92 years of age.

BERLIN, 1922–1923

His father's opposition eased since there was little he could do. The senior de Abravanel sent his son to Germany, where rampant inflation was at its peak in the twenties and good Swiss money would go much further. Here Maurice pursued his musical studies economically and absorbedly.

Recalling his eleven years in Berlin and Germany (1922–33), Abravanel maintains that "the Weimar Republic was just not the Sodom and Gomorrah of the accepted view. It was not like Christopher Isherwood's *I Am a Camera* [the basis for the Broadway musical *Cabaret*]. That is just not true." Germany was, of course, in grave economic trouble during those years,

> but at the same time, especially in Berlin, something incredible was going on: three opera houses playing twelve months a year every night. And what opera houses! The State Opera where Wilhelm Furtwängler conducted one night, Bruno Walter the next, and Richard Strauss the following night—and all conducting the greatest singers in the world. The Kroll Opera with Klemperer contained brilliant ideas and avant-garde stagings. Then there was the Municipal Opera, which was also very, very good, with two orchestras alternating, with the very best soloists and conductors.

Germany and Austria had eighty-five opera houses, each with its own orchestra and professional company. All were full-time companies engaged for twelve months with paid vacations. The orchestras were good-sized—fifty to sixty, except in the big cities, where they numbered 110. "It was a marvelous place to be in my twenties," recalls Abravanel.

Kurt Weill, whose influence on Abravanel would be profound, both personally and professionally, met the young man during Abravanel's first year in Berlin. Weill was twenty-two, Abravanel nineteen, when he became Weill's student. The formal relationship lasted from March of 1922 to June of 1923, but their friendship would be lifelong. In these post–World War I years of runaway inflation, "Weill gave me lessons because he needed the money to survive, not because I had talent," jokes Abravanel. "He already had forty-five students."

By the time Weill was twenty-three he had already studied with Humperdinck and had left the Berlin Hochschule in dissatisfaction, though it was second only to the Paris Conservatoire. From Berlin, Weill had gone to Dessau, his birthplace, where he worked as a coach. But he grew restless, and decided that his future would be as a composer.

Soon afterward he met pianist-composer Ferruccio Busoni, a major figure in the music world who conducted a master class in composition in Berlin and who selected his own students. He chose Weill as one of five. The young Weill's contact with Busoni was enriching both personally and musically, for Busoni was the last of the Franz Liszt–type piano virtuosos who dazzled audiences with their legendary charisma as well as their fabulous techniques.

Busoni had also experimented compositionally with such mini-intervals as one-third and one-sixth tones, and Weill passed the new techniques on to his own students. He taught Abravanel harmony and counterpoint and later told him that of the forty-five students he had learned the fastest. "Harmony and counterpoint are fairly easy if you have a good sense of mathematics. I did my counterpoint exercises in the streetcar going to Weill's place. In those days there were no taxis. Starting with a walk, then a streetcar, and walking again, it took one hour, of which forty minutes were on the streetcar–just the time it took to do my counterpoint exercises," says Abravanel, smiling.

After hearing Weill's atonal avant-garde works, Abravanel was certain even during their first year that Weill was destined to be "a very important composer. But he didn't look it. He was short. He had large glasses, thick lenses, big eyes. Lotte Lenya, whom he met four years later and eventually married, called him *Frosch*, because he looked like a little frog. He was totally unassuming, and as sweet as can be, as kind as can be, as tolerant and patient as can be."

Abravanel recalls Weill as teacher: "I had to buy the Schönberg book on theory of harmony, *Harmonielehre*. He never mentioned it again. Instead, he strictly used the most conservative books, those used at the Hochschule from which he had recently fled in disgust. In spite of his sometimes radical views, he taught the conventional rules, paradoxically." (Schönberg would do the same thing during his years at the University of Southern California and the University of California at Los Angeles [1934–51]. While he wrote avant-garde atonal serial music, his composition students harmonized Bach choral melodies and other basics.)

At Christmas in 1922 Weill conducted his own music for a pantomime called *Magic Night* in a small theater in Berlin. Abravanel was surprised that the music was not atonal but rather light and melodic–"the kind one would expect for a children's ballet. Nothing great, but nice." Abravanel was impressed with Weill's versatility, and Weill told his admiring student, wryly, that Busoni had also attended the performance and had told him that "he had conducted it very well–that was all he said." Not a word about the score from his eminent teacher.

NEUSTRELITZ, 1923–1925

After a year's study, Weill said to Abravanel, "You should get a job in an opera house." The year 1923 was not the rosiest for job-seekers in inflation-haunted Berlin, but the twenty-year-old Abravanel made the rounds of the agencies and happened to drop in at one office at just the right moment. An accompanist had failed to appear for an audition at the Mecklenburg-Streilitz Theater in Neustrelitz, a small town outside Berlin, and Abravanel's professional career began.

When young musicians ask, "How do conductors get started?" he replies:

There was only one way to become a conductor in my day–in the days of Wilhelm Furtwängler, Bruno Walter, Arthur Nikisch, George Szell, William Steinberg, and Dimitri Mitropoulos. The way was very simple: to play the piano well enough and to be a good enough musician to be a coach in one of Germany or Austria's eighty-five opera houses. This meant you rehearsed with singers, helping them learn and sing their parts correctly. In addition, you had to sing the vocal cues while playing the orchestral score at the piano. If you did that correctly, the great day would come when you were permitted to conduct backstage and perhaps relay the conductor's beat to an offstage chorus.

Sooner or later, one of the conductors couldn't go on because of illness, and you would be told–always on short notice–look, tomorrow we want you to conduct this opera! No rehearsal, no run-through with the singers or orchestra–you just walked into the pit and conducted the performance! If you did it right, you got a nod and a little pat on your shoulder. The next time

Abravanel and his good friend Kurt Weill in 1930, with Jacob Geiss, head of the Cassel theater company, and Max Berg-Ehlert, general manager at Altenburg and later at Cassel, who was continually frustrated by the Berlin agents' pursuit of Abravanel for conducting engagements. The four were completing a production of the full-length *Mahagonny*. MAP.

somebody was ill you would be invited to conduct again. And having done that quite a few times and having learned the repertoire with a capital R over a two- or three-year period, you would be ready to begin.

This blithe summary makes it seem almost easy, but the basic opera repertoire at that time included six each by Verdi and Wagner, one or two French (usually *Carmen* and *Faust*) and about fifteen others from the standard repertoire. There were no recordings. There was no radio. "All a would-be conductor had was the piano-vocal score. He couldn't buy orchestral scores. Opera houses rented their scores from publishers, and stamped on the front page was the forbidding notice, *This score restricted for use to such-and-such an opera house. Cannot be loaned or copied under any circumstance!*"

At Neustrelitz Abravanel was far from chief conductor. A general music director headed the staff, followed by the Staatskapellmeister (an "old choir master in favor with a grand duke"), and a choral director, usually a younger man. Then came the first coach, "and then, me," says Abravanel, who was assigned a few choral rehearsals, "which I did pretty well."

Once as the "fifth man" he was asked to conduct something backstage. It also went well. Then he conducted while playing the piano during the Christmas pantomime. That too "went pretty well, but that's all there was," he said, recalling his discouragement. "I had no actual out-front conducting assignments." Then, in a legendary episode, conducting was thrust upon him when he was barely twenty-one years old.

On January 15, 1924, I went to a nearby town about three miles away from Neustrelitz. It was cold. I was to accompany the opera company's tenor in a concert there. He and I walked the entire distance, to and from. It was bitter cold! No one had a car or motorcycle in Germany in those days. And only a few even had bicycles. And it was bitter, bitter cold!

As we returned home to Neustrelitz, my tenor exclaimed, "That's strange! There is a little bit of red on the horizon!" As we drew closer, we could see that our theater was burning down! It was around midnight when we got close. It was horrible, watching it burn down before our eyes.

So there was no more theater. In Germany that did not automatically cancel the musicians' contracts. Their contracts were valid because it was a state theater–building or no building. Shortly afterwards, the majority of the remaining musicians asked me to conduct them in the Schloss [castle]. Why me? I don't know. Anyhow they "elected" me.

The other four conductors at the theater quickly got jobs elsewhere. I was still only twenty-one and very happy to conduct concerts in the castle, for I knew nobody. I had no other job. So I conducted the remnants of the pit orchestra in two concerts a week for ten weeks.

I had never officially conducted any orchestra–except for students in Switzerland. The musicians had instructed me at the outset that they wanted no rehearsals. So I conducted without any rehearsals, and it went very well. I even got a little pay, because they charged admission.

Abravanel's youthful inexperience was in evidence on one occasion when, responding to the musicians' request for "new" music, he programmed a piece by Mussorgsky. "Ah! I

was so stupid!" he exclaims. "It was in six flats! I didn't know that while six flats meant nothing for a pianist, they were murder for a string player, or a flute player, or an oboe player! So when I began to conduct, all hell broke loose. After that fiasco, the musicians suggested, 'Perhaps we should rehearse once in a while.' "

A rather unusual problem the young conductor encountered had to do with the French occupation of the Ruhr in post–World War I Germany. The French were naturally very unpopular in the Germany of the twenties. "To have a French accent in Germany at that time was a death warrant," Abravanel says, "and so I learned to conduct without ever opening my mouth, which endeared me to the musicians no end. . . . I knew anytime I tried to explain something during rehearsal they would feel 'Here is that Frenchman!' and would hate me; so I learned to conduct very clearly, which cut the necessary speaking to a minimum."

While Abravanel was being initiated into the mysteries of dealing with musicians, as well as the complexities of Puccini, Verdi, and Wagner, he encountered Weill accidentally.

One night I went to the theater in Berlin, and there was Kurt Weill! I had never written him, nor he me, and the phone didn't exist for people like us in those days. We met at intermission. He spoke first: "Well, how have you been doing?" I told him I was very proud to be seen with him, for he was an established composer. Further, I mentioned that my music director had okayed an all-Hindemith concert, thinking he would say, "Bravo! That's my boy!"

Instead Weill growled, "All-Hindemith, eh?" followed by a few invectives: "This trash and that trash!" He was mad as hell!

Abravanel realized later that the furious response was because Hindemith and Weill, avant-garde allies, had fallen out. "Weill was mad and naturally jealous because I was his man, and here I was planning to conduct an all-Hindemith concert."

THE YOUNG CONDUCTOR, 1925–1933

After Abravanel had conducted twenty concerts at his musicians' request, he moved to Zwickau in 1925 as choral director. Zwickau, in Saxony, was the birthplace of composer Robert Schumann, but was not Abravanel's favorite city: "You have never seen a place like it," he recalls. "If you could go there, you would understand why Robert Schumann went mad and was so depressed and melancholy all his life. It is a mining town. If you go outdoors at eight or nine o'clock your collar becomes black with soot. I remember one April day, seeing one tree with a few leaves. I stopped and almost cried."

The times were exciting for Abravanel, however, even if the location wasn't ideal: "On the train from Berlin I went out to get some fresh air, and there was Weill coming out of the diner. We sat in his compartment, and he expressed incredibly new and strange opinions about opera. Anything since Mozart was out. All operatic composers should use Mozart's *Magic Flute* for a model." Abravanel was "flabbergasted, because I was just in the process of getting Wagner, Strauss, and their contemporaries into my blood."

In Germany Weill was now a recognized success as a composer. His greatest triumph had come with the premiere of *The Protagonist* in 1926, his one-act opera staged in Dresden, where Richard Strauss's operas had been performed.

"Weill had told me all about the production and invited me to come to the premiere. I was there," says Abravanel, "and I was transfigured."

Abravanel was "consigned" to Zwickau, "that horrible place," for two years. He describes the principal conductor as "also horrible." Operettas were the big money-makers then. Abravanel was assigned the operetta repertoire and conducted very successfully. Because of his success with the light operas, he was next appointed regular conductor at a much better theater in Altenburg in 1927.

In Altenburg the twenty-four-year-old Abravanel auditioned a group of singers for the theater. Among them was Friedel Schacko, a refined and cultured young German ambitious to pursue an operatic career. Friedel fell in love with the young conductor during rehearsals for *Ariadne auf Naxos*, and she had high hopes for the effect of his influence on her career.

At an after-performance party one night, an official introduced them to the gathering as "Mr. and Mrs. Abravanel," unaware that they were not married. They did marry soon afterward, although Friedel's father was opposed to the match.

Friedel's mother was the noted German soprano Hedwig

Newspaper photograph of Friedel Schacko shortly after her marriage to Maurice Abravanel. MAP.

Schacko, who, it was understood, had had an affair with Gustav Mahler. The possibility that her father might have been the great composer rather than a German military officer delighted his wife, says Abravanel. Friedel, who later converted to Catholicism and changed her name to Marie, continued to sing supporting roles. Her voice, according to Abravanel, was "nice but not an operatic one."

That year Abravanel also saw Weill again. His friend had written another stage work, *The Royal Palace*, and was preparing it for an audition with the Kroll Opera in Berlin. The libretto was by Ivan Goll, who was also the publisher of the French magazine *Surrealism*.

The Royal Palace is a mixture of play, pantomime, and cinema. It is set on an Italian lake, where a fashionable woman is surrounded by three men: her wealthy husband who bores her, a shallow former lover, and a romantic future lover. She is depressed; her husband sends her on a trip through Europe. This fails to help her, and she drowns herself.

"Weill was not a good pianist nor singer, but he had a way of playing his own music that was totally convincing." He received the nod from the Kroll Opera, and *The Royal Palace* premiered March 2, 1927. It was "intelligent" and very "novel," joltingly avant-garde Weill. Abravanel was upset during the scene changes, when instead of a curtain, the stage directions called for enormous spotlights aimed directly into the audience's eyes. After the performance Abravanel complained to Weill: "Having those noisy spotlights on stage while your music is being played is disgraceful!" and later he commented, "I have always felt that way about music. Nothing should be allowed to interfere with it."

Weill's *The Czar Has Himself Photographed* was first performed in 1928. In sharp contrast to the tragic tone of *The Protagonist* and *The Royal Palace*, *The Czar* is comic.

The clever plot deals with conspirators conniving to kill the Czar. They arrange for him to sit for his photograph, to be taken by a beautiful conspirator. What better way to kill the Czar than to have him pose and—then—bang! from the camera? "In the opera," Abravanel recalls, "it doesn't work out that way. Instead, the Czar finds the lady photographer very charming and says, 'I've had my picture taken millions of times. I would like to take your picture. Sit down. Smile.' Bang!"

Instead of the usual operatic love duet with scoring for a large orchestra in the manner of Wagner, Strauss, or Puccini, Weill's duet called for no orchestra at all. Abravanel was bowled over by the novelty: "Only a phonograph recording! Weill wrote a tango and had a small band record it. And when the love duet comes—four minutes of phonograph recording!" Once again, Weill had seized the spirit of the avant-garde.

That same year Weill also completed what would become his most popular work. Bertolt Brecht wrote the book for this modern adaptation of eighteenth-century English composer John Gay's *The Beggar's Opera*. Weill had begun *The Threepenny Opera* while he was still composing atonal music.

This seems paradoxical, for in *The Threepenny Opera* he "tried for structures that were as simple as possible—so unlike the style of his sophisticated and complicated teacher, Busoni." Weill had already enjoyed success in his new, simple style, however, in *The Czar Has Himself Photographed*.

Weill had been influenced in this shift toward simplicity by reading Verdi, and he decided to reduce his music to its simplest form, believing with Verdi that, "When all things are said and done, the best critics and best professionals never have as good taste as the public. The public can be wrong at times, but in the long run, the public is right."

Nonetheless, Weill did not sell out to the commonplace by writing tunes that everyone—no matter who—would like at first hearing. Abravanel describes Weill's method: "He simply wrote what he wanted to write, conveyed what he wanted to convey, but with the simplest possible means. If he could do it with four-bar phrases, which are easier in some mysterious way for human beings to understand, to follow, and to remember, then Weill would do it in four-bar phrases."

Weill's apparent desertion of the avant-garde puzzled and angered some critics. Some dismissed him with: "Oh well, *The Threepenny Opera* is only one exception because of Brecht. The avant-garde will be back." But Weill didn't go back. He wrote operas that were not as popular in style as *The Threepenny Opera* but which were much simpler than his earlier avant-garde works. *The Threepenny Opera* was destined for enduring acclaim. It ran for years in Germany between the world wars and was an off-Broadway hit for nearly a decade in the fifties. Bobby Darin, Ella Fitzgerald, Louie Armstrong, and other pop singers recorded "Mack the Knife," the hit of the Weill score, still popular today.

Although *The Rise and Fall of the City of Mahagonny*, one of Weill's major works, was premiered October 20, 1930, by the Frankfurt Opera, its beginnings date back to what Abravanel calls the "Little" *Mahagonny*, consisting of six Weill songs with text by Bertolt Brecht. This original abbreviated version was premiered at Baden-Baden in 1926. Abravanel conducted the cast of six singers, including Lotte Lenya. In 1930, Weill expanded this "Singspiel" (a form of German comic opera with spoken rather than sung dialogue) into a full-scale three-act opera, with a Brecht libretto. The setting is an American desert; the story tells of three escaped criminals who discover there the city of Mahagonny, in which the basest instincts of humanity are catered to. The opera was very controversial at the time of its premiere, while the "Little" *Mahagonny* has continued to be performed quite often, particularly in France.

After two years as music director of the Altenburg Opera, Abravanel advanced to the same position at Cassel, a major opera house and his most important position to that time. While conducting there he received his biggest break – the general director of the Berlin State Opera saw him conduct Verdi's *La Forza del Destino* in Cassel on January 16, 1931.

A still-bewildered Abravanel admitted, "I hadn't even seen a performance of *La Forza del Destino* for a year and a half and had never performed it. Never in my life had I seen the score except for this particular performance. . . . But the general director liked it. He gave me the following instructions: 'Take the night train to Berlin now. You rehearse with the singers in the morning. Tomorrow night you conduct *La Forza* at the Berlin State Opera!' " The performance was to be sung in a new German translation by novelist and dramatist Franz Werfel.

Abravanel was overwhelmed. This was the opera house where Richard Strauss conducted "yesterday," Furtwängler "tomorrow," Bruno Walter the "next day" and,

here was I, twenty-seven years old and innocent, having to conduct without any orchestra rehearsal! That night, January 17, 1931, I went to the orchestra pit white as a sheet and conducted the first act, which is short. Afterwards I was told I took the overture's *allegro* "in two" while the orchestra had it marked "in four" in their parts. I took it in a majestic "two" while they were used to a faster "four." In spite of that the whole orchestra applauded me! The Berlin State Opera orchestra!

In those days the orchestra notified the general director whether or not they wanted a conductor to return. If they didn't like a guest, that was the end! If they liked him, it was different. I was accepted by both orchestra and audience. This was my debut at the Berlin State Opera and certainly the most significant single event in my life, to that point. They wanted me there as a permanent conductor. I guest-conducted many times, each time without rehearsal, each time improvising many things.

His conducting appearances with the Berlin State Opera climaxed Abravanel's German "period" – from "fifth" coach to conducting in Germany's leading opera house within eleven years.

These exciting days were cut short by Hitler, who was spreading terror throughout Germany. Many prudent Jewish families were leaving their homeland. There was no longer room in Germany for Kurt Weill, Bruno Walter, Paul Hindemith, Austrian Arnold Schönberg, or, later, Hungarian Béla Bartók and other persecuted Jewish artists from neighboring countries. Abravanel was a victim as well. Both he and Weill left Berlin in 1933 for Paris, where their friendship and professional association would continue. Their departure came only two weeks after Bruno Walter had been forbidden to conduct by the Nazis. He too fled to Paris.

With most of the Jewish musicians in flight, it is ironical that Abravanel was approached about remaining because of the dearth of conductors. "I was not a German Jew," he explains. "And in those early days of Nazism, foreign Jews were not Hitler's immediate target." But they would be, inevitably, and the Abravanels departed for Paris.

PARIS, 1933–1934

In Paris Abravanel met and worked with Bruno Walter, a twentieth-century giant. Walter is the undisputed authority on the works of Gustav Mahler, learning first-hand from the composer and recording much of his insight in his book *Gustav Mahler*. He learned of Abravanel's conducting at the Berlin State Opera and recommended him as guest conductor of the Paris Opera, where he was appearing in a similar role.

Abravanel remembers Walter as "very gentle, never yelling at the musicians, but enlisting their private, personal musicianship. This is much different from the idea most people have of the conductor as a dictator, playing on HIS instrument, that instrument being eighty, ninety, or one hundred human beings. Human beings are NOT an instrument! I know that you can make very good music without compulsion, without dictatorship, and that is the way Bruno Walter made such wonderful music."

Abravanel treasures the memory of Walter's generosity to him. Walter gave him complete freedom as his assistant to cast, rehearse, and conduct Mozart's *Don Giovanni* at the

Maurice de Abravanel

3646
Hartungs Künstlerkarte. Berlin, Kaiserpl. 7   phot. Nehrdich, Cassel

The rising young conductor in 1929. MAP.

The great Bruno Walter, Abravanel's mentor at the Paris Opera. The 1956 photograph is autographed to "Meinem lieben Freund." MAP.

Paris Opera. The rich experience of working with Walter would greatly affect Abravanel's subsequent career. Walter himself moved to the United States as the war approached and reestablished his own conducting career.

Now just thirty years old, Abravanel guest-conducted Pierre Monteux's Paris Symphony Orchestra for the first time on November 26, 1933. It was one of many such engagements in the Paris theaters and concert halls.

George Balanchine also loomed during Abravanel's year in Paris. Recognized as the kingpin of American ballet until his death in 1983, Balanchine was then just beginning to spread his wings in the artistic world of Paris with his first major company. Abravanel was named musical director of Balanchine's *Ballets 1933*, with runs in both Paris and London.

Abravanel's collaboration with Weill also resumed in Paris, where he conducted Weill's ballet *The Seven Deadly Sins*. When commissioned to compose the score, Weill had said: "On one condition–I want voices, and I want a text, not just instruments." Despite the fact that Weill's author, Bertolt Brecht, "had become a Marxist and had treated Weill badly, Weill still wanted Brecht to be the writer," says Abravanel, who maintains that "Weill was never politically inclined but suffered from the abuse he took from Brecht." Weill, as composer, was "the toast of the town" in Paris, while Brecht was "nobody at that time."

In addition to his opera and symphony work, Abravanel conducted smaller "connoisseur" concerts. One of these featured the "Little" *Mahagonny* at Salle Gaveau on June 20, 1933, with two female and four male singers. The women were Lotte Lenya and Abravanel's wife, now listed as Marie Chacko. "It was the greatest thing since [Stravinsky's unveiling by] Diaghilev," Abravanel boasts. The piece was also performed in Switzerland and at Rome's St. Cecilia hall on December 29, 1933.

"Weill was in demand everywhere–the people wanted Weill. So I asked Madeleine Milhaud to translate something from *Silbersee* [*Silver Lake*], Weill's latest work, which had opened simultaneously in 1933 in eleven different German cities, on the night before the Reichstag was burned! Weill's opera closed the next day, and he fled to Paris."

Abravanel conducted the Paris performance of *Silbersee* selections, with soprano Madeleine Grey:

There was a big scandal! Everything seemed to be okay at the end of Madeleine Grey's performance of the three numbers. There were the usual cries of "bis! bis!" which accompany a favorable reaction. But as the applause died down, a lone anti-Nazi voice continued to yell. It was not aimed at the French singer, who had sung in French translation, nor was it aimed at the conductor, for Maurice de Abravanel is a French name. Rather, it attacked Weill, the German composer. With feelings between French and German, plus the rise of Nazism, the anti-Weill outburst grew to near-riot proportions.

Weill and Abravanel were soon to be separated by many thousand miles, including both the Atlantic and Pacific oceans.

Max Reinhart, Austrian stage director and producer, and Franz Werfel, Austrian poet, novelist, and playwright, asked Weill to compose a score for a biblical pageant called *The Eternal Road* and to go to America to work on the project. Recalls Abravanel, "Weill and I never corresponded. But he wrote a desperate postcard to my brother Ernest, asking, 'Where is Maurice? He is the only man alive who really understands my music.' I remember that card," muses Abravanel, "because he wrote it in French, and he wrote 'mon' musique instead of 'ma' musique."

There was no way Weill could have reached Abravanel by letter. In 1934 he had been invited to conduct a season in Australia–Sydney and Melbourne–and he and Friedel were en route to new frontiers Down Under.

"A Greater Maurice," according to a Melbourne weekly.
The drawing is accompanied by a poem. MAP.
When operatic magic / Wafts us on wings of dream,
Through stately songs and tragic / And love's undying theme,
We all, within the bond of / A subtly-woven spell,
Bow to the magic wand of / Maurice D'Abravanel—
A Maestro! A Maestro! / Whom all the world would love to know—
Maurice D'Abravanel.

CHAPTER 2

Down Under, 1934–1936

"The eminent continental conductor Maurice de Abravanel arrived today on the ocean-liner *Maloja*," trumpeted the *Melbourne Star* for September 3, 1934. The three-column by twelve-inch story heralded the long-awaited visit from London of Sir Benjamin Fuller's Royal Grand Opera Company, a wing of Sir Thomas Beecham's Royal Opera Company based at London's Covent Garden opera house. Sir Benjamin headed the arriving group, with Charles Moor as producer and Maurice de Abravanel as musical director.

Abravanel was only thirty-one, but with credentials from both the Berlin State Opera and the Paris Opera, his youth was an asset. His original thirteen-week contract was for opera in Melbourne's Apollo Theater, but he would remain for two years.

Abravanel looks back nostalgically on the voyage from London, through the Suez Canal, to India and, eventually, Australia: "It took six weeks. Six weeks!" he exclaims incredulously. "We left London in late July and arrived in Melbourne in early September!" All the English singers had appeared at Covent Garden. The featured artist was dramatic soprano Florence Austral, ranked as the world's greatest dramatic soprano by Sir Benjamin and by the Australian press. She was flanked by half a dozen other leading English opera stars.

Abravanel's wife Friedel appeared in a number of supporting roles, billed as Freda Shacko. Her roles included Siebel in Gounod's *Faust*, the High Priestess in *Aida*, Inez in *Il Trovatore*, and a young shepherdess in *Tannhäuser*. Sir Benjamin Fuller's press release noted that Freda had made her first appearance on the concert platform in Paris and had subsequently made her operatic debut in Germany. A poster described her as "the fascinating brunette soprano," born in Portugal, who had studied in Germany and Paris. One press release noted that she was "the daughter of the famous singer Hedwig Schacko. Mrs. de Abravanel is married to the conductor." The press also referred to her as "the charming young continental singer."

The Australian press had some problems with Abravanel's surname. In Europe it had always been *de* Abravanel, his family name. While some Australian newspapers followed the European lead, his name was often misspelled Maurice d'Abravanel. Sir Benjamin Fuller's Royal Grand Opera was frequently referred to in the press as the British National Opera Company, which Abravanel actually preferred.

All the operas were sung in English. Abravanel describes the Australian music public as "quite insular" at that time, but immensely interested. The press coverage was astounding. King-size reviews and feature stories with large photographs abounded. A two-column by ten-inch caricature shows Abravanel flourishing his baton, a great mop of jet-black hair flowing in its breeze.

The season's opener, *Aida*, drew the following prophecy from the *Herald*'s Therold Waters: "If everything comes to the standard . . . of maestro Maurice de Abravanel who had

The *Sun* announces the arrival of the Abravanels and tenor Octave Duo on the Melbourne Express. MAP.

to prepare so intensively within a fortnight, there should be no limits to the season's success." Other operas were *Tosca*, *Madame Butterfly*, *The Valkyrie*, *Il Trovatore*, *Rigoletto*, *Faust*, *Die Fledermaus*, *Tannhäuser*, *Tristan und Isolde*, *The Barber of Seville*, *The Flying Dutchman*, *Samson and Delilah*, and Bizet's then rarely staged *Pearl Fishers*, a well-balanced selection from the standard repertoire.

Overnight Abravanel became one of Melbourne's best-known faces. A feature profile typical of many appeared in the weekly *Table Talk* on October 4: "An excitable volatile manner, a shock of coal black hair, horn-rimmed glasses that light up at moments of musical stress with an unholy fervor, and a broken accent. Broken? Yes, decidedly, smashed into hundreds of little bits! Put the whole thing together . . . and you have Maurice D'Abravanel, the Portuguese conductor of the Opera Season. . . . I don't think I've ever seen anyone so 'all there.' "

The opera-goers loved the Wagner as passionately as the critics did. The Melbourne *Sun* commented on *The Valkyrie*'s opening: "The night provided genuine triumphs for Maurice de Abravanel. The textures he obtained were not only rich throughout, but the opulence of the dynamics, the potency of his climaxes were very seldom, indeed, permitted to obscure the melodic purport of the grand voices. . . . " Abravanel, the *Sun* noted, was presented with a laurel wreath at the opera's end by members of the orchestra. The 1934 Melbourne season was a triumph.

At the end of the original thirteen weeks in Melbourne, the opera company moved to Sydney for a two-month season.

Abravanel and producer Charles Moor went to Sydney ahead of the troupe. They had to be ready for the gala opening eight days later on December twelfth. As in Melbourne, the opener was *Aida*. Abravanel remembers the pressure: "Preparations for the season were very strenuous. Only a handful of key musicians from our Melbourne orchestra and chorus made the journey. The remainder had to be selected in Sydney." Even under such conditions, *Aida* was a hit and

"Action by M. Maurice de Abravanel as seen by Gurney, the *Herald* cartoonist, during a rehearsal of his symphony orchestra at the Town Hall. This famous European conductor will present his first Melbourne concert tonight." MAP.

was followed by *Tannhäuser*, *The Valkyrie*, *Tristan*, *The Flying Dutchman*, *The Pearl Fishers*, and *Samson and Delilah*.

On March 9, 1935, Abravanel and the company returned to Melbourne, where the original orchestra and singers rejoined the company in an opening *Flying Dutchman*, followed by productions from their repertoire through May.

During the summer of 1935, Abravanel turned to the heretofore neglected realm of symphony orchestra concerts.

He was the first to assemble and conduct an "Australian" orchestra. True, there was an opera orchestra in Melbourne, but there were still only the rudiments of one in Sydney, and the same was true of other metropolitan areas. Australian symphony lovers had occasionally been rescued by rare appearances of the Philadelphia Orchestra and one or two other major ensembles, with occasional visits by eminent European and American guest conductors who worked with a local orchestra assembled for two or three concerts.

However, Melbourne and Sydney boasted orchestras subsidized, as in Europe, by the national government and administered by the Australian Broadcasting Commission (ABC), whose concerts were solely for radio broadcasts. Abravanel was charting virgin territory when he planned short symphony concert seasons in both cities.

The Melbourne Symphony Orchestra's summer series was held in the Town Hall rather than at the opera's home in the Tivoli Theatre. Designated as Celebrity Concerts, the series began May 24 and continued for several weeks, adding a new dimension to Melbourne's cultural life.

In Sydney, Abravanel assembled what was billed as the "Professional Orchestra," and the concerts were welcomed by public and press alike.

It was at one of the Sydney concerts that the youthful prodigy Yehudi Menuhin appeared with Abravanel. Amazingly, Menuhin played not two but three violin concertos, one of J. S. Bach's, the Bruch, and the Brahms. Abravanel may be the only conductor ever to have conducted Menuhin in three concertos in a single concert! That summer he also conducted the Perth and Adelaide ABC Radio orchestras.

Returning to his home base in Melbourne, Abravanel led the Melbourne Symphony in two particularly successful concerts in Town Hall. The souvenir program tags the maestro as "the eminent continental conductor." The concerts were

Abravanel rehearsing the first "Australian" orchestra in 1935. MAP.

Yehudi Menuhin played with Abravanel during the pioneering season in Australia. The young American autographed this photograph in French. MAP.

sponsored by the Melbourne *Herald*, which gave Abravanel more press coverage in two weeks than he would later receive in a much longer period with the Utah Symphony.

The late Australian composer-pianist Percy Grainger told the press, according to Abravanel, that "symphony orchestras are absolutely unnecessary. There is only opera and instrumental soloists." Shortly after this interview, continues Abravanel, "Grainger played the Grieg Piano Concerto with the Melbourne Symphony in an apparent change of heart."

Abravanel also was invited to conduct live concert performances of opera over the ABC from January through May of 1936. Among the operas broadcast were Wagner's *Parsifal*, Borodin's *Prince Igor*, Mozart's *The Marriage of Figaro*, Puccini's *Manon Lescaut*, and Ralph Vaughan Williams' unfamiliar *Hugh the Drover*.

Cartoon of Friedel "Hastening down the aisle with a change of shirt for the maestro. . . . " MAP.

Sydney's *Argus* raved: "De Abravanel Triumphs in Stirring Valhalla Music: Mr. de Abravanel's employment of violent dynamics and bold colour contrasts made a most arresting climax to the work. From the striking opening sequence of the third scene with which the performance began last night, the orchestra responded ably to its young conductor, who soon is to seek wider fields at the Metropolitan Opera house."

The reviewer's last statement referred to an unexpected development. In mid-spring of 1936 Abravanel had received a letter from Eric Simon, European talent scout for the Metropolitan Opera. The Met's general director, Edward Johnson, knew of Abravanel's European experience. "The Met was looking for someone who could handle both the French and German repertoires," Abravanel recalls. "My ties with both the Berlin State Opera and the Paris Opera were what they were looking for. Recommendations from Bruno Walter and Wilhelm Furtwängler, a pair of the world's most distinguished conductors, apparently clinched the deal." He was surprised at the Furtwängler letter, however, which was unsolicited. "Apparently he became aware of my work at the Berlin State Opera. Of course I knew Walter intimately, having worked with him in Paris."

During his two years in Australia, Abravanel had become the dominant music force Down Under at a youthful thirty-one to thirty-three years of age. He had built the existing opera tradition into a strong cultural force. In addition, he had given impetus to symphony orchestras in the principal cities. "He could have been elected to Parliament," was the assessment of one writer.

He was now ready for the New World – six weeks away by ocean liner.

CHAPTER 3

New York City, 1936–1947

After two successful years in Australia, Abravanel welcomed a new challenge. When the letter arrived from the Metropolitan Opera Company offering him a three-year contract, he quickly cabled his acceptance. Excited at the prospect of conducting at the Met, of course, he also looked forward with anticipation to the opportunity of living in America. The Met was the country's most prestigious and, in some ways, only genuine opera house. By the early autumn of 1936, at thirty-three, Abravanel had already conducted the Berlin State Opera and the Paris Opera, and now the Metropolitan Opera, three of the world's most illustrious musical institutions; and he was the youngest conductor the Met had ever signed.

Abravanel's Metropolitan debut was a revival of Saint-Saëns' *Samson and Delilah* on December 6, 1936. The cast, headed by Gertrud Wettergren and Rene Maison in the title roles, also listed Ezio Pinza, the company's principal bass, as the High Priest.

Although he had lost contact with Kurt Weill during his two years in Australia, Abravanel located him soon after arriving in New York and gave him a ticket to his debut. Weill came backstage at intermission and greeted him with "Well, Maurice, this is not too good—only about on the level of

Frankfurt. It doesn't compare with Berlin or even Leipzig or Dresden!" This frank assessment was not too encouraging for his young friend's debut in the New World, "but," agreed Abravanel, "I'm afraid he was right."

The Met had a fourteen-week season. The advertising streamers for the 1936–37 season list Maurice de Abravanel as one of five conductors, each conducting his specialties. Ettore Panizza conducted Verdi and Puccini; Gennaro Papi, Rimsky-Korsakov's *Le Coq d'Or* and Leoncavallo's *I Pagliacci*; Artur Bodansky conducted Wagner; and Wilfred Pelletier, Thomas's *Mignon* from the French repertoire.

Abravanel was a "swing" man, with expertise in both the French and German repertoires. Evening and Saturday matinee performances were at the Metropolitan Opera House, except for Tuesdays, when the company performed a variety of out-of-town engagements. *Samson* was repeated at Philadelphia's Academy of Music on January 5, one month after its premiere. Abravanel conducted the same cast, which also performed on a later Tuesday at the Brooklyn Academy of Music, as well as in Hartford, Connecticut. He also conducted "specials" at the Metropolitan, including Wagner's *Ring of the Nibelung*.

On February 3, 1937, Abravanel conducted a production of Offenbach's *Tales of Hoffmann*, memorable for its stars Gladys Swarthout, glamorous mezzo-soprano, and baritone Lawrence Tibbett. (Both were among the first opera stars to sign Hollywood contracts.) The following week Abravanel

Oil painting of Abravanel during his New York period by Theo Fried. Walter J. Russell photograph in MAP.

Wagnerian soprano Kirsten Flagstad, one of the legendary opera stars Abravanel conducted during his seasons at the Met. MAP.

ple performances at the Met and were repeated out of town on Tuesday nights. He conducted *Tannhäuser* twice – on January 5, 1937, with the legendary Lotte Lehmann (as Elizabeth), Richard Bonelli, and Ludwig Hofmann; and on March 19, when Mme. Lehmann and Ludwig Hofmann were joined by Lauritz Melchior, the day's leading heroic tenor, singing the title role.

The opera Abravanel conducted most during his first Met season was *Lohengrin* – six times, including New Year's Day 1937, once each in January and February, and three times in March. The cast was usually headed by the reigning Wagnerian soprano of the day, Kirsten Flagstad, who appeared as Elsa in five of the performances. She was usually joined by Lauritz Melchior as Lohengrin and Ludwig Hofmann as King Henry.

At the age of thirty-four, Abravanel had conducted the world's leading opera stars: Flagstad, Melchior, Hofmann, Lehmann, Pinza, Swarthout, Tibbett, Pons, Crooks, Bonelli, and Jagel. His second season at the Met was much like the first, as he rotated conducting roles with the other four conductors, working mostly with the same artists.

Abravanel describes his years at the Met as a feverish "rush through rehearsals." There were no new operas produced in New York in those days. They were too expensive. Met singers also resented new or unfamiliar scores, which would have meant long hours and tedious work, especially for those who did not readily read music. "On the other hand," says Abravanel, "if you did something from the standard repertoire like *Il Trovatore*, the singers didn't want to rehearse, saying 'Oh, we already know *Trovatore*.' "

Abravanel established a legendary record for endurance at the Met:

> Seven performances of five different operas in nine days! Never equaled before or since! But that's all that it means. I make no claims for the performances musically or artistically, but endurance – yes! That record still stands. Stranger was the fact that I received rave reviews during those nine days. The New York *World Telegram* critic went so far as to write that it was not Flagstad, Lauritz Melchior, nor Ludwig Hofmann, but, rather, the conducting that made the *Lohengrin* great, with the right tempo for the first time in twenty years.

conducted another charismatic star, coloratura soprano Lily Pons, in Delibes' *Lakmé*, with tenor Frederick Jagel and Ezio Pinza. *Lakmé* was repeated in Philadelphia on February 16, and a warm relationship grew between Abravanel and Lily Pons and her husband, conductor André Kostelanetz.

Massenet's *Manon* was Abravanel's fourth French opera. He conducted four performances that season, on January 16, February 13, and March 17 and 19 with exquisite Brazilian soprano Bidú Sayão as Manon. Baritone Richard Bonelli and tenor Richard Crooks appeared with her in leading roles.

Abravanel was assigned two Wagner operas during his first season, *Tannhäuser* and *Lohengrin*. Both received multi-

Abravanel admits that the critics panned him after that: "I guess I was conducting too often and someone didn't like it."

During his two seasons at the Metropolitan Opera he had continued to be billed as Maurice de Abravanel. In 1938 he dropped the "de" permanently. "They were always losing my mail, because they sometimes filed it under A and sometimes under D." His name became one of the easiest to find in the telephone directory, and "Abravanel" is the first chapter of Hope Stoddard's *Symphony Conductors of the U.S.A.*

BROADWAY

Always a champion of Weill, Abravanel had early asked his boss, Met director Edward Johnson, "Why don't you perform operas by Kurt Weill?" "The man thought I was crazy," recalls Abravanel. One night in New York in 1938, toward the end of Abravanel's second year at the Met, Weill asked,

Will you come with me? I'm going to play *Knickerbocker Holiday* on the piano for some sponsors and Balanchine. So I went. Maxwell Anderson, author of the play, was there, along with playwrights Elmer Rice, Robert Sherwood, Sidney Howard, all members of a group of writers determined to bring exciting new ideas to the Broadway stage, and, of course, Balanchine, who Weill hoped to get to choreograph the dances. Listening to a new work was exciting and reminiscent of my years in Germany, where no opera house could hold its head high without presenting several new works each year. It was so exciting to contemplate helping to build something new, not just repeating *Lohengrin* or *Lakmé* or *Tannhäuser* or whatever, but helping with something new that might be better or longer-lasting because of what I may have done for it.

Later that same night Abravanel amazed Weill: "Kurt, I would like to conduct *Knickerbocker Holiday!*" Stunned, Weill answered: "You're crazy. You don't give up the Metropolitan Opera for Broadway!" "I don't care," was Abravanel's retort. And that was that. It was a surprising decision, but Abravanel meant it. He resigned his three-year Met contract at the end of the second year. Weill signed him as conductor for *Knickerbocker Holiday* as well as his subsequent Broadway musicals, and thus began a new relationship for the two old friends.

A grateful Walter Huston, star of *Knickerbocker Holiday*, signed this photograph "To Maurice, whose patience and thoroughness had been a great help to an aspiring Singer." MAP.

Abravanel had been disappointed by the Met's lack of rehearsals and bored by its static repertoire. He was disillusioned with the entire system. In contrast, Broadway's vitality and the possibility of participating in shaping new works promised a new world of excitement.

Years later, Abravanel drew contrasts between grand opera and Broadway musicals:

On Broadway you aim at a long run. You polish and get things exactly right. In opera the aim is not so high. Lack of rehearsals makes finished and polished performances impossible. Unnecessary cuts in the music are made for frivolous reasons. As a result, the finished product is artificial. In spite of the tampering, it is the musicals, paradoxically, that are given the best staging advantages: best sets, best costuming, best everything.

Abravanel became once again one of the problematic Weill's most eloquent interpreters. He supported Weill's abrupt shift from an atonal technique in his successful early years in Berlin to the "simple" style of his later Broadway shows. "How could Weill write so simply at the same time other composers were striving to sound more and *more* modern?" Abravanel asks. "How could he throw away every 'modern' technique and write as simply as he could, ignoring his former friends who would have nothing to do with the new Weill? He wanted to write music the public could understand."

Abravanel early discovered that Broadway's first rule is financial success, and that the backers of a show want assurance that it will have a long run and be a money-maker. Out-of-town tryouts are one of the most reliable shapers and predictors of success. New Haven, Boston, Hartford, and Philadelphia were *Knickerbocker Holiday's* tryout cities. Abravanel recalls: "There was an exquisite little number in the beginning of Act Two. Little Dutch maidens came onstage and swept the streets. Exquisite music by Kurt, exquisite lyrics of Maxwell Anderson, exquisite girls with exquisite voices and exquisite figures! It was exquisite—except they didn't buy it in Hartford! And so, OUT!—after just one performance the number was out! There was no applause, nobody laughed, nobody looked. It was OUT!" Broadway never saw that number.

Walter Huston, distinguished stage and screen actor, and father of director John Huston, had been engaged to play Peter Stuyvesant in *Knickerbocker Holiday*. "He didn't have the kind of memory needed for Maxwell Anderson's long speeches," Abravanel recollects. The greatest song in the show, and one of Weill's all-time best, was "September Song," whose hauntingly beautiful melody is still popular today.

"When [Huston] heard the music of 'September Song,' " Abravanel smiles, "it didn't stay in his head. The intervals are complicated, as you know. I sat at the piano, having just finished my years at the Metropolitan Opera with Lauritz

Melchior and all those great singers. I was anxious to work with Huston, but he couldn't get it. I played it again and again for him. He was very patient. Kurt Weill was listening outside the door. He knew a star could refuse any song and was very concerned."

Abravanel recalls the cast's great rapport and support for one another during the last three days of rehearsal with Ray Middleton and Dick Colnear, both recognized stars, and Huston, then relatively unknown. *Knickerbocker Holiday* was Joshua Logan's first important directing for Maxwell Anderson. He cut page after page from Huston's part, but Huston remained "awfully nice to everyone. As a result, when he got stuck with his lines or music, the whole chorus cheered him on. Everybody loved him."

"Huston was determined," continues Abravanel. "He apologized for being slow, but he couldn't memorize it. It simply wasn't in his ear. But in the fourth week—we were opening in Boston three days later—Huston and I were rehearsing when Maxwell Anderson said: 'I wish Huston would give up and you would just play it with the orchestra.' I said, 'Max, be patient—he will be marvelous!' Actually, I didn't know whether he would be, but somehow on opening night he actually knew the song, and it stopped the show."

A 1938 recording of Huston singing "September Song" became a classic and is a collector's item today. His vocal delivery is similar to Richard Burton's in *Camelot*, effective and unforgettable. This particular recording, conducted by Abravanel, is still heard regularly on the nation's radio stations. Huston, who returned to making films, later achieved stardom in Hollywood, receiving an Oscar for his supporting role in *The Treasure of the Sierra Madre*, starring Humphrey Bogart. Logan went on to become one of Broadway's most successful directors.

"The show ran in 1938 and was strongly anti–New Deal," says Abravanel. "It received terrible reviews because everyone in New York at this time was pro–New Deal." Theatergoers ignored the reviewers, and the show was a hit. At least one observer disagreed with the enthusiastic audiences, however. Abravanel recalls: "I was conducting a rehearsal of *Knickerbocker Holiday* when Friedel burst in bitterly with 'That is horrible music! It is terrible!' " Her husband had not been able to arrange a starring contract for her at the Met, and in 1938 Friedel was ready to move on.

The celebrated German conductor Otto Klemperer had moved to New York and was the biggest-name conductor on the music scene. "Friedel left me for Klemperer," admits Abravanel, recalling that Klemperer accompanied her in a Carnegie Hall solo recital.

The Abravanels separated in 1938, and two years later Friedel traveled by train to Nevada for a "Reno divorce." She and Klemperer were together from 1940 to 1942.

Abravanel still thinks of his first wife with affection. "She is a very refined woman, very intelligent and aware of what is going on in the world generally. . . . I have sent her money every month ever since–to this day. And not just alimony, which simply would not take care of her needs, but more."

For Abravanel, *Lady in the Dark* is Weill's most memorable musical. It boasted an unbeatable foursome in Moss Hart, author and director, Ira Gershwin, lyricist, Abravanel, music director, and Weill. This was one of the few times George Gershwin's brother-lyricist had written for anyone but George.

The musical's plot was ahead of its time. It is 1940 and the principal character is a successful but troubled business executive. She consults a psychiatrist and then dreams of her younger years; the acts are called dreams. Weill's musicals were works of art in their genre, and he cautioned detractors not to dismiss Broadway as "lowbrow." Then, too, in 1940, it was most unusual to have psychoanalysis as the basis for a Broadway show. "Not one person out of ten had even heard that word nor Freud's name in those days," says Abravanel. "Everyone feared the show would be a big flop!"

Gertrude Lawrence had been selected for the leading role by Moss Hart and Ira Gershwin. Since Weill knew that Miss Lawrence could sing, her choice was unanimous. She had enjoyed great success in London, having starred for years in *Charlotte's Review*, which later came to New York. She enjoyed a great career on Broadway through her final appearance as the original Anna in Rodgers and Hammerstein's *The King and I*, which premiered in 1951.

"Beatrice Lillie, Gertrude Lawrence, and Jack Buchanan– all in the same show," Abravanel recalls. While some of Broadway's biggest names were in *Lady in the Dark*, a relative unknown was to emerge as its greatest star. The cast called for a young photographer in a supporting role. In a

small nightclub called La Martinique at Sixth Avenue and Fifty-seventh Street, Hart found a stand-up comic named Danny Kaye. Abravanel recalls that "his role had several songs. It became apparent during the four weeks' rehearsals that Danny couldn't perform well–even in rehearsals–without a nightclub-like audience. He began to sag, but Gertrude Lawrence, a magnificent human being and actress, helped him to relax."

The ironies piled up, particularly in view of Danny Kaye's subsequent phenomenal career and permanent niche in American life. "Quite soon in the game," says Abravanel, "Danny's

From "woiking goil" Gertrude Lawrence, star of *Lady in the Dark*, a flirtatious autograph to her conductor. Maurice Seymour photograph in MAP.

Danny Kaye and Maurice Abravanel, the old friends together many years later in Salt Lake City. Rolf W. Kay photograph in MAP.

first song was cut. Well, that often happens. Then his second song was cut." Abravanel sat down beside a downcast Kaye during a break. "Maurice, if they cut the other song ["It's Never Too Late to Get Married"] there's no part left. I might as well leave." Soon afterward, the "Mendelssohn" was also cut. "Danny, you still have the 'Tchaikovsky,' " said Abravanel. The "Tchaikovsky" was a thirty-five-second song in the third "dream," with lyrics limited to polysyllabic Russian names. In that scene Danny was a ringmaster, whip in hand. Coming to the footlights, as called for in the score, he recited at breakneck speed, and with his innate sense of timing, his only remaining song.

A spontaneous roar of applause from the opening night audience in Boston greeted his final note. His song literally stopped the show. Rather than going into the encore the audience wanted, however, Abravanel pushed ahead.

Gertrude Lawrence was good-naturedly piqued by Kaye's enormous success. During the next Saturday's matinee, Kaye was in the middle of the "Tchaikovsky" and suddenly realized that no one was looking at him. Out of the corner of his eye he saw Lawrence mouthing his entire song while sitting in a swing. "She resented being upstaged even for thirty-five seconds," recalls Abravanel.

It happened again during the evening performance. Kaye was upset and struck back. When it was her turn to sing "Jenny," he was standing behind her and started to mimic *her*! She realized that no one was listening to her. Later Kaye remembered, "There I was at the footlights with all that applause, thinking I was going to be fired. I'm sure Gertrude will ask them to fire me!"

But she was an old pro and fought back instead. "She improvised an entirely new 'Jenny,' in the style of lyricist Ira Gershwin," Abravanel recalls, "and put in a few bumps and grinds–unknown on the 1940 stage. Her applause was many times Danny Kaye's. And that's the way it went in each succeeding performance. The rivalry made it a big hit!"

The show moved to New York. "Opening night was a huge success and Danny was instantly the toast of the town," yet he always remained "the same marvelous person as before." The next day Abravanel saw Kaye's agent, Martin Liebman, walking down Park Avenue. He was the organizer of the Music Corporation of America (MCA), the leading management firm in the theatrical world. "Isn't it marvelous about Danny Kaye?" was Abravanel's greeting. "I've seen the reviews, and they're marvelous!"

Liebman replied tersely, "I gave them [the show's management] three weeks' notice!" In those days, performers signed either a normal contract, which management or artist could break with two weeks' notice, or a run-of-the-show contract, which remained in effect for both artist and management as long as the show was running. Gertrude Lawrence and perhaps one or two of the other leading artists had signed run-of-the-show contracts.

A totally unknown Danny Kaye had signed a normal contract for a minimum salary–"a pittance," in Abravanel's words. So his manager gave notice and immediately obtained a new contract for three times as much money. He requested

Albert and Lucy Menasse Carasso in Paris. MAP.

it only through June first, when Kaye was signed immediately by Hollywood.

Two of Danny Kaye's most popular recordings, both novelties conducted by Abravanel, were "Minnie the Moocher," and "Dinah." Kaye cleverly mispronounced Dinah as Deenah throughout: "Deenah, is there anyone feenah, in the state of Caroleena," etc. "Minnie the Moocher," up to the time of Kaye's recording, had been the property of band leader Cab Calloway.

At about the time of the *Lady in the Dark* opening, Abravanel received a phone call from Albert Carasso, who had recognized his name as Salonikan. The two men discovered that Salonika was indeed their common birthplace. Carasso had emigrated from Paris a few years earlier and had established a successful import-export business. As their friendship progressed, Abravanel gave Carasso piano lessons.

At the Carasso home the Abravanels met Lucy Menasse, Carasso's Parisian wife, the daughter of a pearl merchant, and their sons, Roger and Pierre. Abravanel recalls a musical evening in April during which Albert accompanied Friedel

in an impromptu recital. "One week later," remembers Abravanel, "Albert Carasso was dead, a victim of cancer!"

The Abravanels became very close to the widowed Lucy. She asked Maurice to oversee her husband's business until Albert's brother could take over. It was with Lucy that Friedel first discussed the possibility of divorcing Maurice.

After the divorce, Lucy and Maurice became even closer. "Here was Lucy, a widow who couldn't speak English and with two young sons to care for." The three remained friends, however, and according to Abravanel, "Because I am not a writer, Lucy carried on the correspondence with Friedel."

These were the war years abroad, and during an emotionally eventful 1940 Abravanel also received the news that his mother had died at the age of seventy in occupied France.

A tattered yellow entertainment page of the New York *Herald-Tribune* for Tuesday, February 10, 1942, reveals an exciting, diverse Broadway. A large ad hails Gertrude Lawrence "in the best musical in town! *Lady in the Dark.*" The show was now well into its run.

The alphabetical listing by show titles heralds 1941–42 as one of Broadway's best seasons. Vincent Price and Judith Evelyn were starring in *Angel Street*, Boris Karloff in *Arsenic and Old Lace*. Eddie Cantor was packing them in at *Banjo Eyes*. Clifton Webb and Peggy Wood were playing *Blithe Spirit*, and *Café Crown* featured Sam Jaffe. For variety there were Gilbert and Sullivan and the Jooss Ballet. George Jessel and Sophie Tucker were stopping the show in *High Kickers*. Directly below *Lady in the Dark*'s ad is one for Danny Kaye's musical *Let's Face It*. Kaye had left the original cast after his smashing debut and a short run, and after an even greater success in Hollywood, he was now back on Broadway starring in his own show with Eve Arden and Kenny Baker.

Life with Father was enjoying a long run featuring Howard Lindsay. Shakespeare was represented by *Macbeth*, starring the unforgettable Maurice Evans and Judith Anderson. *My Sister Eileen* was enjoying its first run. George Gershwin's *Porgy and Bess* starred Todd Duncan. Other shows included Olsen and Johnson, Carmen Miranda, and Ella Logan in *Sons O'Fun*; C. Aubrey Smith in *Spring Again* and Mary Boland in *The Rivals*; and, at the bottom of the page, *Watch on the Rhine* with Paul Lukas. Broadway has enjoyed many great seasons since 1942, but few can match this, and in its midst was Abravanel.

The *Chicago Daily Tribune* for Friday, October 25, 1940, announces that Grace Moore, center, her protégée Dorothy Kirsten, and "new opera conductor" Maurice Abravanel are in town to appear in the Chicago opera. MAP.

Weill's next Broadway success was *One Touch of Venus* in 1943. The plot centers around the goddess Venus, who actually comes to life and falls in love with a simple barber. Mary Martin created the role of Venus, and John Boles and Kenny Baker also starred. Ogden Nash wrote the lyrics, and he always got his laughs with a razor rather than an ax. Abravanel tells of one: "A gossiping society lady has a line ending 'She looks like a Titian,' followed by the question 'beaut or mort?' Nobody laughed, not a single person in those thousand seats!" The following Monday night someone finally laughed, and Abravanel turned to the audience from the orchestra pit and applauded. After a performance of *One Touch of Venus* Abravanel recalls that an attractive older, but not elderly, woman tapped him on the shoulder as he was leaving the pit. "Young man, you have the makings of a great Mahler conductor!" The prophet was Alma Mahler Werfel, the widow of Gustav Mahler (who had married the German author Franz Werfel).

In 1945 the legendary Billy Rose signed Abravanel to conduct his extravaganza *Seven Lively Arts*. Rose had bought

Abravanel conducts the opening of *Seven Lively Arts* before a glittering audience which includes Jim Farley, behind the Maestro, the Bennet Cerfs, the Moss Harts, and many of the other leading members of New York's artistic community. MAP.

the Ziegfeld Theatre and was determined to make it "the largest showplace since the Roman Empire." Tickets were fifty dollars, which included champagne, and Rose had commissioned seven Salvador Dali paintings depicting the Lively Arts for the downstairs lounge.

Each of the musical's seven scenes evoked one of the Muses of ancient Greece, the daughters of Zeus and Mnemosyne. These goddesses presided over song, the many types of poetry, the other arts, and also the sciences. Webster lists ten muses, three more than Billy Rose called for.

Many of the great names in the entertainment world starred. Beatrice Lillie, Bert Lahr, Bill Talbor, Dolores Gray, plus a number of younger stars, as well as jazzmen Benny Goodman, Red Norvo, and Teddy Wilson were in this Billy Rose spectacular. Moss Hart and Norman Corwin wrote sketches. Rose had planned for Leopold Stokowski to conduct, but he insisted on a two-week limit. So, says Abravanel, "Rose hired me, even though I said I wanted to close after four weeks."

Rose had commissioned all the music except for the ballet, which he wanted Weill to compose because of the enormously successful ballet in *One Touch of Venus*. Weill refused: "I would like to do the whole score. That would interest me." Rose's reply: "I have Morton Gould and Cole Porter for the show tunes." Rose then asked Weill, "Who is the best ballet composer?" Abravanel recalls Weill's tongue-in-cheek answer: "Kurt said, very innocently, 'Stravinsky!'"

Surprising everyone, Rose commissioned Stravinsky to write the ballet. Balanchine was the choreographer and Alicia Markova and Anton Dolin starred. The production was perhaps too top-heavy and diverse to enjoy a long run, and it is not remembered as one of Broadway's great shows.

DOWN UNDER AGAIN

In January of 1946, ten years after his first visit ended, Abravanel was lured back to Australia. He returned a conquering hero.

Abravanel's trip came just as America's aircraft industry was shifting from military to civilian travel and offered a striking contrast to the leisurely six-week ocean voyages to and from Australia in 1934 and 1936. When asked, "Were you on the maiden voyage?" Abravanel answers, "The *pre-maiden* voyage. The plane was a huge converted military plane. There were only six of us aboard. Two deplaned in Europe somewhere. The rest went on to India and Ceylon, from where we hopped to Australia."

Abravanel was to conduct two series of symphony concerts sponsored and promoted by Sydney's *Daily Telegraph*. He and what one reporter called the "*Daily Telegraph* Orchestra" received a dazzling promotion and advertising campaign. Of course the orchestra was not the *Telegraph*'s. It was the Sydney Orchestral Society, which had become a fairly standard ensemble since Abravanel's appearances with it in Sydney in the thirties.

Three months prior to the opening concert of the series, Lindsay Clinch, under a New York dateline of October 13, 1945, wrote a five-column feature which appeared in Sydney's *Daily Telegraph*: "Maurice de Abravanel, who will open the series of ten concerts in Sydney next January, is regarded here as America's most versatile conductor." He then noted the Maestro's many-faceted experience at the Met, in Berlin and Paris, and on Broadway and included a two-column pencil-portrait.

Abravanel and his manager, Andre Mertens of Columbia Concerts, plot Abravanel's route to Australia in 1946. Ben Greenhaus photograph in MAP.

Throughout January 1946 the *Daily Telegraph* ran one and sometimes two promotional stories daily. The January 24 edition splashed a two-page spread and feature article surrounded by nine action photos of Abravanel and members of the orchestra in rehearsal.

The opening concert, on Sunday evening, January 25, filled Sydney's Town Hall to overflowing. All concerts were to be on Sunday evenings, a time which was controversial at first but became very popular. The next morning's *Daily Telegraph* carried large photos of crowds queuing up for two blocks and Town Hall's foyer packed with hopeful standees. A five-column headline read "Queue Waits Three Hours for Concert Seats"; another, "Hall Packed for Abravanel Concert." The January 26 edition included a full page of sketches of Abravanel in many podium poses, which even today look familiar.

In his *Telegraph* review of the opening concert Kenneth Wilkinson made some keen observations: "During the eight [*sic*] years Maurice Abravanel has spent in New York conducting at the Metropolitan Opera and elsewhere, his style has considerably matured. Last night he gave the *Funeral March* in Beethoven's *Eroica* a performance full of supreme dignity. The *Eroica* needs, above all, a virile, relentless, indomitable attack. . . ." The *Eroica* was a personal favorite of Abravanel's, and it is not surprising that it was featured at Sydney's opening concert. In later years it would become the Utah Symphony's single most-performed work.

Even more popular with the audience was the second, an all-Russian concert: Glinka's *Russlan and Ludmilla* overture, Prokofiev's *Lieutenant Kije* suite, with Stravinsky's *Firebird* and Tchaikovsky's *Pathétique* Symphony as the second half. Once again, a five-column streamer: "Hall Packed for Abravanel's Second Concert," "Three-hour Wait for Concert Tickets," and "Hundreds Unable to Secure Seats."

As a special gesture he also presented one program of work by Australian composers exclusively, which was received with pride. "Big Ovation Given to Australian Symphony" and "Audience Recalls Conductor Three Times" greeted the newspaper's readers. Subsequent concerts inspired these lines: "Exquisite playing by strings," "Abravanel's fine work in *Tristan*," "Another Triumph for Abravanel."

He displayed courage in programming Beethoven's Ninth (*Choral*) Symphony and again drew plaudits from both audi-

Abravanel with Wilfrid Lawson, concertmaster of the Sydney Symphony, a toast to the success of the Maestro's return to Australia in 1946. MAP.

ence and critics: "Inspiring Symphony, . . . [T]his was not a performance by an orchestra plus soloists and choir. . . . It was a vast symphonic scheme in which the voices were bent and disciplined to the orchestral pattern. . . . The finest choral achievements that Sydney has heard for a long time. The soloists adapted themselves flexibly to Mr. Abravanel's virile treatment of the music, and achieved some skillful effects of balance and shading."

The concert series ended on March thirty-first. Abravanel went out in a blaze with Mozart's *Eine Kleine Nachtmusik*, Beethoven's Fifth Symphony, Brahms' *Haydn Variations*, and Ravel's *Daphnis et Chloé Suite No. 2*. All were Abravanel favorites that would receive multiple performances in the Salt Lake Tabernacle during the Abravanel years.

Four rave reviews appeared the following day. The *Sun's* A. L. Kelly wrote: "A fact that has emerged clearly during . . . this orchestral series. .. is the advance that Maurice Abravanel has made in his directorial art since he conducted here ten or twelve years ago; able *chef* of orchestra though he was in those days." He went on to cite Abravanel's "greater elasticity without any loss of his characteristic energy." The sponsoring *Telegraph* roared: "20,000 Attend Sunday Concerts. Full-House Sign Up for Eighth Time!" In addition to the news

"Good Will from the Antipodes." Acting Mayor Vincent R. Impelliterri of New York City accepts an Australian flag from Maurice Abravanel, brought back from his 1946 tour as "a symbol of friendship and appreciation of the kindnesses shown to Australian service men by the citizens of New York." C. V. Kellway, Australian Consul General, looks on. MAP.

story, there was a lengthy critical review plus a half-length photo of Abravanel conducting in white tie and tails.

He introduced twelve works never before heard in Australia, including Stravinsky's *Firebird* which, he felt, was his single best conducting job of the series. Prokofiev, Schönberg, Milhaud, and Hindemith—at that time the twentieth century's most eminent living composers, along with Stravinsky and Bartók—were also given their Australian premieres. Abravanel's return trip to Sydney in 1946 was a resounding success.

FAREWELL TO BROADWAY

Street Scene was the last Weill work Abravanel conducted in New York. It opened in Philadelphia late in 1946 and on Broadway early the next year. The book was by Elmer Rice,

one of the group present when Abravanel had previewed the *Knickerbocker Holiday* score with Weill in 1938.

Toward the end of his Broadway–Weill years and between runs Abravanel guest-conducted extensively, from Canada to Mexico. There were several concerts in Montreal and seasons of opera in Mexico City, Washington, D.C., and Chicago, with miscellaneous appearances at Chicago's Grant Park and Manhattan's Lewisohn Stadium.

He always cherished the European and Broadway years with Weill:

> Weill's style did not change as much in America as most people seem to think. He was always his own man, writing his own way. He tried very hard to write "Broadway music," but never really did. If you compare some of the music from *One Touch of Venus* with the Berlin pieces, for example, you'll see that Weill was always Weill no matter *where* he was. He was a great human being as well as a musical genius.

Seven years of the grueling eight-performances-a-week grind had dampened Abravanel's enthusiasm for Broadway. The war was over, and movement and change were in the air. It was marvelous to be in New York, where the world's greatest artists—Bruno Walter, Artur Rubinstein, Fritz Busch, Leopold Stokowski—appeared before the public on successive nights. After a few years, however, even such a continuous round of "greats" performing the best music was not enough to satisfy Abravanel. He had decided that what he wanted was to settle down "somewhere away from all that with an orchestra of my own."

One day in early 1947, while contemplating possible future directions, Abravanel answered a telephone call. Radio City Music Hall's management had been checking into his credentials and were offering him the music directorship. The contract was for $30,000 a year (the equivalent of six figures by today's standards) for five years!

"Would this lead to a permanent conductorship with an orchestra?"

"No, but it might lead to a $200,000 salary by 1952, plus recordings."

"Then no." Abravanel's decisiveness indicated his determination to settle down somewhere and build an orchestra. He knew what he wanted.

CHAPTER 4

Westward Ho!

Because I had those big successes in Germany and the same thing in Paris and Australia long before I reached New York, they all thought I was great, but I thought "I am young. I am enthusiastic. Musicians love me; therefore, they played better for me." But I could not have built an orchestra the way they had been built for me by great European conductors. Then I went to Australia and was able to prove that I could get a pick-up orchestra and make them play very well. I thought now I could actually build a permanent orchestra. Later, as an American citizen, I was looking for a place where I could prove it. Then came Salt Lake.

In the Spring of 1947 the Utah Symphony had just concluded its first season as a fully professional orchestra under the baton of Werner Janssen, a competent musician and conductor with international experience who conducted his own small ensemble of Hollywood studio artists in a few concerts annually.

A Progress Fund of $150,000 had been announced, for use over a two-year period, and $92,000 had been raised. Janssen was signed as Utah Symphony music director with the backing of the local media. He lasted one year. He never became part of the local scene, living in a hotel suite and

The new Music Director and Symphony manager Ruth Cowan visit the Salt Lake LDS Temple Grounds in 1947. MAP.

commuting between Salt Lake City and Los Angeles. Janssen was married to glamorous screen star Ann Harding, and her studied last-minute spotlighted entrances added interest to concerts of the 1946–47 season.

But Janssen had done something far more serious than not fitting in. He had imported twenty key musicians from Los Angeles, making clear his lack of commitment to building a *Utah* Symphony. The word "import" became a dirty one in the far western city striving for cultural richness.

Janssen had resigned at the end of his first season and accepted the music directorship of the Portland Symphony, taking most of the imports with him. Otis Igleman, his concertmaster, went to the Detroit Symphony in the same capacity.

Asked when he had first become interested in the Utah Symphony, Abravanel replied:

> I first read of it in April 1947 in a *New York Times* story about Janssen's resignation. I had come to a point in my career when all I wanted was to conduct an orchestra of my own. I phoned Arthur Judson, my manager, and was surprised at his reaction. "No! You can't go to Utah. It would be a disaster. You have the Mormons fighting the non-Mormons, and no one can do anything!"

In the forties and fifties Judson was czar of the concert world, controlling most of its artists and organizations, including the New York Philharmonic. A very controversial man, he was reviled as a dictator by those not under contract to him. In spite of Judson's power and influence, Abravanel decided to make his permanent home in Salt Lake City and prove him wrong.

Rather than appointing a search committee, the executive committee and the Symphony Board as a whole, under the leadership of President Fred E. Smith, undertook the task of hiring a new conductor. Forty applications were filed within a month, including that of Abravanel, who pursued the position actively. The candidates included Stanley Chapple, who made his career as director of the University of Washington's School of Music; George Sebastian of the Chicago Civic Opera; Jaques Rachmilovich of the Santa Monica

The Abravanel family in Salt Lake City. Roger and Pierre Carasso both enrolled at the University of Utah. MAP.

Orchestra; Antonia Brico, who was conducting in Denver; Karl Krueger's associate at Detroit, Walter Poole; Nikolai Malko; Ann Kullmer, who had an all-woman orchestra in New York; and Walter Hendl, assistant conductor of the New York Philharmonic.

As a prelude to the final decision of the Board, President Smith, Vice President Mrs. John M. Wallace, and Symphony Manager Ruth Cowan traveled to New York in early May to interview Rachmilovich and Abravanel. Smith concentrated on Rachmilovich. The final list was headed by Abravanel and Hendl and included Wilfred Pelletier, Guy Fraser Harrison, Stanley Chapple, Hans Lange, George Sebastian, Walter Poole, Ann Kullmer, David Van Vactor, and Alexander Smallens.

Abravanel, who was visiting his friend Anne Jeffries at the Ritz Hotel when they arrived, remembers,

> the lovely ladies . . . who came all the way to New York to meet me. I invited them to a recording session with the Columbia Symphony and a performance of *Street Scene*, which I was conducting eight times a week. They seemed very impressed. So later, at their invitation, I stopped over in Salt Lake on my way to San Francisco, where I was guest conducting. They took me to City Creek Canyon, and I saw those mountains. . . . I loved the valley and the mountains. . . .

On May 24 there were five semifinalists on the list accepted by the executive committee: Rachmilovich, Sebastian, Poole, Hendl, and Abravanel. The list was cut further to Hendl, Sebastian, and Abravanel, with Hendl and Abravanel the survivors on June 11.

At a meeting of the Symphony Board on June 16, the members present—President Smith, Vice President Wallace, Morris Rosenblatt, Oscar Heppley, and Gail Martin—voted to recommend to the full Board that Abravanel be offered a one-year contract. The full Board approved this recommendation unanimously and Abravanel signed the contract the following day.

Although the pace was grueling, with the "rush through rehearsals" at the Met and eight performances a week on Broadway, life in New York had its pleasures. During this period Abravanel enjoyed close friendships with many glamorous stars of the opera and the Broadway stage, including

Dorothy Kirsten, Anne Jeffries, Grace Moore, one of the first opera divas to reach stardom in Hollywood, and Lily Pons, the Met's leading coloratura soprano, many of whose recordings he conducted.

But when the opportunity in Utah came, Abravanel says "I thought only of marrying Lucy, whose deeper qualities made her the ideal wife and companion." They were married in Richmond, Virginia, on September 20, 1947.

Symphony rehearsal during Abravanel's first season with Governor Maw, at far left, in attendance. MAP.

FRESHMAN YEAR

Abravanel was determined and committed from the beginning to building a Utah Symphony with Utahns. During his first season he limited imports to seven key principal artists: Leonard Posner, concertmaster; Paulo Gruppe, principal cello; Napoleon Cerminara, first clarinet; Allan Fuchs and Norman Fuchs, first and second horns; Morris Norkin, principal bassoon; and John Swallow, trombone.

Posner had been concertmaster of New York's Radio City Music Hall orchestra, the most sought-after post in New York after the Philharmonic. Gruppe had been a member of the Belgian Trio. Cerminara was a veteran orchestra musician and had played eleven years with the Philadelphia Orchestra under Leopold Stokowski. Allan Fuchs came from the Pittsburgh Symphony's horn section. Norkin and Swallow were freelance musicians in New York.

After auditioning and signing his key replacements, Abravanel arrived in mid-October to commence rehearsals and plunge into his first season. He brought Lucy, his bride of several weeks, who would soon endear herself to her adopted city. They purchased a modest bungalow just below the Douglas School on Thirteenth East and Seventh South, in a comfortable but not exclusive neighborhood, and lived there permanently.

Lucy Abravanel was a steadfast supporter and champion of her husband. Ever-present at concerts and concert-related occasions, she was also a charming hostess to a steady stream of guests in her home and played a leading role as adviser to the Symphony Guild. Her sons Roger and Pierre were in school and would join the Abravanels the next year.

Abravanel began with a problem—no rehearsal hall. While the Church of Jesus Christ of Latter-day Saints (LDS or Mormon) had made the famous Tabernacle on Temple Square available for dress rehearsals and concerts, it was not available for daily rehearsals. Nor was Kingsbury Hall on the University of Utah campus, which was scheduled for daytime classes. Eighty musicians were ready to go, anticipating with enthusiasm their first meeting with a new conductor. While most had played under Janssen the previous year, some had been members since the orchestra's first official season in 1940.

The first rehearsals were held in the old Labor Temple on Second East Street, but this arrangement did not last. The

An enthusiastic Abravanel rehearsing his orchestra in the fifties. MAP.

Eagles Lodge on West Temple then served for a few weeks. Winter had set in by the time rehearsals were moved to the old Kiwanis-Felt Boys and Girls Club building. The heating system there was inadequate and some musicians rehearsed in their overcoats.

Despite the adverse conditions, Abravanel unveiled the orchestra in the Tabernacle at its first subscription concert on November eighth. The audience numbered only a fraction of what it would later become. The featured work was Beethoven's *Eroica* Symphony. Through Abravanel's thirty-two years, the *Eroica* would top all other works with eleven performances. He programmed it on the opening concert for six different seasons. Abravanel felt a great reverence toward both the *Eroica* and the Ninth symphonies of Beethoven,

Abravanel and Artur Rubinstein at a rehearsal for the great pianist's performance on January 10, 1950. MAP.

and he approached them with seriousness and depth of feeling.

The Abravanel who was to overcome so many obstacles and who was to build such a fine musical organization on local foundations is very much in evidence:

> My beginnings here were very simple. The most important thing for me in the ideal performance is the "total message," even if at the expense sometimes of total precision.
>
> Verdi felt that way. Prokofiev felt that way. Bruno Walter felt that way. Others felt the same.
>
> I felt that way from the beginning. . . . Pianists who were precise and never missed a beat and were cool as an iceberg were not my favorites. I preferred pianists who missed occasional notes in favor of the "total message"—Rubinstein, in other words. I thought he was the greatest even though he missed occasional notes.

During this first season Abravanel signed Rubinstein, the biggest name in the concert world, as guest soloist. He was to play the Brahms Second Piano Concerto with the orchestra on January 3, 1948. The printed program for December 13 announced him as guest artist for the "next concert." Unfortunately, he was forced to cancel sometime during the holiday season, and he did not appear in the Tabernacle until two seasons later, on January 10, 1950. Rubinstein became one of the Symphony's most popular guest artists, appearing with the orchestra five more times in the following years.

Caught without his star attraction for January, Abravanel replaced him with Leroy Robertson's *Trilogy*, the three-movement symphony which had taken the music world by surprise in early November by winning the prestigious Reichhold Award as "the Western Hemisphere's best symphonic work." It had not been performed except by the Detroit Symphony a few weeks earlier at the award ceremonies and broadcast. This would be a Utah premiere for Utah's now-famous composer, and while Rubinstein's non-appearance was disappointing, the novelty of the Robertson work and the glamour surrounding it compensated.

Adding to the orchestra's luster—and listening public—during both the 1947–48 and 1948–49 seasons was a series of radio concert broadcasts presented to live audiences in the University's Kingsbury Hall over radio station KSL. These were not simply repeats of works presented earlier on subscription concerts but programs of the highest quality, some with prominent local soloists. The weekly broadcasts extended over a ten-week period and were sponsored by ZCMI—founded by the Mormon pioneers and for many years the region's largest department store.

Guest artists this first season included violinists Ginette Neveu and Louis Kaufman and concertmaster Leonard Posner. Posner played the Brahms Concerto on both the subscription series and one of the orchestra broadcasts. The glossiest solo concertmaster ever to play under Abravanel, Posner also played Saint-Saëns' *Rondo Capriccio* on a later broadcast.

Pianist Sydney Foster played the Beethoven Third Piano Concerto, and Abravanel programmed Salt Lake City keyboard artists Reid Nibley and Gladys Gladstone in the first of many Symphony appearances for each. Dorothy Eustis soloed in the Grieg Piano Concerto on a KSL broadcast, and Utah piano team Helen Druke and Walter Shaw played both the Mozart and Poulenc double piano concertos as highlights of Abravanel's first season. Cello soloists are rare, but principal cellist Paulo Gruppe was featured during the 1947–48 season in the Schumann Concerto.

Even before his *Trilogy* had brought so much musical attention to Utah, Abravanel had bravely programmed a world premiere of Leroy Robertson's *Punch and Judy* Overture, which gives a pleasant introduction to the Utah composer. Abravanel's audacity at programming Stravinsky in his maiden season in the conservative community was encouraging to

many. Utah audiences welcomed the *Firebird Suite* on January 17, 1948. Abravanel was delighted. Other local "firsts" included Barber's *Adagio for Strings*, Ravel's *Daphnis and Chloé Suite No. 2*, Prokofiev's *Lieutenant Kije*, Copland's *Appalachian Spring*, William Schuman's *Side Show*, and Poulenc's Double Piano Concerto.

Abravanel loves to tell of the indignation of one Symphony Board member who didn't like his "modern" programming:

> In my second concert in November 1947 I programmed three contemporary works. When we were through, a very powerful member of our Symphony Board [Mrs. John Wallace], one of the most powerful people in our state, went to the music critic of one of our local papers and said: "I hope you will write that this is not the music we want to hear—this is a disgrace!" Well, the critic went on to write a lovely review.
>
> Don't you wonder what those contemporary works were? One was brand-new, *Appalachian Spring* by

Abravanel daringly programmed composer Virgil Thomson's *The Seine at Midnight* during the 1948–49 subscription season. MAP.

Copland, one was seven years old, *Adagio for Strings* by Samuel Barber, and the other was William Schuman's *Side Show. . . .* And these are the pieces that a powerful Board member thought were "awful, contemporary, and a disgrace"!

NOSTREBOR

"Leroy Robertson Receives Reichhold Award." "Utah Composer Wins $25,000." "Mormon Sheepherder Wins Top Prize in Western Hemisphere Composition Contest." These headlines galvanized the citizens of Utah in early November of 1947. The Robertson story occupied the music pages of *Time* and *Newsweek* and major newspaper music columns all over the nation. And deservedly–$25,000 was the largest prize in music history! But there was particular meaning for a state that had been founded by a people for whom music and dance were potent forms of religious worship. Utahns of all stripes rejoiced in Robertson's dual recognition–musical and financial.

Samuel Barber, Abravanel, and William Schuman discuss the Symphony's performances of the composers' still-controversial music. Ben Greenhaus photograph in MAP.

The competition, which was open to composers in all nations of the Western Hemisphere, was sponsored by the Detroit Symphony, Dr. Karl Krueger, conductor, and its principal financial backer was Detroit industrialist Henry H. Reichhold.

The $5,000 second prize was awarded to Carmago Guarnieri of São Paulo, Brazil, that country's most distinguished composer. Third prize of $2,500 went to Albert Sendry of Los Angeles, an MGM studio composer. Honorable mentions were given to eleven composers from Canada, Chile, Venezuela, Mexico, Argentina, Uruguay, Peru, and Brazil, lending geographic balance.

This winning entry was by no means a fledgling work by a novice. As Boris Kremenliev observed in *Music of the West* magazine for January 1952: "In 1923 Robertson had won the Endicott Prize in Boston for his Overture in E Minor; his Quintet in A Minor for Piano and Strings won first place in a contest conducted by the Society for the Publication of American Music in 1936; his String Quartet was chosen by the New York Critics Circle in 1944, along with works of Copland and Randall Thompson; his *Rhapsody* for Piano and Orchestra won the Utah Institute of Fine Arts Award in 1945."

Kremenliev, like his fellow critics, commented on the American aspect of the composer's music: "Robertson is particularly interesting to those who strive to predict and understand the future of American music. . . . His important influences have been the mountains, the vast deserts of the West, the wholesome family atmosphere. . . ."

Robertson had been a reluctant contest entrant three years earlier under the pseudonym "Nostrebor." As his daughter Marian Wilson later ventured: "It certainly didn't require an Einstein to discover that Nostrebor spelled Robertson backwards. Contest rules required pen names to insure anonymity. Because the prize was large, this competition drew a field of four hundred. Major composers from Canada, the United States and Central and South America had entered the contest."

Eastman's Howard Hanson, one of the panel of judges, recalls: "*Everyone* entered–big names, hordes of commercial composers from the pops field of Hollywood and Broadway, and young 'tenderfeet' who submitted their ink-wet 'Symphony No. 1.' "

Choosing the winners took nearly three years because of the deluge of entries. Selecting the judges was also a problem, as all of the major composers were also contestants – Copland, Barber, Piston, Sessions, Harris, Chavez, Villa-Lobos, Guarnieri, Ginastera, and scores of others. The first-round judging was done by countries. The United States entries, as Abravanel recalls, were judged solely by conductor Fritz Busch, a refugee from Nazi Germany who, interestingly, had conducted the premiere of Kurt Weill's *The Protagonist* in Dresden in 1926. Robertson had studied violin in Europe with Busch's brother Karl during the early thirties, and the brothers had performed Robertson's chamber works there. The final round included only the winners from each country. The final panel of judges included Aaron Copland, Samuel Barber, Roy Harris, William Schuman, and others eliminated in the first round, with Howard Hanson serving as chair.

Robertson's opinion, confided years after the contest, was that the makeup of the panel of judges during the final consideration probably favored his conservative style. "It was Fritz Busch's influence as a judge that brought me the prize," he declared. "Most awards went to the experimental, avant-garde, fads, or fly-by-night." Robertson had always felt estranged from the "Eastern Establishment" – the better-known, widely performed names in American composition whom he jokingly termed the "Boulangerie," since most had studied in Paris with the legendary teacher-composer Nadia Boulanger. Robertson felt that they dominated all major performance outlets and "inlanders," particularly Mountain West composers, were normally excluded.

Dorsey Callaghan of *The Detroit Free Press* wrote of the *Trilogy*'s "windswept freshness" and of its "American-ness. There are climaxes that are as moving as the snowy peaks of the West that gave it birth; there is a gusty sort of humor that springs only from the American soil." Robertson liked this review best for its sensitivity to his roots.

The *Los Angeles Examiner*'s Patterson Greene reviewed the first Utah Symphony performance on January 3, 1948. He singled out Abravanel, calling his first-season orchestra "surprisingly excellent" and praising his "stimulating direction." Greene also mentioned the indigenous qualities of the *Trilogy*: "The work conveys an overall mood of spaciousness and dignity. It sets off the introduction as solemn as a vista of the Rocky Mountains. . . . The whole work impresses me

Abravanel and "Nostrebor," composer Leroy J. Robertson, whose works the Maestro championed on recordings and in subscription concerts. *Deseret News* photograph in MAP.

as one of the most worthy contributions any American has made to orchestral literature."

Robertson's sudden fame came at a strategic moment in the Utah music world. During the early fall of 1947 Abravanel had met Robertson, had studied his new *Punch and Judy* Overture, and had programmed it for his second concert on November twenty-second. The timing of the *Trilogy*'s award could not have been better. From the outset, Abravanel and Robertson shared ideals and mutual respect and admiration which blossomed into a uniquely cooperative association lasting more than two decades.

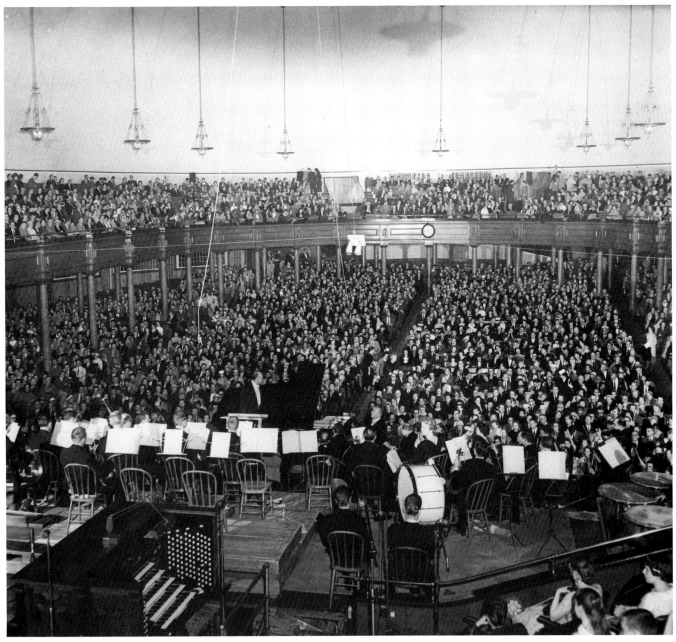

Packed houses like this one, with Jose Iturbe as soloist, made it easy to forget the sparsely-filled Tabernacle of the Symphony's pre-Abravanel seasons. MAP.

Unfortunately, Abravanel remains the sole conductor to perform the *Trilogy*, except for its Detroit premiere. Abravanel was persistent, repeating it again in 1954 and also twenty-two years later as a feature of the 1976 Bicentennial of the American Revolution, five years after the composer's death. In total Abravanel performances Robertson ranks tenth among composers with twenty-eight (one more than Mahler), including several premieres.

PROMISED VALLEY

When Abravanel signed with the Utah Symphony in June of 1947, the celebration of the Centennial of Utah's founding was at its height. Performing arts activity was the greatest in the state's (or Territory's) history, spearheaded by the governor-appointed Centennial Commission chaired by David O. McKay, then a counselor in the LDS Church First Presidency (and later to be president of the church).

The Mormon Tabernacle Choir appeared in an unprecedented series of six Sunday evening concerts. Haydn's *Creation* and Mendelssohn's *Elijah* were performed with guest soloists. Helen Traubel and Leonard Warren, two of opera's leading artists, appeared as soloists in separate concerts. This series was a high-water mark for J. Spencer Cornwall's conductorship, surpassed only by the Choir's first European tour in 1955. Miss Traubel drew the largest crowd of all, singing to a packed Tabernacle. Present for her performance were forty-six state governors who were in Salt Lake City for the National Governors' Conference, hosted by Utah Governor Herbert B. Maw. (The center of attention throughout that conference was New York's Thomas E. Dewey, who became the Republican Party's presidential nominee a year later.)

An unusually large number of name artists also appeared throughout the 1947–48 season on subscription series throughout the state, including those of the well-established Salt Lake Civic Music, University of Utah Master Minds and Artists, and Granite Arts Association. A Centennial Light Opera Company of Utah talent was organized, with Vernon J. LeeMaster as director, and toured the state.

The San Carlo Opera Company of Naples was brought to the University of Utah by Kingsbury Hall manager and impresario Gail Plummer for a week's performances, and a Gilbert and Sullivan troupe entertained for a week at the State Fairgrounds theater.

Promised Valley, an original musical dealing with the Mormon trek west and the settling of the Great Salt Lake Valley, had been commissioned by the Utah Centennial Commission and was to be the celebration's central event, the main attraction.

A successful Crawford Gates, here rehearsing the Rockford (Illinois) Symphony in 1975, fulfilled his early promise. Photograph courtesy of Crawford Gates.

During the summer of 1946, while the Utah Centennial was in the planning stages, Crawford Gates, a twenty-four-year-old Palo Alto native, paused in Salt Lake City on a hot August afternoon en route to Rochester, New York, for graduate composition study with Howard Hanson at the Eastman School of Music. He had just had an automobile accident in the Nevada desert and was waiting for repairs before continuing eastward.

"Why go east and spend all that extra money on tuition, board, and room?" he was asked. "Especially when you can get equivalent or better training right here!" This was a reference to the presence of composer Leroy Robertson on the faculty of Brigham Young University in Provo, Utah.

Gates decided to remain in Utah, and the young composer was introduced to the state in a *Salt Lake Tribune* column on September 30: "The name of Crawford Gates is destined to loom large in the musical future of this region," the author predicted. "Reared in California, his roots are, nevertheless, definitely Utahn, coming as he does from pioneer stock. Music enthusiasts of this area will do well to adopt him 'legally.' "

At about this time another story appeared in the local press announcing that Dr. Lorin F. Wheelwright, production manager of the Arts Division of the Centennial celebration, was flying east to engage a composer for the *Promised Valley* production. Broadway playwright Arnold Sundgaard had already been signed to write the book. The press story heralded the production as a Utah-style *Oklahoma* (whose Broadway success was still ringing in America's ears), but Wheelwright's decision was not a popular one: "An easterner to write and compose the Utah story and score? Don't we have capable writers/composers here?"

In the words of the *Salt Lake Tribune* for October 13, 1946, "The committee owes it to its constituents to exhaust all possibilities in trying to find Utahns to produce these works. For, after all, it is a Utah Centennial." The column suggested some possibilities: Leroy Robertson; Arthur Shepherd, then at Western Reserve University; Leigh Harline, Oscar-winning Disney composer and Utah native; and Gates, Wheelwright, and others.

Things happened fast. The following morning Tracy Y. Cannon, chairman of the Arts Division committee, was on the phone: "Where can we locate Crawford Gates?" The committee wanted to interview him. The young composer was signed for the score of *Promised Valley*. He moved to Salt Lake City after less than a month's study at Brigham Young University and devoted all his time to the musical.

Helen Tamiris, fresh from her Broadway triumph in choreographing *Annie Get Your Gun*, wove her magic with nonprofessional but talented local dancers. She had no qualms about repeating *Annie*'s spectacular Indian dance in *Promised Valley*.

Alfred Drake, star of *Oklahoma* on Broadway, sang the leading role, and young ingenue Jet McDonald sang opposite him. Crowds of more than 180,000 saw the production in the University of Utah's refurbished outdoor stadium. One of the run's most memorable moments occurred when Miss McDonald took a deep breath before hitting a high note and drew in an unsuspecting moth. Both were surprised!

Wheelwright headed the Centennial staff as production manager. C. Lowell (Doc) Lees was director. Gates conducted rehearsals of the marvelously successful musical until other demands became burdensome; then Jay Blackton, one of Broadway's busiest conductors, was called in to take over. Blackton was an old pro, having conducted *Oklahoma*, *Annie Get Your Gun*, and other Broadway hits.

Gates was important to Abravanel, who was in and out of town during *Promised Valley*'s run. Gates had insisted that his orchestral score be played by the Utah Symphony and not by a smaller pit orchestra. The fact that he had written the score for full symphony orchestra added three weeks' welcome salaries to the orchestra's schedule. Abravanel invited Gates to guest-conduct the Symphony in the Tabernacle as a feature of his freshman season, and on February 14, 1948, the composer conducted his Suite from *Promised Valley* with the Symphony and the chorus from the musical.

CHAPTER 5

Academic Overture

"The University of Utah invites the Utah Symphony to make its home on our campus and join with the University in enriching the cultural life of our state." President A. Ray Olpin's amplified voice filled a hushed Tabernacle, the audience bursting into spontaneous applause. The announcement came March 13, 1948, at the intermission of the Symphony's next-to-last concert of Abravanel's first season—a season throughout which his innovative ability had been tested, not only in programming but in patching together an orchestra and rehearsal facilities as well.

None of the strain showed as he took his bows that night. The University's A Cappella Choir had just sung the first Utah performance of Beethoven's Ninth with the Utah Symphony, in a program dedicated to the fledgling United Nations. The soloists were all Salt Lakers: Ruth Clawson, soprano; Annette Dinwoodey, contralto; Ray Brimhall, tenor; and Harold H. Bennett, bass.

The student choir, conducted by Richard P. Condie, included a number of young singers who would play important roles in the arts in Utah: Herold L. Gregory, who became executive director of the Utah Symphony, and his wife Mary Ethel Eccles; twins Janice and Jewel Johnson (Cutler); Claire McMaster; Margaret Hewlett; Vernie Swenson, veteran Tabernacle Choir member; John Marlowe Nielson and Kenly

Whitelock, University music staff members; Orson D. Wright, a local dentist; University librarian Mary Jane Hair, and others.

The Ninth (*Choral*) Symphony, the highlight of the season, was the first of a steady stream of collaborative performances by the Symphony and University choruses. Subsequent seasons always included one or two choral-orchestral masterworks—a total of fifty-eight performances of thirty separate works during the Abravanel years. Important spin-offs were commercial recordings of twenty-five joint works, two of which received Grammy nominations.

The March 14 *Salt Lake Tribune* called President Olpin's invitation "another step in perpetuating the Utah Symphony" whose "members . . . greeted the announcement with enthusiasm. The main advantage," continued the *Tribune*, "would be providing a 'home' for the Symphony and a practice hall. It would make members of the orchestra available to the University staff for private instruction."

After the concert, Abravanel said in an interview: "I am thrilled, absolutely thrilled, with the invitation of Dr. Olpin. . . . I think it could be the greatest step yet taken to help build the orchestra. It would be extremely beneficial to the University as an enlargement of its cultural program. The University must not be just a training school, but an institution for advancement of culture."

Olpin's invitation was not precipitous. He, Abravanel, and composer Leroy Robertson had huddled for weeks. Olpin was new to his presidency, having been inaugurated in 1946.

This portrait of the conductor is stamped "Sol Hurok presents . . . " MAP.

Already he had acquired expertise in dealing with Capitol Hill and the local power structure. He had taken giant steps in transforming what admittedly was a liberal arts college into a full-scale university. The four-year medical school had graduated its first class in 1944, and the first Ph.D. programs and expansion of the graduate school were behind him. Some of the nation's leading scientists, educators, and scholars in the humanities had responded to his invitation to join the faculty.

New professional schools were being organized. Olpin had been readying a College of Fine Arts and sensed the wide popular support for attracting and attaching Abravanel and the Utah Symphony to the campus. Moreover, he wanted to sign Robertson as chairman of the new music department, and he wanted to accomplish all this in one fell swoop! Robertson was at his peak, the toast of the national press.

The advantages of the affiliation for the orchestra were clear. Abravanel had no rehearsal hall except for dress rehearsals in the Tabernacle the night before each concert. Orchestra musicians never knew whether they would be rehearsing in the Moose or Eagles Lodge, the Labor Temple, or the Kiwanis Boys and Girls Club.

These deplorable conditions had caused Robertson and Abravanel to discuss the "University connection" seriously. Abravanel was convinced that a permanent "home" on campus should be pursued and Robertson agreed: Abravanel would encourage President Olpin to appoint Robertson chairman of the music department, and both he and Robertson would lobby Olpin to offer the campus as the Symphony's home. Olpin, for his part, recognizing a masterstroke, tied up the loose ends, cleared the proposal with key advisers, and went public before the Tabernacle audience on March thirteenth. Hailed in both the music and academic worlds as a unique coup, this move by a delighted President Olpin meant that his was the only university in America that could boast a "major symphony orchestra-in-residence."

A large "temporary" World War II barracks building on campus was hastily remodeled during the summer to accommodate rehearsals. "It doesn't look like much," noted one musician, "but the sound is good."

One particularly fruitful aspect of the Symphony–University collaboration was the appointment of the orchestra's principal musicians as music department adjunct faculty, which provided an "instant" conservatory-type artist faculty for student performance majors.

Prior to the Olpin invitation, University music students majoring in any performance specialty had been forced to travel to either coast for expert instruction. Now, with Utah Symphony artists on campus, it became possible to obtain a degree in violin, viola, cello, contrabass, flute, oboe, English horn, clarinet, bassoon, French horn, trumpet, trombone, tuba, harp, or percussion.

Both students and adjunct faculty clearly benefited. Symphony principals earned a modest added income during those early lean years. They also formed a Utah String Quartet, a Woodwind Quintet, and a Brass Ensemble, each offering quarterly public concerts.

Robertson marshalled the University music department's choral forces: Richard Condie's A Cappella Choir, William Peterson's Girls' Glee Club, and J. Marlowe Nielson's Boys' Glee Club. The combined choruses totaled 400, and they spent the entire autumn quarter 1948 rehearsing Beethoven's *Missa Solemnis*. The transition to such a concentrated dose of Beethoven from the lighter, popular college "glees" posed

The University's choral directors—from left to right William Peterson, Richard P. Condie, Leroy Robertson, and John Marlowe Nielson—rose to the challenge of providing well-trained singers to perform with the Utah Symphony. MAP.

problems. Doubly so with the *Missa Solemnis*, which is admittedly the most difficult major choral-orchestral work in the repertoire. To move from their usual lighter fare to Beethoven's loftiest work for chorus and orchestra was hard and frustrating work rather than fun for the college students.

Joint rehearsals were held in Kingsbury Hall with Robertson conducting from the stage and singers seated in the auditorium. Abravanel took over the rehearsals a few days before the performance.

Kingsbury's stage barely accommodated the eighty-member orchestra. A platform for the musicians was built over the small orchestra pit, extending over the first rows of seats, while the singers were seated uncomfortably on stage on bleachers borrowed from the Field House.

Rehearsal in December 1948 for Beethoven's *Missa Solemnis*, a major undertaking and the first in a distinguished series of choral-orchestral collaborations between the University's singers and the Symphony. MAP.

The performance on December 10, 1948, was a noteworthy beginning for the orchestra's association with the University. The musicians played sensitively, and the singers sang enthusiastically. Abravanel had underscored the University–Symphony association at the season's first Tabernacle concert on November 6, 1948, opening with Brahms' *Academic Festival Overture*, "in honor," read the program, "of the Utah Symphony's affiliation with the University of Utah."

During his thirty-two-year tenure, Abravanel gave Brahms' *Academic Festival Overture* eight performances in a continuing gesture to the University. He usually conducted it as a program-opener for a University-related concert, such as the 1950 centennial commemoration of the University's founding. Faculty in that Kingsbury audience rose and joined in the universal German college song "Gaudeamus Igitur," which climaxes the overture.

The joint choral-orchestral history of the Utah Symphony with University choruses is impressive. Bach's *B Minor Mass* and *St. Matthew Passion*, Beethoven's Ninth Symphony and *Missa Solemnis*, Verdi's *Manzoni Requiem*, and Handel's *Messiah* are among the repertoire's most distinguished works. Abravanel himself never conducted the *Messiah*, because locally it was considered the sole property of the Salt Lake Oratorio Society and presented annually in the Tabernacle during the Christmas holidays, at first with a pick-up orchestra, later with the Utah Symphony and guest conductors.

Leroy Robertson, left, Alexander Schreiner, back to camera, and Abravanel with Eugene Ormandy on the University campus in September 1964. The Philadelphia Orchestra was in town to record with the Mormon Tabernacle Choir, and the author asked Abravanel to invite Ormandy to speak to the students. MAP.

Abravanel conducted multiple performances of many masterworks with chorus. Beethoven's Ninth, Verdi's *Requiem*, and Mahler's *Resurrection* Symphony were all heard five times. The only indigenous work, Robertson's *Book of Mormon* Oratorio, also received five Tabernacle performances plus additional ones in Ogden, Provo, and Logan, Utah. Although it was not performed in the Tabernacle, Crawford Gates's choral-orchestral score for the LDS Hill Cumorah Pageant was recorded by the Utah Symphony, with the Brigham Young University A Cappella Choir and soloists.

More novel were Honegger's *King David*, *Judith*, and *Joan of Arc at the Stake*, the latter with guest artist Hollywood actress Dorothy McGuire in the title role; Handel's oratorios *Israel in Egypt*, *Judas Maccabaeus*, and *Samson*; Dubussy's *Blessed Damozel*; Milhaud's *Pacem in Terris*; Vaughan Williams' *Dona Nobis Pacem* and *A Sea Symphony*; Berlioz' *Childhood of Christ* and *Requiem*; Bloch's *Sacred Service*; and Stravinsky's *Symphony of Psalms*.

From 1948 to 1961 the University's student choral organizations comprised the official Utah Symphony chorus and were listed as the Combined University of Utah Choruses.

SUMMER FESTIVAL

The "best show in town" during the summers from 1948 to 1965 was alfresco, in the University's Stadium Bowl, which had been built in 1947 and inaugurated with the state Centennial's *Promised Valley*. The director, C. Lowell Lees, chairman of the University speech department (which at that time included theater) and director of the University Theatre, sensed a crescendo of public enthusiasm for continuing outdoor summer productions.

Olpin's spring coup in bringing Abravanel and Robertson into the University spelled "Go" for a Summer Festival. A scientist unabashedly dedicated to the promotion of the arts, President Olpin appointed a Summer Festival Committee chaired by himself. All meetings were held in his office, and he exercised strong interest in the selection of operas, musicals, and guest artists. His influence was not sufficient, however, to convince the committee that the musical *Rio Rita*, a favorite of his and Mrs. Olpin's, would ever go on the boards.

Rio Rita was produced on Broadway in 1927, the same year as *Show Boat*. The latter was a significant landmark in musical theater. *Rio Rita* was much less successful. The Olpins, living in New York at the time, loved it, but Lees and Abravanel felt it was outdated and insisted on more current shows. Levity prevailed in committee meetings as Olpin persistently nominated *Rio Rita* from the twenties.

Throughout its history, Lees and Abravanel were the Festival's central figures. The original Summer Festival Committee numbered nine and was increased to ten when Willam Christensen joined the faculty in 1951. He had been signed as choreographer for the summers of 1949 and 1950. The following year he left his San Francisco Ballet Company and moved to Salt Lake City with exciting new ideas for the campus.

The first University of Utah Summer Festival featured Jerome Kern's *Show Boat* and Shakespeare's *Midsummer Night's Dream*, with the original and rarely performed Mendelssohn score. Abravanel conducted both from July 14 to 27, 1948. The total attendance was an impressive 44,661.

From 1949 to 1965 the Festival format remained the same—an opera coupled with a Broadway musical. Receipts from the musical usually helped to defray the opera's deficit. Grand operas were usually scheduled for half as many performances as the musicals. Yet on the basis of nightly attendance, many of the operas outdrew the Broadway shows: *Carmen* over *The Great Waltz*, *Faust* over *Promised Valley*, *Tales of Hoffmann* over *The Merry Widow*, and *Samson and Delilah* over *Kiss Me, Kate*. But admittedly, it was the musicals that sold the season tickets, produced the large opera audiences, and paid the freight.

Problems were bound to develop over the years. From the outset there were expected points of friction between artistic directors and business managers. Olpin named Gail Plummer, longtime manager of the University Theatre and Kingsbury Hall (and manager of the formative Utah Symphony in pre-Abravanel days), Festival business manager. This led to artistic versus business clashes between Lees and Plummer and/or Abravanel and Plummer. Each of the three had a direct pipeline to the president, who somehow jockeyed his way through, seeming to revel in personal contact with "artistic temperaments." Although one of the "troika," Christensen managed never to be drawn into these arguments; he remained neutral, an arbitrator, oil-on-the-water.

There was also conflict, usually low-keyed but sometimes spirited, between Abravanel and Lees, particularly concerning opera, which Abravanel felt was his area of expertise because of his European, Australian, and Metropolitan experience. Lees saw opera as theater. A compromise was finally reached. Abravanel got top billing in opera, Lees in musicals.

The Summer Festivals were exciting for the campus and popular with the public. They were a stepping stone for Utah's most celebrated vocalist, Glade Peterson, who was launched from several Festival roles to New York and on to his permanent position as the Zurich Opera Company's leading Puccini tenor for over a decade. The Festival's most memorable production was *Faust* in 1950, which received national attention for its breathtaking three-level sets and strong musical cast. Although the signing of a young Beverly Sills by Abravanel for $500 each for *Traviata* and *Aida* received no public notice at the time, it now looms large in light of Miss Sills' subsequent stardom.

The glamour and good press coverage of the Summer Festivals overshadowed a more important aspect, at least for Abravanel and the orchestra—the addition of two weeks' payroll to their slim eighteen-week contract season. Abravanel worked patiently to expand the season from the eighteen

Rehearsal in the University stadium for one of the Summer Festival operas. *Deseret News* photograph in MAP.

The Summer Festival Troika and a friend. Willam Christensen, Abravanel, Lowell Lees, and the first master's candidate in ballet, Karen Cheney Shores, in the old barracks used for ballet classes, about 1956. MAP.

weeks his first year to a full fifty-two weeks with paid vacation by the time he resigned in 1979.

The Summer Festival died a natural death in 1965 as its strongest advocates left the scene. Olpin retired in 1964, his departure followed a year later by that of Lees, who left to head the Pasadena Playhouse and went on to chair the Rutgers University theater department. He returned to Salt Lake after retirement and taught an evening course for the theater department. The main stage of Pioneer Memorial Theatre was named for him. He died in 1973.

MR. C

Ballet master Willam Christensen returned to his native Utah in 1951 after decades of success climaxed by national recognition of his San Francisco Ballet Company. Later he admitted that he had been "testing the climate for the performing arts in Salt Lake City." After two Summer Festivals, he decided "the water was fine." Lees announced on November 27, 1950, that Christensen would be returning permanently; and on May 1, 1951, he accepted a University appointment as professor of ballet. He set to work choreographing the 1951 Summer Festival productions of *The Great Waltz* and *Tales of Hoffmann*. This leap from the glamorous

professional world to academia was daring, but Christensen knew exactly what he was doing. "The presence of a professional symphony orchestra" was an all-important factor in his decision.

Christensen soon became "Bill"; every local newspaper's copy-desk invariably changed "Willam" to "William." (The same pattern inevitably transformed "violoncello" into "violincello.")

Christensen joined Abravanel and Lees in a Summer Festival artistic triumvirate. He avoided the frequent and heated artistic arguments, focusing instead on adding high quality to heretofore semiprofessional choreography. Olpin ran interference with courage, vision, and fortitude. While his invitation to the Utah Symphony to make its home on campus had brought protests from some quarters, Christensen's hiring inspired a now-famous newspaper headline: "What? A Toe-dancer on the University Faculty?" This expression of outrage was Governor J. Bracken Lee's.

Nor was it only politicians; some simon-pure academics on the faculty questioned the propriety of Christensen's appointment. "Ballet doesn't belong on a campus." "No other university has a ballet program," some argued, and "besides, Christensen has no degrees!"

But Christensen hadn't returned solely to choreograph Summer Festival operas and musicals. He had come home with an imaginative plan that was to influence ballet training throughout America. He aimed for an absolutely new concept in American ballet: a baccalaureate curriculum demanding rigorous professional studio training coupled with and enriched by university liberal arts and sciences studies. The Bachelor of Fine Arts (B.F.A.) degree in ballet was approved by the Regents in 1953; the wheels of academe, greased by Christensen's enthusiasm and the vision of other key University figures, sped the new degree on its way.

Almost overnight, ballet became the most cosmopolitan program on campus, with all fifty states and several foreign countries represented among its students. The most surprising artistic event of that first year was Christensen's public introduction of his student corps to a Kingsbury Hall audience. There was no choreography, no program as such. Instead, Christensen simply had his dancers go through their barre exercises and practice routines. It was novel and charming; everyone was delighted and curious as to what he would do next.

In 1955, just two years after the baccalaureate degree was approved, Christensen scheduled, with some trepidation, Tchaikovsky's *Nutcracker*. He had choreographed and directed the first American performance of the complete ballet in San Francisco in 1944. Christensen's *Nutcracker* was destined to be his greatest success by all odds. It has played annually in Salt Lake City and on tour during the Yuletide season to more than a million people. Christensen insisted from the outset, against pressure from business manager Gail Plummer, that the full Utah Symphony play the score. The *Nutcracker* added two weeks' salaries to Abravanel's musicians' contracts and expanded further in later years. Coupled with two additional weeks during the Summer Festivals, their contracts were already increased by a month. During these early, difficult years, ballet productions and Summer Festivals were godsends to the Symphony.

Abravanel conducted all performances annually, playing one of the world's most danceable *Nutcrackers*, from 1959 to 1969, when he retired from conducting ballet. He was succeeded by Ardean Watts, the Symphony's associate conductor, through 1983. Watts made some observations in the *Salt Lake Tribune* in December 1979: "Looking back at how *The Nutcracker* has grown over the years, I sometimes wonder what would have happened if Maurice Abravanel, Bill Christensen, and C. Lowell Lees had not taken the gamble the first year. It obviously has altered the course of ballet here. It is the strongest income-producing ballet for every company in the country that presents it." Watts also recalled how Abravanel hated to give up conducting it: "He had retired from ballet conducting, but he still loved doing *The Nutcracker*. He hated to let it go."

A short time after joining the University faculty, Christensen organized the Utah Theatre Ballet Company, a semiprofessional spinoff from the University ballet department. Aided by a Ford Foundation matching-funds grant of $175,000, this company was reorganized as the Utah Civic Ballet in 1963. The grant provided $35,000 annually from 1964 to 1966. The redoubtable and energetic Glenn Walker Wallace, longtime ballet patron and one-time president of the Symphony, became president of the Utah Civic Ballet in 1963 and headed the successful financial drive to build a professional company.

In 1968, at the request of the Federation of Rocky Mountain States, the company's name was changed to Ballet West, a move intended to portray the company as representing not only Utah but the entire West. It soon was recognized as one of the nation's five largest professional companies and praised by *Dance Magazine* as "America's third finest." The company has won international acclaim with European and Far Eastern tours, but to the observers of the region's cultural development, Ballet West will always be the creation of William Christensen, aided and abetted by Utah's principal backers of the arts, headed by Maurice Abravanel.

Somewhere along the way Christensen became, affectionately, "Mr. C." Made Professor Emeritus at the University in 1971, he was recalled to active status in 1981 and rejoined the faculty in an exciting new ballet curriculum combining the University faculty and resources with Ballet West's artistic staff and a special Christensen-trained "junior" Ballet West.

The "University connection" launched by Abravanel, Olpin, and Robertson in March of 1948 was to prove one of the most creative associations in American music. The groundwork was now laid for the remarkable Contemporary Music Festival and for decades of precedent-setting collaborations between art and the academy.

CHAPTER 6

Crisis

In November of 1947, on the heels of his first two concerts, Abravanel received a long-distance call from Houston Symphony officials: "Will you come to Houston as music director of the Houston Symphony?" They offered to increase his salary substantially.

"They promised me the moon," he recalls. "They told me money was no problem in Texas and that I could engage whatever musicians I wanted from Los Angeles and New York."

Abravanel advised Utah Symphony president Fred E. Smith of the offer in late January. Smith had also received a Houston call and declared, "We're folding, Maurice. The Utah Symphony is folding! My advice is to accept their offer." Board member Morris Rosenblatt appealed to the conductor to stay, however, offering generous patronage and continued support. In 1946 the Board had campaigned to raise $150,000 to help underwrite the budget for three years. They had raised only $92,000, however, and the Symphony was now beset by serious financial woes.

Despite Houston's attractive offer and Smith's discouraging prognosis, Abravanel was determined to stay and stabilize the orchestra, come what might. He declined the Texas

All the Maestro's considerable persuasive powers would be needed during the financial crisis of his second season in Utah. MAP.

invitation, although the Houston group indicated that they would return later with another offer.

As a young man, Fred Smith had pursued an operatic career. He had sung some roles at the Metropolitan Opera and was considered quite expert in German opera, but he gave up that financially precarious life to success in banking. He was President of the First National Bank of Salt Lake City and a director of First Security Corporation from 1931 until his death in 1963.

In 1940 Smith had become president of the Symphony Board, and under his leadership that group upgraded the Symphony in 1946 from a semiprofessional community ensemble without a regularly planned season to a group of fully professional musicians with an eighteen-week contract season.

During the summer of 1948 Smith had tendered his resignation from the Board. Abravanel regretted his decision, as Smith was completely in sympathy with Abravanel's long-range plans for gradual, certain growth toward excellence. Even though they had worked together for only one season, their association was treasured by Abravanel, who dedicated a concert to his friend's memory on October 14, 1964. A Smith favorite was featured, Richard Strauss's *Death and Transfiguration.*

Smith's officers had included Glenn Walker Wallace as vice president, Seymour Wells as treasurer of both the Symphony and Utah Art Institute boards, and Gail Martin as

The opportunity to launch a new musical lured Abravanel back to Broadway briefly in 1949. Stars Priscilla Gillette and Brenda Lewis join author/composer Marc Blitzstein and the Maestro in a discussion of *Regina*, based on Lillian Hellman's play *The Little Foxes*. Although the Utah Symphony season began a little late that year, the state basked in the reflected glory of Abravanel's Tony Award for the year's "Best Musical Direction of a Musical." Committed to Utah, Abravanel had turned down the invitation of Lerner and Loewe to conduct *Brigadoon*. MAP.

Glenn Walker Wallace, Symphony Board President during the financial crisis. *Deseret News* photograph.

secretary, with a number of distinguished citizens serving as directors. A new Board would have to weather a severe financial crisis.

Mrs. Wallace was named as acting president. She had been a strong, energetic Symphony officer and board member since 1922, when she was elected president of the Salt Lake Philharmonic Society, a Symphony predecessor. Her interest in ballet dated at least from the same period. George D. Pyper's *Romance of an Old Playhouse*, the story of the old Salt Lake Theatre, notes that "Glenn Walker Wallace appeared as *danceuse*," in a production of the Emma Lucy Gates and B. Cecil Gates Opera Company. She was elected Symphony president on October 1, 1948, with Calvin W. Rawlings, Salt Lake attorney and civic leader as first vice president, Utah Supreme Court Justice J. Allan Crockett as second vice

president, and her husband, banker and civic leader John M. Wallace, as secretary. The Board, Abravanel, and the musicians would face the crisis squarely, unflinching in public regardless of their private feelings and conflicts.

A special concert dedicated to the LDS Church in appreciation for the continued use of the Tabernacle opened the season on November sixth. LDS President George Albert Smith attended and made a brief intermission response.

Morris Rosenblatt, chairman of the Symphony Board's finance committee, announced a series of Dedicatory Concerts for the Utah Symphony Progress Fund. His message was upbeat and optimistic: "Through the support of industry, the utilities, municipalities and special groups the current season of the Utah Symphony is going forward. . . . " Heading the list of sponsors were the LDS Church, the public utilities, Salt Lake County, and Kennecott Copper. Rosenblatt's idea was sound, but Abravanel recalls that it actually netted little money. Most sponsoring organizations were really being honored for long-standing services "in kind."

Later in November, Symphony manager Ruth Cowan told Abravanel that there wasn't enough money for the current payroll. That particular payroll was paid anonymously by Board member James L. White, a civic leader and supporter of the arts, and disaster was temporarily averted.

At the beginning of the season, the treasurer's statement for the previous year had revealed a deficit of $15,000. On December 8, the Board voted to request a deficit appropriation of $10,000 from the State Board of Examiners. The examiners deferred the request for consideration by the new state legislature scheduled to convene in several weeks. Mrs. Wallace and Morris Rosenblatt stepped in with a $10,000 loan.

When the orchestra played the sixth concert of its ninth subscription season on January 22, 1949, the financial crisis had deepened. The following day the music page of the *Salt Lake Tribune* warned: "The Utah Symphony is sick financially. Musically it glows with health but when it comes to meeting biweekly payrolls . . . it is usually a matter of eking out an existence. . . . It is within the realm of possibility that our excellent orchestra might 'fold' because of the tremendous financial burden of maintaining it on a full-time basis."

The Utah Legislature met in regular session in January, on the heels of the inauguration of Governor J. Bracken Lee, former mayor of Price, Utah, succeeding popular two-term governor Herbert B. Maw. Governor Maw had recommended and the Legislature had passed deficit appropriations in some previous years. Several Board members assured Abravanel that Governor Lee would follow suit, but those who knew Bracken Lee feared that this might not be the case.

Mrs. Wallace phoned Abravanel on Thursday, January twenty-eighth. Abravanel remembers well that "she and Symphony manager Ruth Cowan had been directed by the Board to attend the orchestra's rehearsal next day to notify the musicians that the Symphony was 'dissolved.'" During a 1986 interview for University television station KUED, Abravanel recalled the situation as if it were yesterday:

As a candidate for governor, J. Bracken Lee had been approached by some Board members and had promised to support a deficit appropriation for the Symphony. Then he reneged on that. There was no deficit appropriation. . . . Those Board members felt then that Governor Bracken Lee, after his election, had double-crossed them, which he had, no question. They knew they could

not raise any more money because they had tried for three years to reach their goal of $150,000.

When I heard that Mrs. Wallace and Ruth Cowan were coming to the rehearsal the next morning to tell the musicians it was all over, I said to the ladies "please don't say it's all over, because that is illegal. We have a term contract with the musicians. They have a contract . . . and are committed to us. So are you committed."

They answered "what can we do? We have no assets," which was true. It was clear that the state would not come through, and the city and county could not give more. . . . The public had been asked for donations for three years, so how could they be asked for more?

What could be done? I convinced those Symphony officials not to come to the rehearsal. "If you come, I will be very embarrassed and will have to tell the musicians to disregard what you say. It's illegal, so please don't come". . . .

I told the orchestra "I believe this community is basically a very exceptionally decent community. You have not been paid to walk off the job; that would only be hastening . . . the finality of the Board's decision, and if they cannot raise the money while you play concerts, how can they if you stop playing concerts?"

This didn't exactly convince them. I just told them the facts of life as I saw them. I told them I would be there as scheduled eight times a week. I would understand if anybody could not come because he had to buy the groceries for his family. We had eighty musicians at that time. I told them if I only had twenty-eight, I would play Haydn and Mozart—but we would play!

First horn player Allan Fuchs told a Board member that "Maurice could be black-listed" by the American Federation of Musicians and never again permitted to conduct any union orchestra for insisting on continuing rehearsals and concerts without paying his musicians.

Concertmaster Leonard Posner requested a meeting with the entire board of directors to further plead the musicians' case. The "imports," the orchestra's key personnel, were understandably nervous. (By the 1948–49 season, first clarinet Napoleon Cerminara had been replaced by Herbert Blayman and first trumpet Stewart Grow by Herbert Eisenberg.) The remaining seventy-three musicians were Utah natives or long-term residents for the most part and were disposed to be more patient. It was only Abravanel's persuasive reassurance that the Utah Symphony Board would meet its contractual commitments that kept the newcomers from jumping ship.

The desperate Board considered canceling the season's three remaining concerts, but Abravanel and some Board members insisted on finishing the season. The "imports" refused to play in the Ogden matinee on February 19, however, although Abravanel prevailed upon them to play the Tabernacle concert that same evening. Mrs. Wallace attended both Ogden and Salt Lake concerts.

On February 3, 1949, representatives of the Board appeared before the Joint Appropriations Committee of the Utah Legislature, and "an almost constant vigil of nearly two weeks was set up in the legislative halls at the State Capitol." According to *Deseret News* music critic and political reporter Conrad B. Harrison, "Mrs. John M. Wallace, Symphony president, headed the move, and, along with Mr. Abravanel, members of the board and other orchestra supporters worked 'round the clock' during that period."

A deficit appropriation request of $50,000 was agreed upon. Calvin W. Rawlings, perennial Democratic national committeeman and the Board's first vice president, told the Committee that "the Symphony would 'fold' if it didn't get an emergency appropriation. He said the deficit was already $35,000 and an additional $15,000 would be needed. Unless this money is forthcoming from the Legislature, the orchestra will go into bankruptcy and be forced to liquidate after the Saturday night [February 5] concert!" wrote Harrison.

A number of leading citizens appeared before the Appropriations Committee to endorse the deficit appropriation, including distinguished American composer Roy Harris, then in residence at Utah State Agricultural College (now Utah State University), Morris Rosenblatt, and President A. Ray Olpin, then also a Board member.

Rawlings requested an additional appropriation of $100,000 for the 1949–51 biennium to cover deficits of $50,000 each for two future seasons. According to Harrison, the Appropriations Committee "Took this under advisement and suggested the emergency appropriation be taken directly to the floor of the legislature."

This was February 5, a day of intense political maneu-

vering which concluded with a regular subscription concert in the Tabernacle. Few in the audience were aware of the orchestra's perilous situation. The many legislators in attendance heard one of the Symphony's most exciting performances when Bloch's *Schelomo* was performed for the first time in Utah, with the fine Spanish cellist Gaspar Cassado.

On Monday, February 7, a bill calling for $40,000 (rather than the $50,000 requested) was presented to the Utah Senate by two of its most capable and respected members, Senators Mitchell Melich (R., Moab) and J. Francis Fowles (D., Ogden).

Symphony faithful had flocked to the State Capitol en masse to lobby for the bill—noisy and uncompromising and obviously infiltrated by "fringe" groups seeking political advantage. After some cheerleading in the rotunda they crowded into the Senate gallery. Composer Leroy Robertson, a folk hero to many rural senators because of his international recognition, was invited to the floor to speak. He gave an impassioned plea for the deficit appropriation and received an ovation from senators and gallery. He was impressed and excited by his reception, remarking to friends at the session's conclusion: "I think I could run for governor." In the heady flush of the occasion, he was deadly serious. In the heat of the moment both houses passed the bill with huge majorities. The House voted 46 to 12 and the Senate 20 to 3. The Symphony crowd left light of heart, thinking they had won the war.

Emma Lucy Gates Bowen, Utah's grande dame of music and hostess of memorable soirees honoring visiting celebrities, local artists, business and church leaders, held forth that same evening in her spacious home. Abravanel and his wife Lucy were among the guests. Abravanel recalls that "Emmy Lucy" introduced them to "a distinguished church leader, J. Reuben Clark, Jr., of the LDS Church First Presidency." After some introductory conversation, Abravanel mentioned that the Legislature had approved the Symphony's deficit appropriation. "They did, did they?" was President Clark's response.

At this time President George Albert Smith was not in good health, and President Clark was the Church's powerful voice. Naturally, Abravanel was most anxious to win his support for the orchestra. As it happened, Clark was fond of inviting guests to his home to listen to hours of opera record-

The Orchestra. MAP.

ings, but he did not like symphonic music and also happened to be adamantly against subsidies for the arts.

The following day a two-column, twenty-one-inch editorial appeared in the *Deseret News*: "The state should not be asked to assume and should not assume the burden of meeting this year's deficit of the symphony, nor of hereafter main-

taining it, a plan which reports say is in the minds of some." The editorial recognized that:

some of those who were the original proponents and sponsors of the symphony movement, to the effect that the deficit must be met, seem to show they thoroughly understand the situation and that they are determined to meet it in order to satisfy their feelings as to the need of the community for cultural uplift. . . . From what we know of the sponsors we are persuaded they are amply able to assume this burden and carry it.

But if the wealth of the city is not prepared to finance the enterprise, it should be postponed until the conditions change.

The writer also compared the Mormon Tabernacle Choir with the Utah Symphony, suggesting that the famed choir had had no need of subsidy in its near-100-year history, so "why should the symphony?" The rather naive editorialist was unaware of their two "different worlds," the Choir being a purely volunteer group, and the Symphony a professional organization with a union contract. In comparing their financial operations, he had entirely missed the point.

The editorial accurately pointed out that "the Church has been generous, furnishing the Tabernacle [for dress rehearsals and concerts], with heat and light, without any charge" save for clean-up. Abravanel and the Symphony, ever-cognizant of this generous thirty-three-year gesture, expressed profuse appreciation through the years.

The pro-Symphony lobbyists lost the war although they had won the initial skirmish. Not only did they have President Clark to deal with, they had not reckoned on brand-new Governor J. Bracken Lee's own philosophy on such matters. The day after the *Deseret News* editorial he vetoed the appropriation, and his veto was upheld in the Senate on a party-line vote of 13 to 10. Even though the Democrats held majorities in both houses, they fell short of the necessary two-thirds or 16 votes in the Senate.

When Abravanel is asked "What *really* happened?" he quotes State Senator Mitchell Melich: "It was very simple. President Clark simply told Orval W. Adams [a Church banker] to call on Governor Lee and explain their position." While Melich's version is accurate, Lee would have vetoed the bill regardless, as a matter of his personal political views. The Board members who had counted on the new governor's support had been quite mistaken.

Shortly after the Lee veto was sustained, the *New York Times* commented:

The Utah Symphony, one of the few orchestras in the country which received any form of government support, has lost its state grant. Governor Bracken Lee vetoed the $50,000 appropriation proposed for the 1948–49 season and there is no chance of any more government aid for at least two years. To counteract the loss, a drive is being conducted for $100,000 – seventy per cent of this being sought for next season, with the rest to make up deficits.

Maurice Abravanel, conductor the last two years, is taking a hand in the campaign. He feels that, since private individuals no longer have the means to be lavish patrons, corporations are the logical ones to replace them in upholding the arts that cannot fully pay their own way. He has been on a visit to the East to call on corporations with interests in Utah, asking them if they will help support the symphony.

In the flurry of the crisis, echoes of the Houston Symphony's offer to Abravanel were heard. Frances G. Bennett recalls a visit to Houston at the time:

The Abravanels at home in Salt Lake City. Newspaper photograph in MAP.

In 1949 my husband [Wallace] was President of the National Association of Manufacturers, a full-time job for a year, involving a lot of travel. I went with him on his first trip through the South, and one of his stops was Houston, Texas. The wife of the N.A.M. director, who lived there, asked if I would like to go with her to the symphony concert.

I was delighted, as I always enjoy a good symphony concert. . . . She said they had been looking for a new music director for the symphony and they had spent the previous year with guest conductors, trying to find the right person. . . .

I asked her if she would mind telling me what the offer had been. She told me, and I remember being surprised to hear how large it was. I told her I was sure we couldn't have offered Abravanel that much. . . . I was curious to know just what our own offer had been. Dave Romney was the business manager of our symphony at the time and a very dear friend. When I returned home, I asked him how much Mr. Abravanel was being paid. He told me, and it was just half of what Houston had offered!

Dave said that Mr. Abravanel said although the Houston Symphony was an excellent one, that he was a "pioneer" at heart and admired our spirit and would enjoy building a symphony of his own in Salt Lake City.

Adversaries Abravanel and Governor J. Bracken Lee appear to have declared a temporary truce. *Deseret News* photograph in MAP.

In retrospect, Governor Lee's veto may have rallied Symphony officials and music lovers to renew the fight. An indignant Abravanel, "mad as Hades," resolved to do battle "like an 1847 pioneer" in this "greatest challenge" of his forty-six years. He announced that he had refused the Houston offer and was going to remain in Utah to fight for the orchestra and for Utah's cultural future.

In his Symphony program column for February 19, Jack Goodman wrote, "despite the most severe mental and financial strain . . . members of the Utah Symphony Board have spent sleepless nights and busy days endeavoring . . . to raise funds from . . . public and private sources."

The veto was history, and the Symphony was back to square one. There were no payroll funds and no paychecks for several weeks. The imported principal musicians met to inform Abravanel that "They would not play any longer without payment of salaries called for in their contract."

During this critical period Abravanel was naturally much concerned with the musicians' union:

> I talked to the then secretary of the local union, Ben Bullough. God bless his soul! Ben said, "Mr. Abravanel, my duty of course would be to stop the whole thing right away, but I'm going out on a limb. I'm going to look the wrong—the *other*—way. We have tried to have an orchestra here for one hundred years, and we have had a few concerts for a season, or maybe four or five concerts, and then it would stop. Now for the first time we feel it might stick. We might have an orchestra. And if we stopped it now, we might never have one. If they cannot raise that money while you continue to play the concerts, obviously they could not raise it if you don't play concerts. Therefore, go ahead! I'm going to close my eyes."

If the Utah Symphony members had done what most union locals would have demanded, "to stop playing because they were not paid," it would have taken "another five or ten years before we would have had an orchestra again," Abravanel concludes. He admits it was a real risk, but also a chance that had to be taken. "Unions sometimes have very silly rules, make very stupid decisions, but I must say for the local union there that it has been fully cooperative."

"Mrs. Wallace and her husband then pledged a note . . . to help cover existing salaries owed," recalls Abravanel. "It covered about half the amount due." The remainder was forthcoming from other Board members and friends of the Symphony, "big" and "little" people who were anxious for the orchestra to return in the 1949–50 season.

All the musicians were paid, but at the end of the season the principals severed connections with the orchestra. Posner went to Toscanini's NBC Symphony and later to the University of Texas at Austin; Allan and Norman Fuchs went to the Metropolitan Opera Orchestra and the Pittsburgh Symphony, respectively; Herbert Blayman also joined the Metropolitan Opera Orchestra; and Herbert Eisenberg and John Swallow went to Radio City Music Hall.

The financial crisis consumed so much time and energy of the Board, management, and orchestra personnel, to say nothing of the media, that the music was sometimes lost in the shuffle. There were important performances throughout Abravanel's stormy second season, however.

The *Missa Solemnis* performances with the University choruses represented a high-water mark. The mere fact that this intricate, difficult, demanding Beethoven masterwork could be attempted meant that all the great choral-orchestral music was within reach. Roy Harris conducting his Third Symphony (termed America's "greatest" by Koussevitsky) reminded audiences that one of America's distinguished composers was in residence on the Logan campus.

Abravanel had initiated his series of live broadcasts from the Kingsbury Hall stage. (Musically the concerts were a success, but the audiences tended to listen at home.) The February performance of Bloch's *Schelomo* by cellist Gaspar Cassado had been outstanding, and the March 5 program was typical of Abravanel's best programming, featuring Prokofiev's *Classical Symphony*, Tchaikovsky's Violin Concerto with Isaac Stern, and Beethoven's Seventh.

In an upbeat full-page letter that appeared in the program for the March 19 concert, Mrs. Wallace referred to "a successful close of the ninth season of the Utah Symphony Orchestra," reminding symphony-goers that the orchestra had begun officially in 1940. She continued: "We are looking forward to next season with a feeling of encouragement. We are indeed fortunate to have Maurice Abravanel as Musi-

Abravanel with popular guest soloist Isaac Stern. Martin Zwick
photograph (MZPC).

cal Director for the coming year." She then announced, "Beginning this spring the Utah Symphony Board will conduct an
annual campaign for funds. Every possible effort will be made
to maintain the high standard set during the past two years
under the inspired leadership of Maurice Abravanel."

In his column the next day, *Deseret News* music critic
Conrad B. Harrison reported Abravanel's extemporaneous
remarks at the concert's conclusion: "He simply restated his
faith in the orchestra and the people in the face of serious
troubles, and this speech brought the crowd of 4,000 to its
feet, cheering. One subscriber observed: 'They probably could
have paid the entire deficit if they'd passed the hat after that
speech!' "

Abravanel conducting in a classroom. MAP.

CHAPTER 7

A Four-letter Word? Contemporary

One of the most exciting University–Symphony collaborations was an outgrowth of Abravanel's dedication to contemporary music – a daring undertaking given his conservative mainstream audiences.

For his second subscription concert, in November 1947, he had programmed Aaron Copland's brand-new *Appalachian Spring*, Samuel Barber's *Adagio for Strings*, and William Schuman's *Side Show*. Abravanel says, "Not a bad choice for a young man, eh? All three composers became world renowned. The first two works, in particular, are now an accepted part of the repertoire."

Responding to the same program that had aroused Mrs. Wallace's ire, George M. Gadsby, a Board member and head of Utah Power and Light, telephoned Symphony manager Ruth Cowan the next morning: "Will you tell Mr. Abravanel, if that's the music he's going to play, don't expect one penny from us!"

Abravanel phoned right back. "I understand you didn't like the contemporary music last night and said not to expect a penny from you."

"No!" he retorted. "And let me tell you, Salt Lake City doesn't like it!"

Abravanel countered with, "Isn't that economic boycott?" "Economic boycott" was a forbidden phrase in those early years of Harry Truman's Fair Deal. "Gadsby reconsidered and came to our manager the next day with a personal check as a peace offering!"

Some of the community's leading musicians were also offended by "new" music. "Dr. Lorin Wheelwright told my manager at the Rotary Club that Rotarians were up in arms! And that he took his wife home after the concert and played 'Annie Laurie' to get rid of the bad taste."

Abravanel phoned Wheelwright: " 'Look, if you want a whole evening concert of ballads, "Annie Laurie," *Countess Maritza*, *Oklahoma* – anything you want, I'll play it in Kingsbury Hall, if you get Rotary to guarantee one thousand tickets at two dollars each.' That was the end of that." It was also the end, essentially, of serious complaints about programming in the Tabernacle.

Abravanel took a giant leap into contemporary music in 1958 when he and Olpin agreed to the University's cosponsoring two pairs of contemporary concerts annually in Kingsbury Hall. The Festival of Contemporary Music was born and continued throughout Abravanel's tenure and beyond to 1982.

Originally, Abravanel had envisioned the concerts as a "connoisseur" series. (In fact, he conducted an initial program of Bach's Brandenburg Concertos.) The University felt that the contemporary series was the arts' counterpart to research in the sciences. President Olpin often described the works Abravanel programmed as "exploring new frontiers."

Initially, the concerts were offered as "specials" on campus. In 1974 they were moved from Kingsbury Hall to the Tabernacle and included as an option on season tickets. The

Aaron Copland conducted his own work in the Contemporary Music Festival in 1966. MAP.

Abravanel with his friend, composer Henri Lazarof, winner of the La Scala Prize of the City of Milan and Composer in Residence of the City of Berlin, in June 1973. MAP.

University continued its cosponsorship, however, and a music faculty committee served as advisers. More than 160 new works were introduced to predominantly youthful audiences.

During the early years of the Contemporary Festival, Abravanel pointedly expressed appreciation to Olpin for sponsoring the campus series. After the orchestra's opening number, Abravanel would face the Kingsbury Hall audience and shout "Is President Olpin here? Ray, are you out there?" And he would ask that a spotlight be turned on Olpin. To the audience Abravanel would then announce: "This is the man who, although a scientist, yet enthusiastically promotes the arts." Reluctantly, President Olpin would get to his feet and acknowledge the applause.

Many times, however, Olpin's busy schedule would not allow him to attend. Abravanel would still call out: "President Olpin, are you out there? Ray, where are you?" Then, with a twinkle in his eye, he would say: "He must be at the basketball game!" (another campus activity Olpin passionately supported).

Middle-tier University officials often expressed concern that the hall was only slightly more than half full each night. Abravanel, on the other hand, was elated: "We are attracting larger audiences to contemporary music than in most larger cities."

The first three years' programming is impressive. Most of the twentieth century's major works were performed, and most were not included on a subscription series: Stravinsky's *Apollo*, *The Fairy's Kiss*, *Pulcinella*, *Song of the Nightingale*, Octet for Winds, and Concerto for Violin and Orchestra; Prokofiev's *Romeo and Juliet*, *Lieutenant Kije Suite*, *The Love for Three Oranges*, *Scythian Suite*, *Overture on Jewish Themes*; Milhaud's *La Création du Monde*, *Le Boeuf sur le Toit*; Berg's *Wozzeck* excerpts; Webern's *Six Pieces for Large Orchestra*; Bartok's *Music for Strings, Percussion and Celeste*; Copland's *Our Town*; Ives' Symphony No. 2; Kennan's *Night Soliloquy*; Barlow's *The Winter's Passed*; and Phillips' *Concert Piece for Bass and Strings*. And this is only the first three years' repertoire. The pace continued for twenty-four years, through 1982.

In all, 164 performances of 162 works (only Berg's *Wozzeck* and Gould's *Soundings* were repeated) were given their first local performances in the University's Festival of Contemporary Music. Not surprisingly, Stravinsky was the most performed composer (sixteen), followed by Prokofiev (ten) and Copland and Ives (eight each). Not a "major" composer but a definite Abravanel favorite was Henri Lazarof of UCLA (six). Receiving four performances were Béla Bartók, Ned Rorem, Samuel Barber, Alban Berg, Leonard Bernstein, Crawford Gates, Darius Milhaud, and Sir William Walton.

Sixty-three other composers' works received from one to three performances each.

There were valuable spin-offs. Sixteen "local" composers were heard, among them Crawford Gates, Leroy Robertson, Ned Rorem, Theodor Antoniou, Ramiro Cortés, Alexei Haieff, John LaMontaine, and Vladimir Ussachevsky. All but Gates were composers-in-residence on the University of Utah campus. Cortés and Ussachevsky also had works performed in the Tabernacle subscription series, and Cortés (who died in 1984) later in Symphony Hall as well.

The Contemporary Music Festival challenged the Symphony musicians. MAP.

Abravanel conducted all concerts during the Festival's early years, but eventually he shared the podium with several guests. The orchestra's associate conductor, Ardean Watts, appeared eight times. Gunther Schuller conducted three times, Aaron Copland and Henri Lazarof twice each. Lukas Foss, Crawford Gates, Joseph Rosenstock, James DePreist, Ralph Laycock, and Sarah Caldwell each conducted one concert.

Aaron Copland, dean of American composers, made two visits, conducting much of his own music by request. He first guest-conducted on January 25 and 26, 1966, in Kingsbury Hall. An honorary doctorate was conferred on him by President Olpin on that occasion.

Ten years later, on March 19, 1976, he conducted an all-Copland program for a packed Tabernacle as a feature of Utah's observance of the Bicentennial of the American Revolution. He had been invited months in advance to compose a brief fanfare for the occasion. His response read: "I would love to write a fanfare, but I'm sorry – I'm all 'fanfared' out!" He was seventy-six at the time.

Lukas Foss, American composer-conductor, raised a ruckus when he appeared as the Festival's guest conductor in 1968. He programmed his own *Baroque Variations*, which Abravanel had heard at Lincoln Center with the New York Philharmonic under Bernstein. "The president of the Philharmonic gave Lucy and me two chairs next to him in his box. So there we were. This was a new piece, a world premiere by Lukas Foss." Foss was a brilliant young musician, one of music's "naughty boys" of experimentation and dissonance. Abravanel recalls "Bernstein's magnificent performance of Mahler's Sixth Symphony, the program's major work. Magnificent – never heard it better in my life. But preceding the Mahler was Lukas Foss's piece called *Phorion*, with the very poetic idea of a dream with waves bringing music and taking them back." Abravanel was startled: "When the piece began, it was the E Major *Prelude* of Bach, and I was so furious that if I had not been sitting next to the Board President, I would have yelled, 'Leave Bach alone! Do whatever you want, but leave Bach alone!' "

In spite of what Abravanel thought of his treatment of Bach, the Maestro invited Foss to conduct a pair of contemporary concerts in November of 1968. "I would like you to perform your *Baroque Variations* [of which *Phorion* is the second]." Surprised, Foss asked, "Really – the whole thing?"

Abravanel and Dr. Billy Taylor, who soloed in the Tabernacle in the world premiere of his own *Suite for Piano and Orchestra* in 1973. MZPC.

Abravanel answered, "Yes, I would love you to. I strongly feel that interested young people in the community should have the opportunity to know what young people who are really not mad – called composers – are composing. Even if they don't like it on first hearing, they should give it a try."

Abravanel recounts Foss's visit:

Well, I came to the Lukas Foss dress rehearsal. I am very near-sighted. I really hadn't seen what had gone on onstage at the Lincoln Center premiere . . . so I discovered for the first time here at the Kingsbury Hall dress rehearsal that Lukas Foss not only had an electric organ, but at one point he also used a garbage can! When I saw that I thought, "Oh, what luck we're not in the Tabernacle for this concert!"

Can you imagine the garbage can in the percussion section in the Tabernacle or having to tell Lukas Foss, "I know, artistically, it's indispensable, but still this is basically a religious building." Censorship! "Personally, I'm all for it, Lukas, but the nation's press might say: 'Those bad Mormons, like Abravanel, are censoring.' " So this is how far out some contemporary composers go with percussion instruments. Garbage can in B flat!

President A. Ray Olpin presents Maestro Abravanel with an honorary doctorate in 1957. MAP.

Abravanel never faltered in his commitment to contemporary scores in the regular Tabernacle subscription series. His record compares favorably with that of any other major symphony. The Contemporary Music Festival on campus complemented and enriched the Tabernacle series. Abravanel conducted fifty-three world premieres of works by American composers, many of them from the West. In 1971 he received Columbia University's Alice M. Ditson Conductor's Award honoring the conductor who most encouraged contemporary American music.

The complaints of Mrs. Wallace and Mr. Gadsby in the fall of 1947 hadn't restrained Abravanel from playing Stravinsky the following January seventeenth. He concluded that concert with the first Utah performance of Stravinsky's *Firebird Suite*, which was long overdue in Salt Lake, having been premiered in Paris in 1911. All major eastern orchestras had played it, but it took thirty-seven years to reach Utah. The *Firebird* is rather gentle, considerably influenced by Stravinsky's teacher, Rimsky-Korsakov. Abravanel left the Tabernacle encouraged by its reception and introduced two works of Prokofiev the following two seasons.

In 1950 he was ready to commence his audience's Stravinsky education in earnest. He repeated the now-familiar *Firebird*, which received a noisily enthusiastic reception the second time around. The following season he played *Petruchka* which, despite considerable dissonance here and there, is a bright, sunny work. The crowd loved it. He programmed *Firebird* again in 1952–53 because it had become a favorite.

Two seasons later, 1954–55, when his listeners were thoroughly softened up, he performed *The Rite of Spring*. It was especially well received by the young in the audience, and even their conservative elders said, "It must be good, to have been composed by the same man who wrote *Firebird* and *Petruchka*."

During Abravanel's early years, Symphony rehearsals were held in the evenings because most of the musicians worked daytime jobs for their principal income. This situation continued for twenty years. In 1968, as the result of a Ford Foundation grant contingent upon daytime rehearsals, the orchestra left the campus for the vacated Christian Science Church on South Temple. Later, when it was slated for demolition, the orchestra moved to the old Salt Lake Central (LDS) Stake Cultural Center at 169 South 400 East, then owned by Robert Mason. When the new Symphony Hall opened in 1979, the orchestra had a permanent home at last. The adjunct faculty arrangement with the University, which has benefited Symphony principals, University, and community alike, continues unchanged.

Abravanel treasured his University connection—his professorship, his election to honorary membership in Phi Beta Kappa, an honorary doctor of laws degree awarded in 1957, and his leadership role in so many significant collaborative enterprises. It was a thirty-two-year love affair.

Abravanel with LDS Church President David O. McKay; at the
far right is David Romney, Executive Director of the Symphony.
MAP.

CHAPTER 8

King David

"You mean the University of Utah choruses have not been permitted to sing in the Tabernacle with the Symphony?" LDS President David O. McKay posed this question to a small group around his conference table in the late spring of 1951. Present were David S. Romney, managing director of the Utah Symphony; Leroy Robertson, chairman of the University of Utah music department, Lester F. Hewlett and J. Spencer Cornwall, president and conductor, respectively, of the Mormon Tabernacle Choir, and Thorpe B. Isaacson of the LDS Church's Presiding Bishopric. The latter were administrators of the Tabernacle and Temple Square. President McKay had just succeeded George Albert Smith as ninth president of the LDS Church on the ninth of April.

The meeting had been requested by Symphony and University representatives eager to schedule their 1952 choral-orchestral work in the Tabernacle. From their beginning in 1948, the now-traditional joint Utah Symphony–University Choruses concerts had been performed in cramped, acoustically poor Kingsbury Hall. Beethoven's *Missa Solemnis* in 1948, Verdi's *Requiem* in 1949, and Bach's *St. Matthew Passion* in 1950 had all been performed on the University campus rather than in the Mormon Tabernacle.

Abravanel and Robertson had not requested the Tabernacle for the *Missa Solemnis*, a Roman Catholic mass. However, the building had been requested for the Verdi *Requiem*, a mass for the dead, and for the *St. Matthew Passion*, Bach's dramatic setting of the biblical text dealing with the events leading up to the Crucifixion. Despite the ecumenical nature of both works, the requests were denied. Romney, a friend of President McKay's, happened to mention to Abravanel and others that McKay was often referred to by his inner circle and close friends as "King David." Abravanel immediately seized upon the coincidence and suggested that "our choral-orchestral work in February 1952 should be Honegger's *King David!*"

The timing was opportune, for McKay was in the first few weeks of his presidency. Romney arranged the joint meeting and presented the problem. President McKay was not only surprised but disturbed to hear that University choruses had not been permitted to sing in the Tabernacle. When he asked for an explanation, conductor Cornwall said that the Choir was protective and jealous of its monopoly on the Tabernacle's singular acoustics and didn't want any other chorus to compete with its unique sound.

President McKay was not satisfied. Turning to Romney and Robertson, he reiterated: "Are you saying the University of Utah Choruses have not been permitted to sing in the Tabernacle with the Utah Symphony?" They nodded. The Tabernacle Choir spokesmen protested: "You can't let another choir in the Tabernacle!" The tall, majestic President McKay, his face red against his luxuriant white hair, got slowly to his feet and pointedly asked: "You mean the prophet of the Lord can't permit the University chorus in the Tabernacle to sing with the Symphony?" The meeting was over almost

Beneficiaries of the "University Connection," rehearsing for an early production of the *Book of Mormon* Oratorio. Surrounding composer Leroy Robertson are, from left, Arthur Kent, Sr., Jewel Johnson Cutler, Roy Samuelson, and Kenly Whitelock. MAP.

before it had begun. President McKay opened the Tabernacle not only to Honegger's *King David* but also to fifty-eight subsequent performances of thirty different works in twenty-eight years, through Abravanel's retirement in 1979.

Abravanel and Robertson planned to follow *King David* with Robertson's *Book of Mormon* Oratorio the following season. Interestingly, the oratorio had been "commissioned" by President McKay six years earlier. Robertson composed the work as a major event for the Centennial celebration. He scored it for the Mormon Tabernacle Choir and his BYU Symphony Orchestra, with a sizable part for Tabernacle organist Alexander Schreiner. The oratorio was not premiered in 1947, however, and in fact gathered dust until 1953.

The reasons for this apparent neglect were both political and personal. Naomi Nelson Robertson, the composer's wife, wrote to the author following the passing of her husband in 1971, recalling a dinner twenty-five years earlier in 1946. George Albert Smith had succeeded Heber J. Grant as eighth president of the LDS Church. Early planning was under way for Utah's Centennial commemoration. President McKay was

President Smith's second counselor at the time, and Governor Herbert B. Maw had just appointed him chairman of the Utah Centennial Commission.

One of the Commission's earliest hopes was for a spectacular yet artistic event of genuine excellence. President McKay had just learned of Robertson's oratorio in progress, and as both Commission chairman and Church general authority had arranged a dinner as a sounding board, recalled Mrs. Robertson. "President McKay had us up to his home for dinner, along with President Smith, President [J. Reuben] Clark, and their partners [daughters Emily Smith Stewart and Marianne Clark Sharp]."

As they moved into the living room after dinner, President McKay invited Robertson to discuss his oratorio and to play and sing portions of it. Robertson sat at the piano. "President and Mrs. McKay were very interested as Leroy talked and played bits of it," recalls Mrs. Robertson. "It was late. President Smith went to sleep, and President Clark had no comment. President McKay was the one who was first interested in the oratorio, not President Clark, who showed no interest until after the *Trilogy* won the prize."

During the preceding year, Robertson's BYU Orchestra had joined President Clark in the regular Sunday Evening Church Hour broadcast over LDS-owned KSL radio. Robertson's student orchestra was considered the state's best in those pre-Abravanel days, and Clark, who gave religious talks on the program, shared this feeling, although he was an opera-lover himself and didn't care for symphonic music.

The First Presidency "commissioned" Robertson to complete the oratorio for the Centennial, and a sabbatical from BYU was arranged for him during the academic year 1946–47. "The 'commission' did not include a stipend," revealed Naomi, but was a tacit agreement that the oratorio would be premiered as a feature of the Centennial. The Mormon Tabernacle Choir and the BYU Symphony were to be the performing artists. "Expenses for copying the orchestral parts were underwritten by the University of Utah Research Committee," she added.

In later years Robertson himself always seemed to credit President Clark with commissioning the oratorio. "Not so," Mrs. Robertson maintains. "It was President McKay, from the 1946 dinner with the First Presidency all the way through the oratorio's eventual premiere seven years later in 1953."

Abravanel rehearses with Artur Rubinstein. MZPC.

Robertson commenced his sabbatical in Los Angeles, made some headway, and then returned prematurely to Provo and continued to compose "in a cleaned-out attic, undisturbed, off-campus," according to his daughter Marian. A few months later, Robertson's world resounded with the announcement that his *Trilogy* had been awarded the $25,000 Reichhold Prize as the "best symphonic work in a competition open to the entire Western Hemisphere."

Within months he left BYU and Provo for Salt Lake City, the University of Utah, and, more importantly, access to the Utah Symphony and Abravanel. He did this with some misgivings, for the BYU campus had been his home for a quar-ter of a century. In fact, he expressed some guilt about leaving his church's university on the heels of his international recognition, and he was particularly reluctant to leave his excellent student orchestra.

When the dust had settled, the 1947 Centennial was in full swing. The fate of the *Book of Mormon* Oratorio was uncertain, for Robertson no longer conducted the BYU Orchestra, for which the score had been "commissioned." Complicating the problem, the Mormon Tabernacle Choir had programmed half a dozen concerts with guest artists as its part in the Centennial, and an already tight schedule had become even busier. During this period the Choir also had a policy of no guest conductors, which precluded an appearance by Abravanel.

Robertson's work lay neglected from 1946 to 1953. While Robertson himself understood and endured the complex situation, his friend and admirer Abravanel grew more impatient each year. Finally, in the autumn of 1952, the Maestro announced, "If the oratorio is not going to be premiered by the Tabernacle Choir, we'll go ahead with it!" The result was its world premiere on February 8, 1953. Abravanel conducted the Utah Symphony, University Choruses, and guest soloists in the Tabernacle. Enthusiastically received, the *Book of Mormon* Oratorio was also performed later that season in Provo.

A year later, the work was revived in the Tabernacle at a "special" concert on April 6, 1954. During intermission the

Abravanel with Dorothy McGuire, a stunning Saint Joan, in December 1956. John Swope photograph in MAP.

author recognized two distinguished American composers in the audience: Halsey Stevens and Ingolf Dahl, both faculty members at the University of Southern California. After the concert Stevens and Dahl, chatting with the author, praised the Tabernacle acoustics, the orchestra, Abravanel, and the oratorio. "Robertson feels neglected and isolated from the mainstream of American music. Particularly, he feels shunned by the eastern establishment," observed the author.

Stevens and Dahl immediately took exception. They had flown to Salt Lake as members of Robertson's Ph.D. examining committee to audition, evaluate, and approve the oratorio as his proposed dissertation (which USC subsequently accepted in fulfillment of the doctoral dissertation requirement). "Robertson could never have it so good elsewhere," they maintained. "He has it 'made' here, with his own resident orchestra whose conductor is willing to put his baton on the block for him. And how many performances has Robertson had here? One or two a year! No one in the eastern establishment or on the West Coast can boast as much."

Stevens and Dahl knew first-hand. Their own performances by major West Coast orchestras were minimal. In contrast, during his tenure Abravanel conducted twenty-eight performances of Robertson works. Some were repeated, and twelve were world premieres.

STABILIZATION

"No other major symphony orchestra can boast a State Supreme Court Justice as president," observed a prominent Board member when Judge J. Allan Crockett was elected to fill the unexpired term of Glenn Wallace, who resigned in 1951. As a member and vice president of the Art Institute (now the Utah Arts Council) Board, and concurrently as a Symphony Board member, Judge Crockett had been a longtime Symphony supporter. He was elected president of the Art Institute, the state's official funding agency for the arts, in 1949, and while his term as Symphony president was short, he continued as an influential Board member until 1953. Judge Crockett became Chief Justice of the Utah State Supreme Court and enjoyed a long and outstanding career on the bench.

After two relatively short-term presidents, Raymond J. Ashton's eleven-year span (1952–63) provided more continuity than the young orchestra had ever known. One of the

West's most distinguished architects, Ashton possessed an innate love of beauty and the arts. Prior to his election as Board president, he too was a member of the Art Institute Board. Ashton moved quietly but surely, carrying out the wishes of Abravanel and the Board. During his decade at the helm, the Symphony organization stabilized. The orchestra began to make its presence known among its American counterparts, and its recordings began to have an impact on both the national and international markets.

This was a period of welcome change from the wild days of financial crisis, and the Board itself and management matured as well. Herold L. (Huck) Gregory succeeded David Romney as manager in 1958, bringing youthful enthusiasm, dedication, thoroughness, and an unquenchable love for music—a combination rarely found in management.

Major figures in the building of the Utah Symphony, about 1959. Seated, from left, Fred Smith, Abravanel, and Raymond J. Ashton; standing, Lee Flint and Huck Gregory. MAP.

ENTER MAHLER

During the venturesome fifties Abravanel conducted the first Utah performance of Gustav Mahler, whose gentle Fourth Symphony with Salt Lake's Blanche Christensen as soprano soloist in 1951 was the harbinger of an oncoming Mahler flood. A dazzling array of guest artists appeared: Rubinstein returned twice, and Milstein, Horowitz, and Piatigorsky all made return visits. The Verdi *Requiem*, Mahler's *Das Lied von der Erde*, and Robertson's Oratorio from the *Book of Mormon* were performed. Metropolitan Opera tenor Jan Peerce sang the title role in Handel's oratorio *Samson*, which was also recorded (Vanguard). Robertson's *Passacaglia* was commissioned for the Athens Festival, where it was premiered by the London Symphony in 1955 through the efforts of Alice and Christopher Athas, Salt Lake Greek-Americans and long-time Utah Symphony supporters.

Abravanel continued to program contemporary music on the Tabernacle series, and by the time he slyly included Stravinsky's *Rite of Spring* in the 1954–55 season, he had completely won over most of his essentially conservative audience.

Other fifties highlights included Isaac Stern performing Dvořák's Violin Concerto, Alexander Schreiner premiering his own Organ Concerto, Grant Johannesen in Bartók's Second Piano Concerto, Zara Nelsova premiering Robertson's Cello Concerto, Heifetz playing the Tchaikovsky Violin Concerto, Honegger's *Joan of Arc* with Dorothy McGuire, and the first season of the University's pioneering Festival of Contemporary Music. Guest artists of international stature and provocative symphonic scores indicate the high level of Abravanel's programming during his first full decade with the Symphony.

Two historic nights in 1960 were high-water marks for the Symphony, the Utah premiere of Mahler's Second (*Resurrection*) Symphony, and the guest-conducting appearance of the pre-eminent twentieth-century French conductor, walrus-mustached Pierre Monteux.

The Mahler climaxed the 1959–60 season on March sixteenth. Abravanel had introduced Mahler to his Tabernacle audience with the Fourth Symphony in 1951 and *The Song of the Earth* in 1953. The First Symphony followed in 1954 and *Song of the Wayfarer* in 1956. Finally, he coupled the Adagietto from Symphony No. 5, one of Mahler's most ingratiating movements, with the lengthy, dramatic Second Symphony, which deals with the Day of Judgment and the Resurrection—made to order for a Tabernacle audience. It was a triumph.

One of a handful of twentieth-century conductors revered by Abravanel and the musical world for his mastery of the French repertoire, and for his humanity, was Pierre Monteux. He had been scheduled as a guest conductor in 1958 but was called to fill in with the New York Philharmonic for an ailing Dmitri Mitropoulos. Monteux's visit in February of 1960 was a marvelous experience for the orchestra and a prize opportunity for Abravanel to show off his musicians to the

Abravanel with Nathan Milstein.
MZPC.

Pierre Monteux rehearses the Utah Symphony in the University
Music Hall, now Gardner Hall. MAP.

eminent octogenarian. His all-French program included
Debussy's *L'Après-midi d'un Faune*, Ravel's *Rapsodie Espagnol*,
a Lalo overture, and Berlioz' *Symphonie Fantastique*.

The audience cheered Monteux and the orchestra long
and loud. The press followed suit the next day. As critic for
the *Salt Lake Tribune*, the author was surprised to receive
angry phone calls and a letter or two for "writing too
enthusiastically" about the spirited eighty-five-year-old
Monteux. Most originated with Symphony Guild members
dedicated one hundred percent to the Utah Symphony and
Abravanel. They apparently felt that praise of Monteux
reflected unfavorably on Abravanel by comparison. Of course
it was actually the highest of compliments to Abravanel that
his orchestra sounded so beautiful under the baton of this
legendary figure.

. . . AND LADIES OF THE GUILD

The Utah Symphony Guild has always been "a driving
force whose members," in the words of its first president,
Becky Almond, "have always . . . played a vital role in fur-
thering the Symphony cause."

Although Maurice and Lucy Abravanel moved to Salt
Lake City in October of 1947, the Guild was not formally
organized until 1953. "During those early years, however,
the women were not idle. There were Symphony Soirees,
receptions, musical teas and many delightful events given to
support the orchestra," she recalled in a series, "Our Femi-
nine Allies," in the orchestra's 1969–70 programs. Subsequent Guild presidents also contributed to this series. Miss
Almond credits a long list of "cultural and civic-minded
matrons who sponsored those important early functions."

Abravanel rehearsing
with cellist Gregor
Piatigorsky. MZPC.

In November 1951 a Women's Symphony Committee, a forerunner of the Guild headed by Mrs. L. J. Hays, sponsored a meeting at the Governor's mansion. Then, "Preceding the 1953–54 Symphony season a gathering of supporters was held at the home of Lucy Abravanel. Mrs. Harold K. Beecher suggested we organize a conventional Guild . . . as in other states." At this meeting Becky Almond was elected the organization's first president, along with a slate of enthusiastic, dedicated officers.

From the beginning–during the six formative years and throughout her life–Lucy Abravanel played a dominant role. "From behind the scenes it was Lucy who realized the importance of the dedicated efforts of local women who would work for the good of the Symphony," wrote Almond.

Twenty-four presidents (listed in an Appendix) have strengthened the Guild, which has become the orchestra's most powerful auxiliary.

An effective, influential Ogden Symphony Association has been the orchestra's mainstay in Ogden's six-concert seasons. Its president and the Guild president traditionally have been members of the Symphony Board, sometimes of the executive committee.

The members of both organizations sponsor symposia prior to each subscription concert, luncheons for distinguished guest artists, and receptions and teas. They participate actively in fund drives and would play a prominent role in the passage of the bond issue that made the construction of Symphony Hall possible.

Gustav Mahler's *Symphony of a Thousand*, performed by the Utah
Symphony with the University choruses on December 6, 1963.
Deseret News photograph in MAP.

" . . . of a Thousand"

" . . . Moreover, we have discovered a new Mahler conductor of stature and sympathy in a day when such men are precious indeed," declared Thomas C. Marsh in the July 1964 issue of *High Fidelity*. "This is not only a remarkably well-engineered stereo recording," he continues, "it is also by far the best monophonic version [of Mahler's Eighth Symphony] ever made, extraordinarily rich and lifelike even in single-channel form."

Marsh was writing of the Vanguard recording of Mahler's *Symphony of a Thousand*, which Abravanel conducted for the first time on December 6, 1963, in the Tabernacle, with approximately 800 performers, including seven vocal soloists, an expanded orchestra, the combined University of Utah Choruses, and a large children's chorus from the Salt Lake schools under the direction of music supervisor Vernon J. LeeMaster and five of his elementary and junior high school teachers.

The audience reception was overwhelming, surpassing anything else in Abravanel's sixteen years in Utah. When the record album was released six months later, it was featured by most of the nation's record reviewers. It also created a stir overseas. While the orchestra had been recording since 1952, it was this recording of Mahler's *Symphony of a Thousand* that brought Abravanel and the Utah Symphony national standing and international recognition. It also brought Abravanel the Mahler Award of the Bruckner Society for 1965.

As Marsh declares, "Abravanel asks for a lot. He is deeply involved with this music, and he plays it not for surface or show but for content. . . . Much of Bruno Walter's skill as a Mahler conductor was his ability to fuse the composer's scores into solid architectural forms, and this power Abravanel also possesses."

The Eighth's triumph was the young orchestra's first real high point. Even today the recording is one that the nation's music critics and serious musicians refer to when assessing Abravanel's leadership of the orchestra. The Eighth's recognition and warm reception in the national press assured the Utah Symphony's subsequent recordings of serious consideration and high-level reviews.

Its huge dimensions make the Eighth extremely difficult to perform. While Abravanel conducted Mahler's Second (*Resurrection*) Symphony five times in the Tabernacle, he programmed the Eighth only once more after the 1964 recording—in 1978, one year before his resignation.

From the December 1964 issue of London's *Records and Recording* came a two-page story under the byline of Robert Angles. "Symphony of a Thousand" read the headline under a three-column photo of the Tabernacle performance. "This new recording fills a gap and . . . triumphantly, for it fulfills all the hopes that one has long nursed for the undertaking of such a project," writes Angles, who credits "the American Vanguard Company with taking up the challenge and succeeding magnificently."

. . . I was continually astonished at the balance and the clarity of the stereo sound. . . . Now, at last one has Mahler's Eighth Symphony impressively captured on disc and can savor and appreciate it far more satisfactorily than the occasional public performance will allow. . . .

. . . Abravanel presses home Mahler's heaven-shaking intentions with all the daunting might and main at his disposal; the attack never falters . . . [the performers] are magnificent in precision and sonority, topped by exultant brass. . . . It is his overall control of Mahler's vast canvas and his forces that I find most impressive. . . .

The English reviewer's enthusiasm continues: "By any standards the Utah Symphony is a first-class ensemble," and he praises each section. "Would that our top British orchestras could boast such clean, reliable trumpets and full-bodied

Soloists for the *Symphony of a Thousand. Deseret News* photograph in MAP.

French horns. Make no mistake, this is a great orchestra and it is backed by their amateur choirs whose enthusiasm is matched by their competence."

Angles concludes, however, that "The overall success . . . undoubtedly rests with Abravanel; it will be a long time before I hear anything to match the glory he conjures from the final pages of the Eighth, setting the seal upon a great Mahler performance that marks a major event in the history of the gramophone."

The *New York Times* and the *Herald-Tribune* also gave prominent space to Mahler's Eighth. The *Times*'s Raymond Ericson calls the orchestra "enterprising," and estimates the total number of performers at 850, which is close to Vanguard's figure of 900:

> Solving the physical problems is to the credit of both Vanguard's engineers and Mr. Abravanel, but the conductor goes beyond that to give a coherent, carefully paced reading. . . . Mr. Abravanel's recording makes all the points in the Mahler score. For this the listener should be grateful, since a superior recording is not likely to come along for some time.

Ericson praises the orchestra and choruses, and among the soloists he singles out "Miss Christensen [who] stands out for the ethereal sound of her final solo, as Mater Gloriosa." Blanche Christensen, a Salt Lake artist, was Abravanel's leading soprano soloist in most of the major choral-orchestral performances from the 1948 *Missa Solemnis* in Kingsbury Hall to its Tabernacle revival in 1968, two decades later.

Writing in the *Herald-Tribune*, Herbert Kupferberg opens with a light touch: "Apparently a lot of people in Salt Lake City are imbued with the idea of making music. A tremendous crowd of them has been gathered together by Maurice Abravanel to record Gustav Mahler's *Symphony of a Thousand*. That 'thousand' represents a slight exaggeration, but only a slight one, for Vanguard says that close to 900 performers actually participated. . . . "

"Was the labor all worth while?" Kupferberg answers: "Definitely yes. Mahler's symphony, for all its ambitious scale and curious textual content . . . is a work with both loftiness of spirit and emotional impact. It isn't overwhelmed by its own size. There are moments in this recording where Mahler's music is made to seem almost intimate in its beauty. . . . "

Listening to a playback during a Vanguard recording session. MZPC.

Abravanel and Seymour Solomon, one of Vanguard's owners. MAP.

The Seventh Symphony, recorded in 1966, was the second Mahler recording, sandwiched between the spectacular choral Eighth and Second. The Seventh (Phillips) drew praise from the *Guardian*'s Edward Greenfield in the October 24, 1966, issue, comparing the Utah Symphony's recording and that of Leonard Bernstein and the New York Philharmonic (Columbia) with Erich Leinsdorf and the Boston Symphony Orchestra, recording for RCA.

> Both performances [Abravanel's and Bernstein's] come closer to a true Mahlerian style. . . . Bernstein's power tactics come close to making the great rag-bag of a finale hang together as a virtuoso showpiece.
>
> The amazing thing is that Abravanel with a far less glamorous orchestra (though a very remarkable one as their recent visit [to London] proved) and with far gentler methods makes the impossible finale even more convincing. The shading of mood, the contrast of frenetic excitement with passionate lyricism and Schubertian relaxion, makes the jig-saw construction the more evident, but Mahler, the magician, was relying on just such shading of mood, and by comparison Bernstein seems too tense, unable to relax enough.
>
> True, Bernstein in the two night-music movements produces playing of an almost celestial refinement, but when you hear Abravanel you appreciate fully the benefits of an altogether simpler, less sophisticated approach. . . . In the first movement, too, Abravanel's warmly rather than tensely passionate account of the second subject is far more effective, and the Utah Orchestra's playing can hardly be faulted anywhere. On bargain label and with excellent stereo the set should encourage even those who have been daunted by the work to discover its genuine warmth.

Dika Newlin, distinguished Mahler scholar, guest-reviewed the recording in the June 1966 issue of *The American Record Guide* as "The Mahler Seventh from Salt Lake City." She reminds readers that "the Seventh has not been neglected on records." She mentions earlier European versions: "However, they are easily superseded by this Abravanel recording, which is not only in fine-sounding stereo but also (far more importantly) is the first to be based on the text established in the 1960 critical edition of the score. In fol-

lowing the new score, Abravanel probably has come as close as possible to Mahler's intentions insofar as we can know them today."

Then follows a lengthy discussion of the many modifications by conductor Willem Mengelberg, apparently with Mahler's approval, and Mahler scholars Erwin Ratz, who wrote the preface to the new critical edition, and Vinzenz Hladky, who researched and recommended "sparing use of *tremolo*." Newlin concludes: "Some interesting comparisons no doubt will be forthcoming when Bernstein's version of the Seventh is released. However, if you lack the Seventh in your Mahler collection or if you wish to replace an earlier mono edition, you will certainly not go wrong by choosing Abravanel's now."

The International Gustav Mahler Society in Vienna had found the recordings of Mahler's Seventh and Eighth symphonies by the Utah orchestra "extraordinarily beautiful." In 1966 the Society expressed the wish that the Utah Symphony and Abravanel record all Mahler's works, singling out four symphonies "of which there are no recordings of such quality." Abravanel was made an honorary member of the society, a rare distinction shared by a handful who have championed performance of and dedication to the works of Mahler and Bruckner, including Bruno Walter, Leonard Bernstein, Herbert von Karajan, and William Steinberg.

The following year, 1967, the Utah Symphony's stereo recording of Mahler's Second (*Resurrection*) Symphony was released by Vanguard. One of Mahler's two colossal symphonies for augmented orchestra, large chorus, and soloists, it featured Beverly Sills, soprano, and Florence Kopleff, contralto. The University of Utah Civic Chorale, Newell B. Weight, conductor, joined orchestra and soloists in an overwhelming performance of the climactic concluding movement.

High Fidelity's lead review of the Second in the November 1967 issue rivaled the raves that had greeted the Eighth three years earlier:

> This release on Vanguard's new Cardinal label is truly an astonishing one. From the technical point of view alone it represents a substantial and exciting step forward. . . . [T]he chorus actually seems to be where it should be: behind the orchestra. . . . [T]he balance between the soprano and alto soloists and the chorus

has been perfectly judged, and the final peroration is overwhelming in its grandeur.

. . . [T]he performance too is a breathtaking one. Abravanel's previous Mahler releases were powerful, sensitive, and musical without ever quite scaling the heights of sublimity. Now he has thrown caution to the winds and produced an interpretation of awesome, inspired magnificence.

High Fidelity gives Abravanel's version the edge over Sir Georg Solti's,

whose performance on London [Records] was my previous recommendation. . . . [T]he total effect of Abravanel's reading is greater. . . . [W]hen the shattering moments *do* come they are every bit as powerful as Solti's: the seemingly endless crescendo . . . in the Finale

The Utah Chorale, Newell Weight, conductor, and the Symphony in a joint performance of Mahler's *Resurrection* Symphony on March 29, 1967. W. Claudell Johnson photograph for the *Deseret News* in MAP.

and the ensuing March (where as Mahler once put it, "The earth quakes, the graves burst open, the dead arise and stream on in endless procession") . . . here Abravanel had me leaping out of my chair in veritable terror. . . . [C]onductor and engineers between them have achieved a moment so intense as for once to justify the use, in its fullest sense, of the word "sensational". . . .

. . . There is a mastery of execution, a crispness of ensemble. . . . With this performance, Abravanel has advanced from the ranks of the very good Mahler conductors into those of the great, and the continuation of his series must be looked forward to with the keenest interest.

While these remarkable Mahler recordings had launched Abravanel and the orchestra to the heights of the recording world, they had really hit their full stride a few years earlier when they signed with the prestigious Vanguard label in 1961, recording forty-six discs (thirty-four albums) during the sixties.

Before Vanguard, the orchestra had enjoyed a successful relationship with Westminster Records. Two of the orchestra's

Newell Weight, Seymour Solomon of Vanguard, and Abravanel confer over a score. MAP.

most productive years, 1957–58, found Abravanel conducting a total of fifteen discs (twelve albums) for Westminster—remarkable for a fledgling orchestra just completing its first decade under Abravanel and its first decade as a bona fide entity.

In the Utah Symphony program of December 6, 1958, a full-page ad let subscribers know that "for outstanding Christmas Gifts" they should "give Utah Symphony performances on Westminster Records." Listed in both stereo and monophonic discs and stereo tapes were recordings of Handel, Saint-Saëns, and Gershwin. Reid Nibley soloed in Gershwin's Piano Concerto in F and *Rhapsody in Blue*. He was cited for his "artistry and nimble-fingered piano," and the Concerto in F performance has recently been released on a compact disc as an MCA classic.

High Fidelity praised Abravanel for the first stereo recording of *An American in Paris*, calling it "a fine success from every standpoint . . . , the emphasis being on rhythmic snap and bite rather than on the overblown schmaltz that has done in too many live and recorded versions of this piece. . . . "

All the critics made pointed reference to Tabernacle organist Alexander Schreiner's artistry in the 1958 release of the Saint-Saëns Third (*Organ*) Symphony. The St. Louis *Globe-Democrat* termed the Westminster album "a welcome recording of a work that deserves a fuller hearing." The Hartford *Times* called it "A first-rate recording of an excellent performance." The Cleveland *Plain Dealer* praised the stereo sound and singled out the collaboration of Schreiner and Abravanel as "a combination of artistry which is thrilling."

Rounding out the 1958 recordings—and drawing a major share of the critical praise—was Handel's oratorio *Israel in Egypt*, with the University of Utah Choruses. The *Daily Times* of Gainesville, Georgia, held that the only satisfactory recording to that time was the Bach Guild Records': "Its main drawback was the fact that it was sung in German. . . . Now from Westminster comes an equally fine performance. . . . Abravanel stresses the massive outlines of the music. . . . [T]he music is delivered with dispatch, even elegance. There is an openness and ease of movement in the Westminster performance that make for better Handel than the impressive but too-heavy English performance led by Sir Malcolm Sargent on Angel." The reviewer also praises the acoustics of the Assembly Hall on the Temple grounds in Salt Lake City which "contribute wonderfully to the success of the enterprise here . . . [creating a] beautiful balance between the large chorus and the orchestra."

The Louisville *Courier*'s critic was "especially struck by the excellence of the Utah musicians and singers in *Israel in Egypt*. . . . [T]he choral work is splendid. Perhaps this is not surprising in light of the musical heritage the Mormon church has built, but the quality of the Utah Symphony did surprise me. They have first-rate musicians out in the mountains and desert and great salt flats."

Abravanel drew compliments in Bristol's *Herald Courier*: "Abravanel has a strong affinity for this music, allows the rolling majesty of the many choral numbers to thrill us without letting the situation get out of hand. The orchestra was kept in proper size and gives an ideal accompaniment. . . . Westminster's . . . overall effect is magnificent."

The Utah Symphony's *Israel in Egypt* was noteworthy and attention-getting partially because this was its first American recording. The soloists included five Salt Lake artists: Blanche Christensen, Colleen Bischoff, Dale Blackburn, Don Watts, and Warren Wood. There was also a young artist destined for stardom in the world's great opera houses and concert halls—Grace Bumbry, a protégée of Lotte Lehmann and one of Abravanel's artist students at the Music Academy of the West (his summer residence).

Although it was not widely known at the time, Abravanel's recording ambitions were central to his long-range plans when he signed his contract in 1947. He saw a recording program as an excellent means of creating income and extending the musicians' season as well as an important tool for building the orchestra's stature in the community. Abravanel conducted the orchestra's first recording in 1952—Handel's *Judas Maccabaeus* with three visiting soloists plus local artists Marvin Sorensen and Beryl Jensen.

On April 18 the Assembly Hall on Temple Square was the scene of a special non-subscription event. Most in the audience were unaware that the concert was a dress rehearsal for the orchestra's first-ever recording session on succeeding nights. The University Collegium Musicum performed as the chorus, and while the Handel Society recording didn't overwhelm the critics, it represented another important "first," as it was then the only recording of Handel's *Judas Mac-*

cabaeus. Seven years later, in 1959, Abravanel and his joint forces recorded the work again, for Westminster, in a performance that remains the definitive version.

During the sixties, the Utah Symphony was in the company of the great conductors and orchestras of the recording world. It was not only the Mahler recordings that brought critical accolades. Every new release received universal attention. High on the list were choral-orchestral works with Ardean Watts's University Chorus or Newell Weight's Utah Chorale joining Abravanel and the orchestra in Robertson's *Book of Mormon* Oratorio, Honegger's *King David* and *Judith*, Handel's *Samson*, Milhaud's *Pacem in Terris*, and the Berlioz *Requiem*. All were recorded by Vanguard and all received favorable reviews from critics for major publications.

King David, a favorite of Abravanel and audiences (three Tabernacle performances), elicited these words from *High Fidelity* in January of 1963: "Incredibly enough, this seems to be the first recorded performance . . . since Honegger's own version on a Westminster LP made early in the fifties and long out of the catalogue. If Utah seems like a rather unlikely point of origin, let that deter no one. Abravanel has authority and style, he has trained his musicians excellently well, and the recorded sound is good. . . . The chorus [trained by Ardean Watts] too is excellent except perhaps at the few most difficult moments. . . ."

A break during the recording of the *Book of Mormon* Oratorio in 1961. From left, Doug Craig, David Shand, the composer (behind Abravanel), an unknown recording technician, and Seymour Solomon. MZPC.

Abravanel with his good
friend Darius Milhaud.
MZPC.

The *Saturday Review* for January 26, 1963, hailed "the release of a new and superbly recorded performance of *Le Roi David*" and concludes with "The result is a top-notch recording. Abravanel has developed a splendid orchestra and the Vanguard engineers have recorded it superbly." Soloists included Salt Lakers Jean Preston and Marvin Sorensen with Israeli soprano Netania Davrath. Two distinguished names appeared as narrator, Martial Singher, and speaker, Madeleine Milhaud, the wife of composer Darius Milhaud. The international musical world was clearly impressed, as the Utah *King David* was awarded the Prix du Disque for 1963.

Darius Milhaud's *Pacem in Terris*, which he called a "choral symphony," was recorded by the Utah Symphony, the University Chorus (Ardean Watts, conductor), and soloists in 1964, not long after its premiere in Paris on December 20, 1963. The title "Peace on Earth" was from Pope John XXIII's sweeping ecumenical Encyclical, portions of which Milhaud used as his text.

The Milhauds were old friends of the Abravanels. In Paris in the thirties Abravanel had conducted Milhaud's music, which ranks among the twentieth century's best. The Milhauds had made America their home after the Nazi takeover of France. They came to Salt Lake City for the recording of the work and were guests at the Abravanel home during the week of rehearsals for *Pacem in Terris* and attended the performance.

A pleased Maestro holding a copy of the Utah Symphony/Vanguard recording of Leroy Robertson's *Book of Mormon* Oratorio. MAP.

In his review of the Utah recording Raymond Ericson of the *New York Times* wrote that, "According to the composer, 'to fulfill the ecumenical idea, this text by a Pope, set to music by a Jew, was conducted [in Paris] by Charles Münch, a Protestant.' " Ericson acknowledges the excellence of the orchestra, the University Chorus, the soloists, and Abravanel's direction. Walter Arlen of the *Los Angeles Times* (August 15, 1965) credits Abravanel with both the American and record-ing premieres, stating that, "He leads his orchestra with the authority of Milhaud's collaboration."

Two Leroy Robertson works, the *Book of Mormon* Orato-rio and the Violin Concerto, were recorded in the sixties. Vanguard recorded the concerto with soloist Tossy Spivakovsky on one side of a disc and Stravinsky's Violin Concerto on the flip side. Vanguard's 1961 *Book of Mormon* Oratorio recording has since been superseded by Columbia Records' 1978 release with the Utah Symphony, soloists, and the Mormon Tabernacle Choir, for which the composer had originally written it more than thirty years earlier. Abravanel had hoped to premiere the oratorio with the Tabernacle Choir during his first season, but because of a number of circum-stances, including the actions of mid-level LDS Church offi-cials, this major event was delayed for three decades. In the meantime, Abravanel recorded it twice with the University of Utah Choruses—for Allen Duff Records, a locally-based company, in 1953, as well as Vanguard's superior 1961 ver-sion.

During the 1960's, Abravanel and Vanguard also recorded Varése, Lazarof, Rimsky-Korsakov, Gliere, and more Gershwin. After Mahler, the most-recorded composers during this decade were Vaughan Williams (7), Copland (4), and Bach and Honegger (3 each). Novelties included Erik Satie, Jerome Kern, Leroy Anderson, and nineteenth-century American composer Louis Moreau Gottschalk.

Vanguard was the Utah Symphony's sole label during the 1960's. Vox took over in 1970 and continued through 1975. Vanguard returned in 1974, however, to complete the cycle of Mahler symphonies with releases of the First, Fifth, Sixth, and Tenth (*Adagio*). The Abravanel recordings repre-sent the only complete Mahler symphony series by a single conductor with a single orchestra, and the Fifth won Abravanel and his musicians the Mahler Society's award for the best Mahler recording of 1975.

The Mahler cycle brought so much attention to all par-ties that Vanguard flew its engineers and equipment to Salt Lake City during the 1976 Bicentennial year to record the symphonic cycle of Brahms, including the *Academic Festival* and *Tragic* overtures and the *Haydn Variations*. A year later Vanguard returned to record the seven symphonies of Sibelius.

The sixteen-year Vanguard association concluded at that point. The familiar label was indelibly linked by musicians, critics, and serious listeners with the Utah Symphony. Vanguard's high-quality engineering and challenging repertoire are respected throughout the recording industry. Their marketing practices, unfortunately, did not match their technical skill.

The Utah Symphony switched to Vox in 1970, and 1972 and 1973 saw recordings of Tchaikovsky's complete symphonic works: the six numbered symphonies, the unnumbered *Manfred* Symphony, the single-movement works: the *1812 Overture, Marche Slav, Romeo and Juliet, Francesca da Rimini*, and the seldom-heard *Hamlet* overture fantasy. Vox's final Utah Symphony recording was a four-disc album of music by Edvard Grieg. The major work is his Piano Concerto with soloist Grant Johannesen, and the album includes both *Peer Gynt* suites and a dozen short pieces.

Angel Records' label became the Utah Symphony's from 1975 to 1978. Two recordings received Grammy nominations: Bloch's *Sacred Service* (1972) and Stravinsky's *Symphony of Psalms* (1976), both with the Utah Chorale (Newell Weight, conductor). In a special 1976 Bicentennial release, Columbia joined the Symphony and the Tabernacle Choir for the first time ever. Jerold Ottley conducted joint forces in patriotic favorites, *Yankee Doodle Dandies*, with Robert Merrill as soloist. Columbia Records, a giant in the industry, also recorded the long-awaited *Book of Mormon* Oratorio with the Mormon Tabernacle Choir, soloists, and Utah Symphony under Abravanel in 1978, in what would be his final recording.

The Utah Symphony's local and regional reputation is based upon concert attendance and face-to-face contact with Abravanel and the orchestra and its continuum of sounds. The orchestra's national and international reputation exceeds its local one and is based almost wholly on the stream of recordings originating "somewhere west of Denver." The music world took the Mahler recordings to its heart—amazed that they could have come from Nazareth. All Abravanel recordings received immediate attention and respect. Only a handful of the nation's critics have ever attended a Utah Symphony concert. Many have heard and read of the new hall's marvelous acoustics. But they all "know" and respect the orchestra through the excellence of more than a third of a century of recordings.

None of Abravanel's 111 discs could have been pressed without his far-sightedness and ingenuity. When he had first broached the idea of recordings in the early fifties, he was told it was impossible. Union scale for one hour's recording was three times that for a regular "service" (a service being either a rehearsal or a public concert of any kind). According to Huck Gregory, "There was no way any major recording company would fly men and equipment to Salt Lake City and, on top of that, be required to pay union scale to eighty musicians. Why do so when they have major orchestras in their own backyard?"

Abravanel realized that he could not pay union scale for recording, so in 1957 he called his musicians together and convinced them that recording was vital to the orchestra's growth and recognition. He asked each musician to agree to play for recording sessions at the same rate as regular services. This was unheard of—heretical—in union president Caesar Petrillo's music world at that time. Abravanel sold them on the plan, however, and presented what Gregory described as "Maurice's pioneering Solomonic cooperative recording arrangement with the American Federation of Musicians and the Utah Symphony players."

The idea was so unusual and unique that Abravanel was instructed by the union Local 102, American Federation of Musicians, that a single petition from the orchestra, signed by all musicians, would not suffice. Rather, each musician was asked to write and sign his own petition. This was done, eighty in all. Herman Kennan, Petrillo's successor as national president of the AFM, approved the proposal, and Abravanel and the orchestra were soon recording for Vanguard. One orchestra service was two and a half hours long; recording sessions were three hours each. By agreement, compensation was the same for both.

Gregory points out that on the financial side, "There was virtually no possibility for . . . recordings to yield a cash profit. . . . But recording sessions each year helped to extend the Utah Symphony's season during a crucial period of growth. . . . "

The "cooperative" arrangement continued through 1970, when the orchestra moved from Vanguard to Vox. From this time on the musicians were paid normal union scale. This was not a union action, Gregory points out, but "resulted from pressure from other orchestras, particularly Los Angeles, which felt the Utah Symphony's 'cooperative' plan was unfair competition."

The Utah Symphony under Abravanel recorded 111 discs, including complete symphonic cycles of four major composers, capped by two of the recording industry's all-time artistic successes by critical consensus: Mahler's *Symphony of a Thousand* and *Resurrection*.

Abravanel coming on stage at the Salt Lake Tabernacle. MAP.

CHAPTER 10

The Big Machine

"You *must* go to Greece! You *must* go to Greece!" Abravanel was bending over "By" Woodbury, who spoke with difficulty in a hoarse whisper.

It was 1965; Woodbury had suffered a disabling stroke, but in the few months of his presidency, he had set in place the Big Machine that would launch the Utah Symphony into international prominence by bringing Wendell J. Ashton aboard.

In 1963 Abravanel had suggested to Walter Roche, the Symphony's finance chairman, that By (T. Bowring) Woodbury be named to the Board of Directors. "Roche was always skeptical of new ideas and anything that smacked of expansion. He was tight-fisted," complained Abravanel. Woodbury, in contrast, was known for his aggressive and imaginative business leadership and high-powered innovations in the LDS missionary program. Over Roche's opposition, Woodbury was named to the Board on October 7, 1963.

Woodbury was a powerful, far-seeing, enthusiastic leader and a brilliant administrator. Two years later, on March 9, 1965, he was the obvious choice to succeed John Gallivan as president.

Woodbury brought a self-styled "back-up" man, Wendell J. Ashton, to the Board as his right hand, with the new title of general vice president. The two had worked together before. In 1965, Ashton was one of three principal executives of Gillham Advertising, Salt Lake's oldest agency. He had been asked to serve as state chairman for the 1964 Cancer Crusade and had asked Woodbury, then an executive at Zion's First National Bank, to serve as chairman of the Salt Lake County drive.

But the two went back further than that, to when they attended the University of Utah. Woodbury led a five-piece band that was popular with Salt Lake's college crowd in the 1930's, often playing at the Green Dragon, a night spot in the basement of the Boston Building at Main Street and Exchange Place. Its nightclub atmosphere had attracted large crowds.

Woodbury usually stood in front of his band, clarinet in hand, playing the melody while the orchestra backed him. At times he held his instrument at his side and doubled as vocalist. His rich bass-baritone voice was reminiscent of Big Band leader Ben Bernie, with Bernie's vibrato and Perry Como's shaking head. An engaging personality, natural wit, and sense of humor plus a running line of chatter made a winning combination.

After World War II Woodbury made his professional mark in the Midwest as a prime mover in the rapidly expanding aircraft industry. He was an executive of Culver Aircraft for eighteen years, leaving the business world in 1958 to accept an assignment from the First Presidency of the LDS Church to head a mission in England.

The LDS Church was introducing an experimental accelerated proselyting program that was somewhat controversial at the time. Woodbury's high-powered style in the aircraft industry, plus his personal charm, was made to order for the new missionary program, and it was only a matter of time before he led all mission presidents in statistics. After three years in England, the Woodburys returned to their Salt Lake home.

Woodbury became an executive at Zion's First National Bank and was respected in Salt Lake's business world. Abravanel immediately saw him as a potential Utah Symphony Board member. Two years later he joined the Board.

The minutes show that John W. Gallivan, one-year Board president and publisher of the *Salt Lake Tribune*, presided at his final meeting on March 3, 1965. One of Gallivan's most significant contributions as president came as that meeting approved plans for implementing the musicians' pension fund.

On March 29, 1965 – three weeks later – Woodbury presided at his first Board meeting with Ashton present as general vice president.

Wendell J. Ashton, born and educated in Salt Lake City, graduated from the University of Utah in 1933. He has held many administrative positions in the LDS Church, including General Board assignments. He has been a stake president and a regional representative of the Council of Twelve. In 1972, he resigned his vice presidency at Gillham Advertising Agency to accept an appointment as managing director of the new LDS Public Communications Department. Earlier he had been managing editor of the *Deseret News* (1947–48) and would return there as publisher in 1978.

However, Ashton was a musical novice. "I disliked music so much in grade school that I'd disrupt the classroom so the teacher would make me leave during music," he confesses.

I knew nothing, absolutely nothing, about symphonic music when Woodbury asked me to become his general vice president. I am sure By felt that I owed this to him, since he had served so valiantly in the Cancer Crusade under my leadership.

I really didn't want to serve in the Symphony organization because I had no interest in symphonic music. My wife Belva had always held that I already had too many irons in community service. I was surprised when she told me this was one community responsibility I

should accept. She reasoned that the Symphony represented a broad base of the community – from the professions, various phases of business, all religious faiths – plus a long-neglected cultural aspect of my own life.

Ashton feels that his lack of musical know-how actually worked to the Symphony's advantage:

My lack of sophisticated knowledge of music has been an advantage, since I have always left the programming and the fine-tuning of the orchestra itself to the music director. I have felt that my responsibilities as president and chief executive officer were to see that the Utah Symphony is managed in a businesslike way

The Abravanels and guest soloist Jose Iturbe in 1965. Steve Parker photograph for the *Salt Lake Tribune* in MAP.

and to raise funds. I believe that the greatest responsibility of the Symphony Board is to raise funds, since no orchestra can long remain viable and grow in excellence without a sound financial structure.

He also admits, however, that "Through the years I have learned to love music, particularly that of the old masters."

Ashton refers to "serving at the side of Maurice Abravanel" in glowing terms as "a great joy and pleasure. . . . I have great affection and esteem for him as a man of tremendous character, to say nothing of his superior skills and musicianship. We had never met, to my recollection, until I became first vice president of the Utah Symphony, but since then we have become warm friends." Abravanel, on first meeting him, had observed, "I like that man," and warmly supported his appointment.

When Woodbury and Ashton moved into their key positions, Gina Bachauer had just made her first appearance with the Utah Symphony. A concert pianist of international stature, Bachauer was a national heroine in her native Greece. She first appeared with the Utah Symphony in Rachmaninoff's Second Piano Concerto on March 17, 1965, a week after Woodbury's appointment as Board president. Bachauer took Utah by storm and would solo with the orchestra seven times between this historic performance in 1965 and 1975.

"It was during Gina Bachauer's first concert appearance with the Utah Symphony," reminisces Abravanel. "We were all going to Brighton [in Big Cottonwood Canyon] and had met at our home for drinks before leaving. Gina said, 'Your orchestra must tour Europe!' I suggested that she put it in writing, and she wrote immediately to By Woodbury":

> Before leaving Salt Lake City I would like to tell you what a great happiness it has been for me to play with the Utah Symphony Orchestra and Maestro Abravanel. I have had the privilege of playing with many fine orchestras all over the world, but the special joy I had from the two concerts this week [in Ogden and Salt Lake] comes from a particular quality inherent in the orchestra. Maestro Abravanel has instilled in the members of the orchestra a deep and sensitive love of music which shows in the beauty of their playing and a lovely singing sound reminiscent of the Vienna Philharmonic at its best.
>
> You must be very proud of your orchestra and its great conductor as I am sure you are. Together they make a wonderful combination which should be heard not only all over the United States but throughout Europe, and I hope all true music lovers in Salt Lake City and the whole of Utah will band together to send your orchestra far and wide and show the world what a magnificent instrument has been created in the state of Utah.
>
> Please give to the members of your Board, Maestro Abravanel, and the orchestra my heartfelt congratulations on the great contribution they are making to the spiritual happiness of mankind – through music.
>
> Very cordially,
> Gina Bachauer

Wendell J. Ashton and Governor Calvin L. Rampton confer over a Symphony Day proclamation. MAP.

Guest soloist Gina Bachauer. MAP.

During his first weeks as Symphony Board president Woodbury was indeed ready to consider new ideas, to look beyond Utah, the Western states, and American borders to Europe and the music capitals of the world. Mme. Bachauer did much more than urge the orchestra to "go international"; she arranged for the Symphony to perform at the 1966 Athens Festival. (The formal invitation was issued by a Festival official.)

"By Woodbury and I were thrilled with this invitation," notes Wendell Ashton. "We immediately began to make plans to raise money so the Symphony could accept the invitation. We calculated that we would need approximately $150,000. But just as we were about to begin the drive, By Woodbury suffered a massive stroke in July."

The Abravanels were in Santa Barbara at the time, Abravanel in his usual summer role as director of the Music Academy of the West. When he and Lucy returned to Salt Lake City in the first week of September, they visited Woodbury as soon as possible. His will was unfaltering, even though he could barely whisper "You must go to Greece!" In spite of his physical condition, reports Abravanel, "he lifted my spirits. By Woodbury was the inspiration behind our first overseas tour."

Woodbury and Ashton had built on the solid foundation laid by Abravanel, Huck Gregory, and, later, Shirl Swenson. Together they had created an effective organization with sold-out houses, an enviable national recording reputation, and a deficit-free operation. Now Woodbury and Ashton added a new dimension. A great team, they talked Big Time, thought Big Time, operated Big Time, and planned Big Time. Both were super-salesmen, indefatigable, imaginative, relentless, single-minded. The Big Machine was gathering momentum, and Woodbury's stroke did not slow it down.

Although Ashton had to carry on with an unexpected responsibility, he considered Woodbury a member of the team. Woodbury's name appeared as president in each concert program throughout 1965–66 atop the Symphony Board listing, while Ashton was designated acting president. The following season, 1966–67, with Woodbury still disabled, the Board named Ashton president. Woodbury's name appeared a president emeritus beside Ashton's until his death seven years later on October 18, 1972.

On September 7, 1965, a *Deseret News* headline read: "Symphony Receives Invitation to Athens." A four-column photo at the top of the page showed Abravanel, Ashton, Gregory, and prominent Salt Lake businessman Christopher E. Athas pointing elatedly at a world globe.

The announcement had been made public earlier in the day at the weekly luncheon of the Salt Lake Rotary Club during a program honoring the Abravanels. "Wendell Ashton . . . made the announcement for the Board's president, T. Bowring Woodbury, who is . . . recovering from a serious illness suffered in July," the article read. "The formal invitation was extended in a letter from the secretary general of the National Tourist Organization of Greece . . . and culminated the combined efforts of . . . Greek pianist, Gina Bachauer, who appeared with the Utah Symphony last March

17 and 18, and Christopher E. Athas, Salt Lake business-man who had been highly decorated by the Greek government for his efforts in encouraging . . . friendly gestures between . . . Utah and Greece."

The invitation, addressed to Woodbury, also said: "We sincerely believe that these concerts will be of the highest musical value, and we are certain you will do your utmost to see that the . . . visit to Greece materializes." The invitation was for three concerts in Athens and "at least two other concerts at another major Greek city." Salonika, Abravanel's birthplace, was subsequently named as the "other" city.

The invitation brought a flurry of media activity. Salt Lake newspapers carried major stories plus editorials. TV and radio gave it major-event coverage.

Abravanel called it "a tremendous honor. . . . Athens is one of the most fastidious world festivals, and to receive an official invitation from this organization is exceedingly gratifying." Although the Symphony Board would delay their official acceptance for eight months, until April 1966, when covering funds had been raised, the *Salt Lake Tribune* quoted Abravanel as saying after the luncheon that "Symphony officials had declared 'definitely' that the orchestra would attend the Greek Festival."

Abravanel went even further, according to the *Tribune*, suggesting that "there is a possibility the group will go to the Soviet Union at the urging of David Oistrakh, the famous Russian violinist who appeared last year with the Utah Orchestra in the Tabernacle," and who would appear with the Los Angeles Philharmonic on December 8, Abravanel conducting.

"Munich Invite for Symphony" headlined a *Deseret News* story by music editor Harold Lundstrom five days later, on the heels of the Athens invitation: "The Utah Symphony . . . received its second invitation for a European concert early Sunday morning . . . to play in the Munich Festival. . . . The invitation came from no less an official than the President of Upper Bavaria, Dr. Jur Adam Deinlem . . . , who made the invitation at a Hotel Utah breakfast to Wendell J. Ashton and Neal A. Maxwell, both Vice Presidents of the Utah Symphony. . . . Acceptance . . . is being withheld . . . until it is sure that the Symphony Board can raise the necessary funds. The Board is highly optimistic." In the September 12 piece Lundstrom also revealed that concerts in Berlin, London, and Moscow were being considered.

Abravanel and cellist Zara Nelsova. MZPC.

The Board met on September thirteenth. Ashton read a letter he had composed to solicit federal government assistance for the tour. Governor Rampton had agreed to contact Utah Senator Frank E. Moss, and Ashton reported that state assistance was being pursued as a fund-raising spin-off; he suggested a tour of Symphony supporters to accompany the orchestra.

In retrospect, Ashton writes:

> We felt we could achieve our goal if we could get a $50,000 grant from the U.S. State Department. Democrats were in control in Washington, D.C., and I was a lifelong Republican, having been involved in a number of Republican campaigns. With the help of my good friend, "Mr. Democrat," [Utah attorney] Calvin W. Rawlings, we laid our plans to go after the $50,000. Cal [Governor Calvin Rampton] got in touch with Senator Frank E. Moss, Democrat Senator from Utah, and thus began a struggle to obtain the $50,000. The State Department turned us down, but we kept going back. . . . Finally, Senator Moss got to Vice President Hubert H. Humphrey, and Mr. Humphrey, against the wishes of the State Department, obtained the $50,000 grant for us.

At the November 15 Board meeting, Rawlings reported "an informal commitment of $50,000 from the government." This marked the beginning of specific fund-raising plans for the projected European tour.

"Neither Abravanel nor Gregory really thought we could raise this kind of money for the Athens Festival," recalls Ashton. Neither had James C. Fletcher, president of the University of Utah and a member of the Board. He had gone on record in that first meeting as stating "chances were slim" of getting any kind of federal funding.

Rehearsing in the Tabernacle with soloist Grant Johannesen in 1966. MAP.

Fortunately, their hopes and not their fears proved prophetic. In April 1966 – over a year after Gina Bachauer's informal invitation to the Athens Festival – the Board officially accepted. The State Department grant, approved that month, came with a string, however; it had to be matched with local funds. Fortunately, this was not as difficult as it might have appeared because Wendell Ashton is one of the nation's most effective fund-raisers for the performing arts.

Even while Gina Bachauer was proposing the idea of a tour, another possible funding source had appeared. Board minutes of March 29, 1965, record that "George Kuyper of the Ford Foundation is in the city to explore the possibilities of Ford Foundation grants to American orchestras." Kuyper, former manager of the Los Angeles Philharmonic, visited half a dozen American orchestras "to conduct a preliminary study of the needs, problems and goals of professional symphony orchestras," according to Oona Sullivan of the Ford Foundation staff.

Huck Gregory recalls walking Kuyper over to meet President Woodbury at his Zion's First National Bank office. He also remembers driving the visitor through a wintry Emigration Canyon to his home for an informal but high-powered evening. It was the beginning of a chain reaction that led to the Utah Symphony's greatest financial opportunity. It didn't receive the media coverage it deserved, because at the time it was competing with the approaching European tour, but it soon emerged as the Symphony's overriding preoccupation.

In substance, Kuyper asked the Symphony Board: "If the Ford Foundation should decide to initiate a program to aid symphony orchestras of the United States, what would be the most meaningful kind of help?"

Abravanel and Isaac
Stern. MZPC.

Utah had an answer: "It was Maurice Abravanel who suggested that the most significant assistance would certainly not be a massive infusion of funds that would later be withdrawn, but rather the establishment of an endowment for each orchestra that would yield on the order of $100,000 a year to help defray operating expenses—a sum that could be counted on year after year. This suggestion became the cornerstone of the subsequent $86,000 million program of the Ford Foundation," wrote Ms. Sullivan in a Special Report on the Ford Matching Endowment Grant (reprinted in the Utah Symphony program for March 10, 1973).

"The Ford Foundation subsequently invited us to send a delegation to New York to meet with Foundation representatives and be briefed on their far-reaching program to aid symphony orchestras," Gregory recalls.

Ashton invited Obert C. Tanner, prominent philanthropist and civic leader, to chair the Ford Foundation committee and, with Gregory and Abravanel, Tanner "anguished over what figure we should suggest. It was finally agreed to set our goal at one million dollars to be raised between 1966 and 1971."

"Prior to that New York meeting with Ford Foundation officials," adds Gregory, "I distinctly recall attending a smaller meeting in Salt Lake with Wendell, Obert, Jack Gallivan, one or two others, and myself, who discussed this subject and decided to recommend to the blue-ribbon panel a grant request of $1.25 million. The panel trimmed it to $1 million, and that's how we arrived at that figure." The "panel" was a committee of top civic, government, business, education, and religious leaders.

The genius of the Ford Foundation grants was that the amounts recommended by each orchestra and approved by Ford had to be matched by local fund-raising within five years, from 1966 through 1971. In addition to the funds to be matched, the Ford Foundation also gave direct grants ranging from $75,000 to $640,000 that did not require matching. The Utah Symphony received one of these, for $500,000 ($100,000 a year for five years) earmarked for salary increases. The half-million-dollar non-matching grant is now often overlooked, but it should be added to the larger endowment-plus-matching total of $2 million when the fund-raising efforts of this remarkable group are judged.

The Utah Symphony was one of twenty-five major orchestras, based on total budget, receiving Ford grants. A total of sixty-one orchestras from thirty-three states, the District of Columbia, and Puerto Rico were funded. Matching endowment funds ranged from $2 million for the fourteen largest orchestras (Boston, Philadelphia, New York, etc.) to $75,000 for the smallest (Rhode Island, Fort Wayne, Jacksonville). The Utah Symphony was in the "second fifteen," all of which received $1 million matching endowments, plus $500,000 non-matching funds. It was tonic for the orchestra's ego as well as its pocketbook.

When the Ford Foundation drive was approved and announced, Wendell Ashton records that "Obert [Tanner] and I invited Edward M. Naughton, chairman of the board of the Utah Power & Light Company, to serve as general chairman for the Ford Foundation drive." They not only successfully completed their assignment by June 30, 1971, but exceeded the $1 million goal in the process: a total of $1,053,832 was reported to the Foundation.

The Ford drive was one of Wendell Ashton's most successful undertakings as Board president. "About the time this drive was completed in 1971 (to me the most crucial time in the history of the Utah Symphony since I have been its chief executive officer), approximately eight musicians of our orchestra asked for a meeting with me," Ashton recalls:

> We met, and they expressed some real concerns. They pointed out that they had been serving as part-time orchestra members and many of them had other jobs teaching at the University, secondary and elementary schools. The way the Utah Symphony is developing, they were going to ask to be full-time musicians. Their question to me was: Is the Symphony on a financially sound base, so that they could . . . give up their other part-time jobs and go full-time with the orchestra?

Ashton had come to share Abravanel's twenty-five-year obsession. Through the years, the Maestro had continued to work to add more salary weeks to the musicians' contracts: two or more with the University Summer Festivals, another with the University Festival of Contemporary Music, five to six weeks with Bill Christensen's ballet, recording sessions—anything that could be found or created.

The Maestro exhorts his orchestra during a Tabernacle performance. MAP.

Ashton recalls that the musicians' questions,

took some real soul-searching on my part. My response . . . was that we had not let them down to this point, and while I could not promise them anything that was risk-proof, the Symphony Board would do everything to meet its commitments for a full-time orchestra. . . . The musicians accepted our word, and soon after the orchestra achieved full-time status . . . with the number of weeks of service extending virtually each year until it reached a full fifty-two-week contract.

A regular daytime rehearsal schedule was a stipulated requirement of the Ford Foundation grant. The University's busy daytime class schedule made it impossible for the Symphony to use the Music Hall, then its campus home, on a daily basis, so the orchestra arranged to move to the vacated Christian Science Church at 560 East South Temple.

While the Ford Foundation matching endowment deadline was June 30, 1971, the principal of the trust would not be distributed until 1976. In the meantime, however, Ford-funded orchestras received dividends from the trust, and Huck Gregory puts the annual dividend figure for the Utah Symphony at $130,000. Nationwide, the Ford endowments largely accomplished their primary goals: (1) most orchestras now had their own endowments; (2) orchestral seasons had been extended, providing longer working periods for musicians; (3) basic salaries had been raised; (4) new musical activities had been developed – summer concerts, expanded school and college programs; and (5) concerts were being offered by portions of the orchestras which were more practical for specialized repertoire.

The invitation to the Greek Festival of Music coupled with the Ford Foundation program had brought the Utah Symphony's Big Machine into high gear. Both invitations came during By Woodbury's abbreviated term as president. Both were assumed wholeheartedly and positively by Wendell

Ashton, who was quick to include many other non-musicians in the Big Machine: "Obert Tanner has been a major factor in the progress of the Symphony, both with his time, his energies, and his means. Obert has been one of our greatest supports. He . . . was chairman of the Bicentennial Commission appointed by Governor Calvin L. Rampton. It was this commission that launched the move toward . . . a new Symphony Hall."

Ashton also includes among the stalwarts "Alonzo W. Watson, Jr., a prominent Salt Lake attorney, of the Board of Trustees of Westminster College, and member in charge of legal affairs; Calvin W. Rawlings, major contact with federal officials; Governors Calvin L. Rampton and Scott M. Matheson; and B. Z. Kastler, chairman of the Symphony Board's Audit Committee," who in 1980 helped organize the staff, computerize, and add "other modern methods of management and controls."

From the Utah Symphony staff Ashton praises Huck Gregory as "a dedicated chief executive officer of our staff from 1957 through 1982 and then continuing as Executive Director; Shirl H. Swenson, who would join the staff after our 1966 European tour and take charge of logistics and arrangements for four subsequent overseas tours; and Carleen Landes, office manager, who helped book concerts, acted as Abravanel's secretary, and served as an important liaison with the musicians."

The Big Machine emerged with the internationally acclaimed recordings of Mahler's Eighth, Seventh, and Second symphonies in the years from 1964 to 1967. By Woodbury and Wendell Ashton brought the orchestra a broadened vision of its role worldwide. The first overseas tour, spurred by Gina Bachauer in 1965, became a reality the following year – at the same time the Ford Foundation grant was awarded. The Big Machine rolled with increasing momentum through the sixties and seventies. The middle sixties was really the Golden Era.

The Symphony performs in the Greek amphitheater of Herodes
Atticus, at the foot of the Acropolis. MAP.

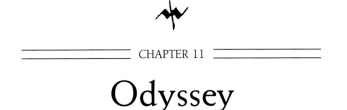

CHAPTER 11

Odyssey

New York City, Athens, Salonika, Belgrade, Ljubljana, Vienna, Stuttgart, Cassel, Wuppertal, Berlin, London, and Albuquerque! This itinerary for the Symphony's first overseas tour, from September 9 to October 2, 1966, captured the imagination of conductor, musicians, and 115 others, including many orchestra spouses and fans.

The Bachauer-inspired invitation from the Greek government to perform three concerts in the Athens Festival became a reality. Two concerts were added in Salonika, Abravanel's birthplace. The tour expanded during the planning stages to four other European countries, and the overseas leg would conclude with a concert in London.

En route to Europe the orchestra helped to commemorate the seventy-fifth anniversary of Carnegie Hall with their first concert in that historic building. To perform in Carnegie Hall was an unexpected honor for the little-known Utah Symphony. Manhattan's major music critics were in attendance on September 10 to compare sounds from the Mountain West with the East's glossy Big Five.

The New York *Post's* Harriett Johnson saluted Abravanel, "whose 26-year-old organization is too interesting to merit only respect." She praised a youthful cello section and took special note of the orchestra's "distaff majority."

Harold Schonberg, one of the nation's top music critics for thirty years, wrote a very objective yet very favorable review for the *New York Times*:

Kicking off (1) the New York orchestral season, (2) a tour of Europe that will last almost a month, and (3) Carnegie Hall's diamond jubilee year was the Utah Symphony Orchestra in its first visit to New York.

Maurice Abravanel, who used to conduct at the Metropolitan Opera [Schonberg had been a young music student in those days] and has headed the Utah Symphony since 1947, conducted, and the soloist was Grant Johannesen, a native son from Salt Lake City and one of America's best pianists.

Schonberg's review is positive for the most part. He praises the orchestra as "an enthusiastic and a well-drilled organization," but points out some weak spots. "Intonation troubles beset the woodwinds and the strings had a raw or shrill rather than a sensuous quality. It could be that the temporary plastic seats in Carnegie Hall have changed the acoustics. . . . Otherwise, the playing was rhythmically accurate, vigorous and full of the special qualities that occur when visitors are in Carnegie Hall, playing their hearts out to make a good impression. Mr. Abravanel is obviously a superior conductor, more interested in the music than in himself. In the Prokofiev C Major Concerto he and Johannesen collaborated as two fine musicians can." Schonberg closed his review by acknowledging the presence of Utah Governor Calvin L. Rampton, U.S. Senators Wallace F. Bennett and Frank E. Moss,

The Abravanels embarking on the Symphony's first international tour in 1966. MAP.

United Nations Ambassador Arthur G. Goldberg, and New York Mayor John Lindsay among those in attendance.

The *New Yorker* magazine's salty Winthrop Sargent devoted his September 17, 1966, column to the Carnegie Hall appearance:

> The orchestra . . . is the kind of orchestra that has been built to achieve a high standard of performance entirely through the methodical efforts of a great conductor. The conductor in question is Maurice Abravanel . . . of enormous experience and authority. He has drilled his orchestra to the point where it some-

times sounds almost like one of the top symphonic organizations of the country. Its personality is responsive, accurate, and wonderfully disciplined. . . . Nothing stands out particularly, the effect being one of carefully coordinated ensemble.

Sargent praised the programming and rated Abravanel's conception of Vaughan Williams' Sixth Symphony as "masterly . . . with the orchestra giving an eminently respectable reading of the work."

The day of the concert, September 10, 1966, was proclaimed Utah Day in New York City by Governor Rampton, and an estimated 1,700 Friends of Utah attended a buffet dinner and reception at the Waldorf Astoria. It was a gala affair attended by dignitaries representing the government, churches, education, and performing arts. An attractive souvenir program for the concert contained letters of greeting from Vice President Humphrey, Governor Rampton, and Senators Bennett and Moss. A photo of President Woodbury, inactivated more than a year earlier, was included with a photo of Abravanel and the orchestra.

The entire New York stay was brilliantly orchestrated. Successful beyond expectation, the concert and associated events launched the Symphony toward Athens with confidence.

Huck Gregory detailed the tour in the April 1967 issue of *Music Journal*: "In all, the Utah Symphony visited five countries outside the United States, travelled a total of 18,000 miles and gave sixteen concerts in three and one-half weeks. It played before a combined audience of 46,300." Gregory revealed that while jets for trans-Atlantic service had to be chartered at least a year in advance, because of the delay in making final arrangements for the tour, the Symphony had only a few months. "After every major airline had said 'No', El Al Israel Airlines made arrangements . . . for a plane from New York to Athens. . . . Our joy was short-lived, however, because an obscure international air agreement provided for *American* carriers only to land at Athens." It wasn't until May 1966 – five months before departure – that a TWA plane was finally chartered.

Hotel reservations also had to be made a year in advance but, as Gregory pointed out, "One doesn't simply reserve rooms all along the proposed route. One waits patiently until concert dates have been definitely set to correspond reasonably to the original itinerary. There was a trade fair in Salonika, for example . . . and the orchestra's travel agent tried for a year unsuccessfully to obtain anything . . . other than a youth hostel, despite petitions by the National Tourist Organization of Greece."

Other sticky obstacles, unknown to most travelers, included the "bass drum problem." With its large wooden case the bass drum would simply not fit into the B-707 at Salt Lake International. United Airlines offered to cargo-freight it to New York for the Carnegie Hall concert, but Gregory says, "It wouldn't fit into the trans-Atlantic plane, either, and had to be returned to Salt Lake City." He concludes humorously: "Everyone should share the experience of borrowing a bass drum in four different languages and six different countries!"

Of the tour's sixteen concerts, the five in Greece were the most exciting and unforgettable. Everyone agreed—Abravanel, musicians, the one hundred fifteen supporters who accompanied the orchestra, and the press. The three at the Athens Festival were performed outdoors in the 1,800-year-old Herodes Atticus Theatre at the foot of the Acropolis—one of the wonders of the world—flood-lighted at night.

In his *Music Journal* account, Gregory describes the Athens concerts: "A combined audience of 14,000 including all members of the Royal Family filled the gigantic outdoor amphitheater for the three Utah Symphony concerts in Athens. Mme. Bachauer herself appeared as soloist for the first concert. The second was an all-orchestra program and the third featured Soviet violinist David Oistrakh."

When Gina Bachauer came on stage to solo in Prokofiev's Third Piano Concerto, the audience welcomed her as a national heroine. The applause was long and sustained. Harold Lundstrom of the *Deseret News*, who reviewed the first two Athens concerts, noted:

> After a half-dozen curtain calls [following the Prokofiev], Mme. Bachauer and Abravanel joined forces again to repeat the finale of the concerto as an encore. . . . [T]he audience demanded still more. Mme. Bachauer obliged by playing a Bach *Aria*.
>
> Though she announced neither the piece's title nor that it was a favorite of the late King Paul, her perfor-

Abravanel with Gina Bachauer, who soloed in the Symphony's first concert in Athens. MAP.

mance was so poignantly moving and impressive that everyone was aware that something deeply personal was involved. King Paul's beautiful widow, the queen-mother, sat, eyes closed throughout the long *Aria*, deeply touched.

Abravanel then led the Symphony in the Overture to *Oberon* of Weber and Beethoven's Seventh, the latter drawing noisy response.

Sandwiched between the first and third concerts starring the Greek pianist and the charismatic Soviet violinist was an all-orchestra evening. Abravanel programmed popular favorites that triggered the orchestra's most enthusiastic receptions. Mendelssohn's popular *Italian* Symphony started things off. Stravinsky's *Firebird* suite was greeted with warmth and, the critics reported, played to perfection. Samuel Barber's subdued *Adagio for Strings* brought a respectful response. But the audience went wild over Gershwin's *Porgy and Bess* suite. Abravanel was eventually coaxed back for an encore—Morton Gould's *American Salute*, the orchestra's most-performed encore of all time. The applause and roar of the crowd continued until Abravanel conducted Leroy Robertson's subdued *Pastorale* from the *Book of Mormon* Oratorio, which also became a regular encore during the tour.

One Athens newspaper carried a four-column photo of Oistrakh and Abravanel smilingly acknowledging applause after the performance of the Shostakovich Violin Concerto, which received a standing ovation at the final concert. The reviews were enthusiastic except for that of the politically rightist newspaper, *Estia*, which took an unusual and unexpected jab at Abravanel's dedication of the concerto's performance to Shostakovich's approaching sixtieth birthday: "The applause should not deflect from the fact that Mr. Abravanel has no right to dedicate anything to any Soviet composer while performing under the Acropolis. . . . The concerto reminds one of cat meows and it was a pity to waste Oistrakh's talent on such 'katzenmusik.' " On this concluding Athens Festival concert with Oistrakh the orchestra also played Brahms' Fourth Symphony and Bernstein's *Candide* Overture.

The two Greek princesses, Irene and Sophia, attended all three concerts and both rehearsals in Athens. Princess Irene subsequently performed twice in the Salt Lake Tabernacle with Gina Bachauer, Abravanel, and the Utah Symphony. On a program billed as "A Royal Evening," she appeared there with Bachauer on February 8, 1969, as duo-soloist in Bach's First Double Piano Concerto. Bachauer soloed that night in Beethoven's *Emperor* Concerto. On January 23, 1971, Princess Irene appeared with Bachauer again, this time in Mozart's Double Piano Concerto. Bachauer also performed the Grieg Concerto, which had brought her first critical acclaim and public success in London's Albert Hall in the late 1940's. Princess Sophia subsequently married King Don Carlos of Spain and is now Queen Sofia.

For the sixty-three-year-old Abravanel the journey to his birthplace in Salonika was a sentimental one. The two concerts there were good musically but drew small crowds. The *Salt Lake Tribune*'s Jim Fitzpatrick explained:

> The turnout in this northern city was nowhere near comparable to those at Athens, but there were reasons for this. In the first place, Salonika currently is the scene of an international industrial fair to which European and many American firms have sent exhibits. It runs during the evening concert hours. . . .

Concertmaster Oscar Chausow, violinist David Oistrakh, and Abravanel take their bows. MAP.

In addition, Salonika is the scene this week of one of those film festivals from various countries. . . . [T]he result, of course, was that the orchestra held the short end of the stick.

Norman R. Bowen, *Deseret News* City Editor, wrote of Abravanel taking,

a half-hour from his crowded schedule to return to the historic White Tower of Salonika to enjoy an ice cream cone as he fondly remembers doing as a child. . . . "The Tower hasn't changed a bit," the maestro happily commented: the only difference he noted was the replacement of the sidewalk ice cream merchants by refreshment stands, but "the nearby neighborhood has not changed."

The second Salonika concert drew a larger audience, however, because Gina Bachauer appeared again as soloist in Prokofiev's Third Piano Concerto.

The orchestra then traveled north into Yugoslavia for two concerts; the first in Belgrade, the second in Ljubljana. An interesting sidelight of these behind-the-Iron-Curtain performances is recounted by Huck Gregory: "Yugoslavian border guards wanted to be sure, for example, that nobody was hiding in the contrabass cases. What is surprising is the fact that under such pressure [of schedules] so little went wrong. Belgrade embassy officials said it was the smoothest, best-organized tour they'd ever seen."

Utah-born Grant Johannesen, who had attained international stature in his twenties, joined the orchestra in Yugoslavia for the second of his solo appearances on the tour. Johannesen played Prokofiev's Third Concerto in both Belgrade and Ljubljana. "His crackling high style throughout had the intense Slavic audience completely mesmerized," wrote Fitzpatrick. The Belgrade concert was preceded by a reception at the residence of U.S. Ambassador C. Bur Elbrick, and the Abravanels celebrated their nineteenth wedding anniversary at the Ljubljana concert.

Then to Vienna, the "music capital of the world" in the eighteenth and nineteenth centuries. The concert was presented in "the greatest symphony hall in the world," the Grosse Musikvereins Saal, home of the Vienna Philharmonic. The Utah Symphony concert was sponsored by the Friends of Music Society, which traditionally presents the Vienna Philharmonic concerts.

Abravanel and Johannesen were singled out for praise by Edward Strauss, conductor of the Vienna Symphony

The Greek royal family applauding the Utah Symphony. Lucy Abravanel can be seen in the third row. MAP.

Abravanel and the two Greek princesses. MAP.

Orchestra: "I am not just making compliments," he said through interpreter Huck Gregory, according to a *Deseret News* story by Donna J. Bowen:

> The orchestra has a wonderful string section and a very good French horn [Don Peterson]. . . . Maestro Abravanel is a musician's musician, not a showman. His movements are for the orchestra, not the audience; he conducts with a sure hand and so easily. Yes, he conducts with precision and without exaggeration.
>
> Mr. Johannesen was excellent. You know it was the first time he had played here, I think. We hear so many pianists but Mr. Johannesen belongs in the top echelon.

Vienna is a haughty city. A minor bureaucrat had complained: "Why are you presenting a concert before the opening of the Philharmonic season? It isn't proper." Still, the concert was a success, the 1600-seat hall was nearly full, and the orchestra was well received.

Abravanel was vexed with one Vienna critic who wrote, "Well, in America you always have to pay the piper. First there was the pops tune [Bernstein's *Candide* Overture] and then that long, lumbering work by a little-known composer." The little-known "American" composer was Ralph Vaughan Williams, England's greatest, whose Sixth Symphony was the main work on many concerts throughout the tour. Obviously Vienna is not the *twentieth* century's world music capital.

Five concerts in Germany followed from September 23 to 27. Stuttgart was the first stop; Abravanel received five curtain-calls. The program included the *Firebird* and Johannesen in the Prokofiev.

Next came Cassel, where in his later twenties Abravanel had been principal conductor from 1929 to 1932. He made a curtain-call speech telling the audience "Salt Lake City like Cassel has wonderful people." He then went on to say that Salt Lake is "the capital of the Mormons" and conducted Leroy Robertson's *Pastorale* from the *Book of Mormon* Oratorio as an encore. It was a gala evening with the burgomaster of Cassel in attendance.

The concert in Wuppertal, an industrial city with a population of nearly half a million, featured Johannesen's Prokofiev again. More important, Vaughan Williams' Sixth Symphony was given its best rendering on the Continent as Abravanel polished it for its long-anticipated London performance.

Then came Berlin and its Philharmonic Hall. Contrasted with Vienna's smaller, acoustically-perfect Grosse Musikvereins Saal, the Berlin Hall is on a grander scale; yet it too boasts excellent acoustics, ranking among the world's best. The Utah Symphony performed there officially as a feature of the Berlin Festival and enjoyed one of its greatest successes. The reviewers were uniformly warm and enthusiastic. Most commented on "die damen" (women) and "junge" (young) musicians. This had also been the case in Vienna, since all-male ensembles are standard in European orchestras. Abravanel's Utah Symphony always comprised around half women (mostly strings) and half men. His musicians were also extremely youthful by European standards. An apocryphal story has Abravanel on the Tabernacle platform after a dress rehearsal: "You know, the Utah Symphony is not just an eighty-member ensemble. At the present time, it has ninety-one members, which includes eleven pregnancies!" One European feature writer humorously called the Utah Symphony "Phil Spitalny's all-girl orchestra," a reference to the popular all-female orchestra of the thirties and early forties.

Many Berlin critics wrote of Salt Lake City as "the capital of the Mormon State of Utah." Without exception they observed that the orchestra "not only gives its regular concerts in the famous Mormon Temple but also serves a vast area of the western states." Berlin's *Die Welt* for September 29, 1966, reported: "It serves an area of over a half million square kilometers" with concert tours in Western America. (Since American tourists on Salt Lake's Temple Square are often confused about which building is the Temple and which is the Tabernacle, it is not surprising that the Berlin music critics echoed the misconception.)

All the Berlin critics devoted generous space to Abravanel as "European-born," as having lived in Germany for thirteen years, been a student of Kurt Weill, spent three years as principal conductor of Cassel's state opera house, and having climaxed his German career by conducting the Berlin State Opera.

Der Telegraf noted that Abravanel "was a guest conductor of the [Berlin] Philharmonic a few years ago. His orchestra, among whom are many women, played with pleasure under his lively, but careful baton direction. . . . [T]he discipline of ensemble left nothing wanting; the sound was supple, fresh and of discriminate colorfulness."

The Symphony in the amphitheater of Herodes Atticus. MAP.

Die Welt praised Abravanel as one under whose "direction the orchestra has developed into an ensemble of sincere musicians whose musicianship is ennobled by their superior orchestral discipline." Stravinsky's *Firebird*, the closing number, "was cheered enthusiastically." The *Berliner Morgenpost*, even more enthusiastically, wrote: "A nearly recording-perfect performance of Stravinsky's *Firebird* Suite closed the evening. But just preceding, Grant Johannesen played the stupendously dexterous and striking solo part of the ever-effective Third Piano Concerto by Prokofiev. . . . It was a thundering success for Johannesen."

The *Kurier*, a Berlin daily, commented on previous "musical visits from Salt Lake City, the capital of the Mormon State of Utah. . . . First we heard the marvelous Tabernacle

Choir . . . whose brave pioneers made their homes between the desert, the ocean, and the rocky mountains. Then during the 1960–61 season of our Philharmonic Orchestra, [Abravanel] . . . stood on the podium. . . . This time he has brought his own orchestral instrument which he himself has developed: the Utah Symphony Orchestra."

Another Berlin daily, *B.Z.*, scolded Berliners:

Snobs, who have until now been of the opinion, that good music is only being made in Berlin and perhaps Vienna, had to lay down their arms. The traveling stars under their 63-year-old conductor, Maurice Abravanel . . . made music with great perfection, virtuosity and candid pleasure of playing.

Pianist Grant Johannesen . . . inspired everyone with Prokofiev's Third Piano Concerto. Above all, as the musicians played, the colorful image of the American teenager dressed in mini-skirt and bobby sox with the knit jacket lackadaisically thrown over the shoulder, just seemed to melt away.

Most of the concerts immediately preceding the orchestra's farewell performance in London featured Vaughan Williams' Sixth Symphony. Abravanel had selected it nearly six months earlier as he plotted his programs for the European tour. While the work was politely received by its Germanic and Slavic audiences, its real destination was London.

The orchestra flew from Berlin to London on September 28, nearly three weeks after departing from Salt Lake International, and performed at Fairfield Concert Hall in Croydon, a London suburb and the site of its principal airport prior to Heathrow. It was the tour's most frustrating, yet one of its most memorable concerts.

The headlines reveal the gist: "Instruments Late, So's the Concert." The *Daily Telegraph* declared: "Delayed Concert a Triumph." The *Times* said "Orchestra Worth Waiting For." The *Manchester Guardian* (now the *Guardian*) simply ignored the unusual delay with the headline "Utah Symphony Orchestra at Croydon." United Press International (UPI) was more flamboyant: "Concert Late? It's Worth Wait!" The *Daily Mail* headed its review with "Why the audience had to wait three hours for curtain up."

Huck Gregory detailed the problem in his *Music Journal* report:

But into each tour some rain must fall. It had already been decided that the instruments should be flown from Berlin to London, but the European shipping agent gave every assurance that land and water shipment would still allow plenty of margin for timely arrival. Not included in his calculation was the fact that the instruments were to arrive at the British port of Harwich without accompanying papers.

Despite the best efforts of the American Embassy, the British Ministry of Labour, the orchestra's European concert agent, Wilfrid Van Wyck, and several British shipping firms, the instruments remained in limbo until a British customs officer took it upon himself to prepare a manifest and send them on their way. But they still had to be trucked through the densest part of London during the rush hour, and as a result the concert was three hours late in starting. . . .

When it became known the instruments were not yet on their way, it became necessary to inform the very large audience that the concert would be delayed for an indefinite period. Those who could not remain were invited to obtain a refund at the box office. Those who wished to stay were assured of a concert, however late.

Following this announcement there was a muffled murmuring as those in the audience decided whether to leave or stay. At this point a very dignified lady arose and said audibly, "These musicians have come all the way from Berlin to play for us tonight. In fact, they've come all the way from the American West. Most of us have only a few miles traveling to get home. Whatever the delay, if they are still willing to play for us I think it would be a shame if we didn't stay to hear them. I for one intend to stay."

It is not possible to know how many knew the identity of the lady – Mrs. Ralph Vaughan Williams, widow of the British composer whose powerful Sixth Symphony was to be the major work of the evening. Half of the audience remained, and it was probably for this London audience that the orchestra gave its best concert of the tour.

Three of London's four newspapers heralded the performance "a triumph." The fourth, the *Manchester Guardian*, which traditionally boasts Britain's top music critics, summed up their feelings: "One hopes now for another visit before long." The conservative *Times* added: "Next time they should stay longer." Gina Bachauer rejoined the orchestra for its London finale, as she and her husband, British conductor Alex Sherman, had a permanent London residence.

The orchestra flew from London to New York and from New York to Albuquerque, where they played two concerts in the University of New Mexico's recently completed concert hall, returning to Salt Lake City on October third. The *Salt Lake Tribune*'s Jim Fitzpatrick hailed the "Old World Tour . . . a slam-bang success." Quoting Abravanel: "Fourteen concerts in Europe. All successes. What other orchestra in America can say this?" Fitzpatrick concludes: "Allowing for musicians' natural bent to hyperbole, Mr. Abravanel pretty well summed up the results of the symphony's first tour abroad."

Salt Lake's Fourth Estate greeted Abravanel and the orchestra as heroes. Newspapers devoted generous news and feature space; television and radio stations aired interviews and news stories. "Triumphant Journey Over for the Utah Symphony" trumpeted the *Deseret News* for October 3, 1966, with a four-column headline and photo of Abravanel, Mrs. By Woodbury, and Wendell Ashton.

Two weeks later Abravanel received a letter from Vice President Hubert Humphrey, who had played a key role in obtaining the necessary $50,000 grant from the State Department. Dated October 19, it read:

> I understand from my good friend Senator Ted Moss that you have just begun your 20th season with the Utah Symphony Orchestra.
>
> You and your orchestra made a great contribution during your trip to Europe, and we all appreciate it. You have performed not only a great service for the music lovers of Europe, but also for the interests of the people of the United States.

The successful 1966 tour set a pattern. Wendell Ashton came away feeling that the Utah Symphony should undertake an international tour at least every four years. He saw to it that major overseas tours became routine: Latin America in 1971, England in 1975, Greece and western Europe revisited in 1977 – all under Abravanel's leadership. After his 1979

resignation the pattern continued with tours under Abravanel's successors, Varujan Kojian and Joseph Silverstein.

SOUTH OF THE BORDER AND EAST OF EDEN

In early October 1970, Ashton announced the itinerary for a Latin American tour. It would begin June 1, 1971, with a concert in Washington's Constitution Hall, followed on June 2 by a return engagement in Carnegie Hall.

The ambitious itinerary of twenty-five concerts in five weeks then sent the orchestra to the Caribbean Islands and from there to Venezuela, Brazil, Uruguay, Argentina, Chile,

The Maestro faces his audience. MAP.

Peru, and Bolivia. The tour would conclude in Mexico on a schedule that was two weeks longer and packed in a dozen more concerts than the 1966 European tour.

U.S. State Department sponsorship came quickly – with no haggling or negotiating necessary this time. John Richardson, Jr., Assistant Secretary of State for Educational and Cultural Affairs, wrote: "We warmly welcome and encourage such tours. Performing arts are a . . . positive means of communicating with . . . peoples of other countries. We would like very much to have the Utah Symphony travel under the official auspices of the Department's Cultural Presentations Program."

The Gerard Concerts Association of Buenos Aires made the tour's general arrangements with Huck Gregory and Shirl H. Swenson, the Symphony's director of development, who would be tour director. Ashton rallied the support group, headed by Governor Rampton, that had guaranteed the success of the Carnegie Hall seventy-fifth anniversary concert.

Governor Rampton responded: "We are proud of the unparalleled record of our fine Symphony and what it has done for Utah. Not only have these musical ambassadors brought the inspiration of great music to every corner of our state and region, but through their . . . recordings and foreign tours they continue to focus favorable attention on the laudable achievements of the people of Utah."

Abravanel, contemplating the proposed tour, said: "The citizens of our state . . . can rejoice about this newest incredible honor. It is truly fantastic that our orchestra is invited to perform in world capitals over twenty times Salt Lake City's size. As with our 1966 rave notices in Berlin and London, we trust our musicians will repeat their achievements next year throughout Latin America."

Preparations began immediately, sandwiched into one of Abravanel's busiest and best seasons. Van Cliburn, Grant Johannesen, Gina Bachauer and Princess Irene of Greece, Gunther Schuller, Roberta Peters, Hans Richter-Haaser, James Oliver Buswell, and the orchestra's principal cellist, Christian Tiemeyer, comprised an impressive array of guest soloists. The successful subscription season in the Tabernacle concluded with a performance of *The Childhood of Christ* by Berlioz on April tenth.

Squeezed into the season's demanding schedule were state and regional tours from March 25 through May 14 that

Rehearsing with Utah favorite Roberta Peters. MZPC.

included multiple concerts in Arizona, New Mexico, and Utah, followed by a flight to Sacramento for the first of four concerts in five days in California. The musicians were exhausted by this hectic itinerary and had only two weeks to prepare their Latin American programs.

On June 1, 1971, the orchestra flew to Washington, D.C., for the first concert in Constitution Hall that evening. Abravanel conducted Ned Rorem's Third Symphony, Brahms' First, and Argentinian composer Ginastera's *Variaciones*, which had been introduced in the March 24 Tabernacle concert. Expatriate Utahns mingled with Abravanel, Symphony officials, and musicians at a post-concert reception hosted by the Honorable Joseph John Jova, U.S. representative to the Organization of American States, and Dr. Rodolfo P. Martinez, executive secretary for Education, Science, and Culture of the OAS, and their wives. Governor Rampton and Wendell Ashton presented awards. The distinguished guests included ambassadors to the United States from Nicaragua, Peru, Uruguay, Argentina, Costa Rica, Panama, Mexico, and Brazil. Nancy Hanks, chairman of the National Endowment for the Arts, was there to applaud Abravanel, who had just completed his first year's service on the Presidentially-appointed panel. It was a glittering beginning for a successful south-of-the-border tour.

The next day the orchestra flew to New York for a return engagement at Carnegie Hall. The Latin American leg followed immediately with two concerts in the Virgin Islands on June 3 and 4.

There were surprises. Huck Gregory recalls a phone call from Florida just before the tour began concerning the chartered plane which was to carry the instruments: "Were you aware, Mr. Gregory, that the president of that airline is in jail at this moment in Equador on charges of smuggling $1 million worth of heroin and gold?" Gregory checked it out and discovered that it was actually $2 million worth! He scrambled and found a replacement.

From Kennedy International they flew to St. Thomas in the Virgin Islands, one of the world's most hazardous airports. In Venezuela two concerts were scheduled in Caracas. The first went as planned, but the sponsors of the second concert "wanted to renege on their commitment and cancel the second performance that evening," Gregory recalls. Abravanel, Ashton, and Gregory met hastily with local representatives, insisting on full payment and the second performance. The concert was played, but Gregory stayed behind, alone, and collected the fee. A Trinidad concert had been canceled before the tour began but too late to change the flight reservations. The musicians enjoyed the unexpected two-day respite in their strenuous schedule.

Brazil was next with five concerts. The first, in Brasilia, brought a "particularly chilling feeling" to Gregory because of all the military uniforms in sight. "Brazil's Belem was undoubtedly the low point of the tour," he says. "It is a dumpy town at the mouth of the Amazon River, on the Equator. It was hot and dirty. Accommodations were terrible. No one slept much that night. Some members, including concertmaster Oscar Chausow, his wife Leyah, and Symphony manager Shirl Swenson walked around all night."

As if in compensation, the concert at Rio de Janeiro was sold out, and the final concert at São Paulo was successful but the schedule hurried. After a brief stopover in Montevideo, Uruguay, the orchestra flew to Argentina for six concerts. "Buenos Aires climaxed the five-week tour," says Gregory. Three concerts were scheduled in the Argentine capital at the grand old Teatro Colon.

After the three successful Buenos Aires concerts, the musicians flew to Cordoba and Mendoza. There was no stopover in Mendoza, and the orchestra left immediately following the concert to fly to Santiago, Chile. Political unrest had prevented the scheduling of a concert in Chile, "although we kept trying right up to the last." After an overnight stop the tour continued with a daylight flight to La Paz, Bolivia.

Bolivia is one of South America's poorest countries, and the Symphony had been unable to find a sponsor for a concert there. President Ashton, not one to give up easily, had persuaded a neighbor of his in Salt Lake City to sponsor the concert.

"If Buenos Aires was the climax of the tour, La Paz was without doubt the high point–14,000 feet elevation!" exclaims Gregory:

> The time to begin was an electrically charged moment. Oxygen masks were ready offstage. Two musicians near Maurice Abravanel were on the alert to catch him if he should falter because of lack of oxygen. Now the official entourage of government and military leaders filed in. Mr. Abravanel stepped from the stage to greet Bolivia's president and our ambassador. Then he stepped to the stage and gave the downbeat: the Bolivian national anthem! A splendid performance. It received enthusiastic applause. And the concert continued.

The special effort was worth it, for the political climate between the two countries was tense. The ambassador praised the orchestra and privately passed on the word that the national anthem, which effectively disarmed all present, "was definitely a coup for the United States."

The musicians hurried to one-night stops and concerts in Colombia, Panama, Costa Rica, and Nicaragua. Controversial Nicaraguan President Somoza (who was later assassinated) hosted a reception for the orchestra after the concert in a beautiful new theater there.

The tour concluded in Mexico City's Bellas Artes hall. The musicians then boarded a plane on July 3 for Los Angeles and home. It had been a long but rewarding trip, one regarded by many as primarily a goodwill venture, and clearly a diplomatic and political success. But music had been its language.

THE SECOND TIME AROUND

Four years later the orchestra made a shorter tour to England, from May 20 through June 2, 1975.

The tour began on May 20 with a successful, sold-out concert at the Kennedy Center in Washington, D.C., attended

Maurice Abravanel

Abravanel conducting
on tour. MAP.

by many political luminaries. The next day's Carnegie Hall concert found many former Utahns in attendance, and the critics praised Abravanel once again for his "solid interpretations" and "excellent programming."

The orchestra flew to Glasgow, Scotland, after the concert, traveling from there by bus for concerts in Newcastle-upon-Tyne, Middlesbrough, Huddersfield, Hemel Hempstead, and Portsmouth. Following the Hemel Hempstead concert, Ralph Vaughan Williams' widow came backstage to greet Abravanel.

During the first European tour in 1966, London's prestigious Royal Festival Hall had not been available, and the orchestra had performed in the suburb of Croydon. Although Ralph Vaughan Williams' Sixth Symphony had been a stunning success at that concert, Abravanel, Ashton, and the orchestra had been disappointed with the location and the hall.

The second time around, the climax of the tour would be a concert in Royal Festival Hall. Lord Thomson, England's legendary newspaper tycoon, had met Wendell Ashton in Salt Lake City in 1974. When they discussed the orchestra's desire to perform there, "Lord Thomson allowed as how he could arrange for the Utah Symphony to play in that most prestigious hall, and he left Utah with that in mind," Huck Gregory recalls. "Sure enough, a date was set in Royal Festival Hall for June 1975. The wheels for another European tour were set in motion."

Gregory details a surprising labor problem with members of the musicians' union during the London stay:

> The orchestra arrived in London early enough to rehearse and have the evening free. Shirl Swenson and I decided . . . that it would be nice if we gave the musicians a free day the next day following the concert. The Symphony picked up the cost of hotels and gave the musicians an extra day's per diem.
>
> Would you believe that a day or two prior to our departure for home there were some players who insisted that they must also be paid for the extra day they were kept on tour.

The musicians' demands continued until their return to Salt Lake City. Scott M. Matheson, then attorney for Union Pacific, was appointed arbiter in the dispute. He admitted that management's cause was just, but according to the contract, says Gregory, "we were not justified in keeping the musicians away from their homes without paying them."

Gregory terms this incident "a pivotal moment in the labor history of the Utah Symphony. Maurice Abravanel lost no occasion to tell us what we should have done—'cancel the tour and lay the blame at the feet of the musicians or union.' Otherwise, he said, the musicians and the union will see it as a victory and be encouraged to push for more and more and more. Whether or not Maurice was right," Gregory concludes, "it was not long until the players' demands grew and grew."

FAREWELL TO A FRIEND

Gina Bachauer died August 22, 1976, in Athens, struck down by a heart attack as she was going onstage to perform with the National Symphony Orchestra of Washington, D.C. One of her last phone calls was said to have been to Salt Lake City to confirm an appearance with the Utah Symphony the next season.

Soon after her death the Gina Bachauer International Competition was organized as a memorial on the Brigham Young University campus under the direction of music professor Paul C. Pollei. The Utah Symphony assumed sponsorship in 1982 with Abravanel as honorary chairman and Pollei as director. It is a major competition attracting young artists from many nations and a fitting monument to a fine artist and person.

This great friend of the Utah Symphony was sorely missed when the orchestra returned to the famous Greek amphitheater on September 19, 1977, to open Abravanel's final international tour. Once again the orchestra received a warm reception for three concerts in Athens before moving on to Salonika.

The emphasis shifted to Germany on this second European tour, which lasted four weeks—from September 19 through October 15, 1977. After the four concerts in Greece came one performance in Linz, Austria, then nine concerts in major cities in Germany: Augsburg, Nürnberg, Mainz, Düsseldorf, and Heidelberg.

Huck Gregory terms the Linz visit and concert unforgettable:

Two good friends,
Abravanel and Gina
Bachauer, embrace dur-
ing a rehearsal in 1972.
MZPC.

Words cannot adequately describe the setting in Linz. The Brucknerhalle is located on the banks of the Danube. Across the river . . . were the lush, green hills dotted with picturesque houses . . . and dark green patches of dense forest. The hall itself was spectacularly beautiful. The orchestra gave a performance equal to the hall's magnificence.

The U.S. ambassador from Vienna hosted a buffet reception for the musicians and special guests that was as lovely as any I have ever attended. In a brief toast he said, "This is one of the finest symphony orchestras I have ever heard. Mr. Abravanel and members of the Utah Symphony, tonight you have made us proud to be Americans."

The tour concluded with five concerts in Spain. Queen Sofia, formerly Princess Sophia of Greece, attended the first Madrid concert and enjoyed a warm reunion with the Abravanels and orchestra officials at the intermission.

Abravanel's programming in Greece and Spain included Mahler's First Symphony, Brahms' Second, Schumann's First, Beethoven's Seventh, Richard Strauss's *Death and Transfigu-*

ration, Rachmaninov's Second Piano Concerto, Bach's Suite in D, and Barber's *Adagio for Strings*.

The 1966 European tour was one of the most significant events in Utah Symphony history. Another was the Ford Foundation grant that required the orchestra to become fully professional with fifty-two-week contracts for the musicians. The third was the monumental recordings of Mahler's Second, Seventh, and Eighth symphonies during these same years. The 1966 tour broadened the orchestra's horizons. Wendell Ashton's hopes for overseas tours every four or five years became a reality, and they were the catalysts for increased excellence and continuing enthusiasm in the orchestra.

Governor Rampton was so impressed with the success of the 1966 tour and its accompanying public relations benefits that he offered to send the orchestra to major Western cities in 1968 on an "industrial development tour," with the state paying all costs except the musicians' salaries. The *Salt Lake Tribune* for Wednesday, June 19, stated: "As far as is known, it will be the first marriage of state government–symphony orchestra–industry anywhere as a promotion tool."

Airport staff sporting Abravanel T-shirts give the Symphony a rousing send-off on September 16, 1977. The fourth international tour would be Abravanel's last as conductor. MAP.

Governor Rampton had made that statement at a news conference with Wendell Ashton and Abravanel. Rampton said to Abravanel in jest: "You don't mind being exploited for crass commercial purposes?"

"We are delighted to be exploited for crass commercial purposes!" beamed the Maestro.

While there had always been frequent short in-state travels, this would be the orchestra's first major domestic tour. They traveled to Seattle, Los Angeles, Santa Barbara, San Francisco, and Portland. The State Industrial Department's promotional staff gave the tour a professional image, and it was a major success.

The orchestra's Hollywood Bowl appearance on June 22 was the most memorable of the week-long tour. This celebrated outdoor concert facility was nearly at its 12,000 capacity as the Utah Symphony opened the 1968 season in perfect weather. Abravanel's programming was daring: Mahler's Second (Resurrection) Symphony, which had brought the orchestra international acclaim. Joining the musicians were the Southern California Mormon Choir, Jean Preston, soprano, and Lili Chookasian, contralto. The performance received good reviews except that Martin Bernheimer from the Los Angeles Times felt that the live performance didn't live up to his expectations, based on the orchestra's recording.

The Seattle Symphony offered its home in the opera house. San Francisco's War Memorial auditorium hosted the Bay City's concert, and Portland's Civic Auditorium welcomed the orchestra. Sandwiched between Los Angeles and San Francisco was a happy stop for Abravanel at Santa Barbara, his summer home, for a concert in the Granada Theatre.

The West Coast was toured again, by bus, in 1970. Huck Gregory describes an awesome itinerary: "It was another three and one-half week tour that took the orchestra to within 60 miles of the Canadian border on the north (Everett, Washington) to within twenty miles of the Mexican border on the south (Brawley, California), crisscrossing the four coastal states in the process." There were twenty-three concerts: two in Idaho, five in Washington, three in Oregon, and thirteen in California.

It was in Southern California during this tour that an "infamous" letter to President Wendell Ashton and the Utah Symphony Board was drafted and signed by every player, voicing displeasure at the course the orchestra was taking and expressing doubt "that Utah could ever field a truly full-time symphony in which its players could earn a living wage." The management was already involved in the vigorous fundraising that would create, at long last, a "truly full-time" Symphony.

Overseas, West Coast, regional, and in-state tours have become integral parts of the Symphony's schedule. Typical of the many regional tours was one to Montana and the other Rocky Mountain states, detailed by Time magazine on March 15, 1976. "Not long ago," Time reported, "Abravanel received a letter from citizens in Dillon, Montana. 'We're just a bunch of cowboys,' he was told. 'Play anything you want.' Replied Abravanel, 'I think you deserve the best.' Dillon was treated to Beethoven's Eroica symphony." The crowd jumped to its feet and roared.

Abravanel loved small-town audiences who came to his concerts with no previous symphonic listening experience, even though hinterland tours, by bus and with unpredictable accommodations, are taxing. "Our reward for this hard traveling is the reaction of a small-town audience when it hears a symphony orchestra for the first time," says Abravanel in Time. "If I could choose how and where to die, I would like it to happen while conducting my orchestra in a place like Dillon, Montana!

============ CHAPTER 12 ============

Big Mo

"Big Mo was always right, even when he was wrong!" Sheldon Hyde summed up Abravanel's constant, unswerving dedication to the Utah Symphony. "If what's good for General Motors was good for America, then what's good for the Utah Symphony is good for Utah" was the spirit that permeated Abravanel's thirty-two-year reign.

Shelly Hyde knew Abravanel as well as anyone, working as the orchestra's personnel manager from 1950 until Abravanel's resignation in April 1979 and beyond. Hyde was one of Abravanel's original 1947 orchestra, playing second trumpet until 1980. He was also one of Salt Lake's better jazz pianists; his second language was jive.

He nicknamed Abravanel "Big Mo" early on. "Big Mo" distinguished him from "Little Mo," Morris Norkin, who was the orchestra's principal bassoonist when Abravanel assumed leadership in 1947. "Big Mo" quickly spread through the orchestra, and Abravanel seemed to enjoy it. World War II had ended. The Battleship *Missouri*, nicknamed "Mighty Mo," was the vessel that plowed through all obstacles. Abravanel possessed this same quality in dealing with political and business leaders, all of whom he worked with effectively on behalf of the orchestra.

In later years Hyde referred to "Big Mo" as "the ol' man," short for "the grand old man." Hyde says the term was not used generally throughout the orchestra but only by insiders and that Abravanel seemed to relish it. "I have been called a lot of other things in my day."

Abravanel was a fighter, a scrapper. All decisions made by him were based on "how does this affect the Utah Symphony?" This singleness of purpose was his trademark throughout his years in Utah. There were skirmishes, battles, wars to be won; political and financial crises to be overcome; public and personal relationships to be tackled, resolved, enhanced; sagging spirits to be lifted. Many problems were quickly solved. Some dragged on to the twilight of his term. Abravanel met them all head-on, solving some even before they surfaced. The situations described here are typical and serve to illustrate Big Mo's determination (and patience) in plowing through sticky and sometimes thorny problems that greeted him on his arrival in his new home.

When Abravanel came to Utah in 1947, the Salt Lake music world consisted of the Civic Music Association's artist recitals, the University of Utah's Master Minds and Artists Series with "name" artists, and the Granite Arts Association's series at Granite High School in Salt Lake County.

The Salt Lake concert organizations were apprehensive at Abravanel's coming. The Utah Symphony had functioned as a professional orchestra since 1940, and Abravanel's first season was the orchestra's eighth. Those behind the heretofore secure Civic Music and Master Minds and Artists expressed concern about the Symphony's effect on their audiences. A cold war ensued that was to last for fifteen years.

Abravanel was completely absorbed in building a major orchestra. His high-quality programming, distinguished guest artists, and exciting performances effected a gradual box-office decline for Civic Music and Master Minds and Artists, whose subscribers defected to the Utah Symphony in increasing numbers each season. In 1962, after a lengthy box-office battle, the Civic Music Association and Master Minds and Artists series joined forces as Civic Music–Master Minds and Artists. Nevertheless, the review in the *Salt Lake Tribune* of Julius Katchen's jointly sponsored Kingsbury Hall piano recital on December 2 included the information that "the 2,000-capacity house was less than half-filled–and with the combined subscription audience." Both series were eventually discontinued, leaving the field to the Utah Symphony, whose Tabernacle audiences increased from half-houses in the late forties to standing-room-only crowds by the mid-fifties.

Some Civic Music and Master Minds and Artists faithful were upset, understandably, feeling that Abravanel and his musicians had indirectly scuttled the solo recital series. Abravanel had no alternative but to drive toward the orchestra's economic stability and artistic excellence.

During the early months of the Symphony's first season under Abravanel, Salt Lake newspapers announced the formation of the Intermountain Symphony, to be based in Provo. The *Tribune* for February 29, 1948, listed Allen Jensen as conductor. He was also at the time the Utah Symphony's principal flute player. Jensen planned to attract Brigham Young University faculty and advanced students, plus some Utah Symphony artists. Don Peterson and Glen Dalby, the Symphony's third and fourth horns, were to be Jensen's first and second horn players. Jensen also named Sam Pratt, Abravanel's third flute, as his first flute. Many more Utah Symphony musicians were also involved. Leading Jensen's Board of Directors was Walter Mathesius, Jr., head of Geneva Steel. Guest soloists were to include Grant Johannesen, Utah Symphony concertmaster Leonard Posner, and Reid Nibley.

Abravanel immediately saw to it that none of his musicians continued with Jensen. Jensen's own contract as first flute was not renewed and Sam Pratt replaced him. The Intermountain Symphony has continued through the years on a redefined basis, with some BYU faculty as conductors, notably Ralph Laycock. It is now called the Utah Valley Symphony.

A few months after the Jensen–Intermountain Symphony press announcement, a seemingly innocuous story appeared in the *Tribune*: "Reed Adams, ambitious local entrepreneur, announces a star-studded concert series." Several top international concert artists were listed, including Heifetz, Rubinstein, Horowitz, and Piatigorsky. Alarmed, Abravanel asked for details, feeling that this series could drain his young Utah Symphony of potential audiences. In 1948 his orchestra was still shaky both musically and economically. Phone calls were made, and no more was heard of Adams's ambitious but impractical idea.

Topping all the Utah concert series of the day was Brigham Young University's. Dean Herald Glenn Clark of the College of Commerce programmed a series of major artists with his magic wand, featuring performers apparently unavailable to his competitors. He also seemed to manage this at reduced fees. The prestigious series attracted many out-of-state visitors. "This was his first love," says his son Richard, "and, in pre-Abravanel days, it was almost the only game in town." Salt Lakers traveled to Provo in droves when a name artist appeared.

Big Mo and Clark were outspoken but friendly rivals from the outset. Clark, with Leroy Robertson, then chairman of the music department at BYU, successfully undertook the herculean task of bringing the Los Angeles Philharmonic under Alfred Wallenstein to Provo for an entire week in res-

The Abravanels with Shelly Hyde, second trumpet and personnel manager of the orchestra. MAP.

idence as a feature of the Utah Centennial. Clark brought this off successfully just a few weeks before Abravanel's opening concert. Abravanel observed Clark's coup quietly.

Neither was Abravanel unduly concerned by Dimitri Mitropoulos's appearances with his Minneapolis Symphony at BYU on April 12 and 13, 1949. Abravanel's position — that

The orchestra and soloist Van Cliburn receive audience accolades in the Tabernacle in the days when standing ovations were rare. MAP.

any major visiting symphony orchestra performing in Salt Lake should be "hosted" by the Utah Symphony – was beginning to take shape, however.

In 1951, the Utah Concerts Council was organized to coordinate the several state concert series, minimize scheduling conflicts among organizations, negotiate for cheaper art-ist fees, and upgrade communication and relations with the public. Members included the Salt Lake Civic Music Association, the University of Utah Master Minds and Artists Series, the Utah Symphony, the Granite Arts Association, the Brigham Young University Concert Series, Ogden's Civic Music Association, and Utah State University's Concert Series.

Strenuous rehearsals often found the conductor in shirtsleeves. MAP.

Council meetings were often tense when they served as a forum for Abravanel and Clark to air their differences. Both were powerful, dedicated to their organizations, determined to consolidate their positions. Neither was willing to relinquish one foot of his territory. Clark held that BYU answered to no one except its own governing board. Abravanel's view was that the Utah Symphony was a state-wide organization, not confined to the Salt Lake Valley. More specifically, he maintained that major orchestras on national tours should be sponsored or cosponsored by the Utah Symphony. He held that this was the pattern in metropolitan areas with major orchestras.

Clark signed the New York Philharmonic for Provo and Salt Lake appearances and booked the Tabernacle for the Salt Lake performance. Because the Tabernacle was also the performing "home" of the Utah Symphony, Abravanel objected. Tempers flared at subsequent meetings of the Utah Concerts Council. Eventually a compromise was reached, and visiting major orchestras were jointly sponsored by Clark's BYU series and the Utah Symphony. (The Utah Symphony eventually assumed sole sponsorship of the Salt Lake Concerts.) It was an interesting, significant tug-of-war between the two, who genuinely admired each other.

Ever sensitive to the slightest threat to the growth and stability of the orchestra, Abravanel took offense in the mid-fifties to a press story about the "re-organization of the Salt Lake Philharmonic." Eugene Jelesnik's ensemble was never a real threat or genuine competition; it was the name and its implications that bothered Abravanel. Jelesnik announced that his Philharmonic was a delayed continuation of the 1913 attempt to re-establish the original Salt Lake Philharmonic Orchestra and that it was twenty-seven years older than the modern-day Utah Symphony, which dates from 1940. Jelesnik's ensemble was a small Broadway-type pit orchestra which presented occasional free "popular" concerts, usually underwritten by the Local of the AFM.

Jelesnik first came to Salt Lake City as leader-violinist of his own traveling salon orchestra, playing in the Hotel Utah Empire Room in the early forties. He liked Salt Lake and remained, first as director of the KDYL radio station orchestra and, in recent years, as talent scout, TV personality, and director of annual USO tours to overseas armed service personnel.

SUFFER THE LITTLE CHILDREN

Close to Abravanel's heart was the idea of free school concerts throughout the state. Werner Janssen had presented five Saturday morning youth concerts in Salt Lake during the 1946–47 season, four in the Capitol Theatre, one in the Tabernacle. Even before Governor J. Bracken Lee's 1949 veto of funds to support the Symphony, Abravanel had tried to secure state underwriting. With none forthcoming, he presented three free youth concerts in 1947 during his first season, one in the Tabernacle, two in the Capitol Theatre. Two years later he expanded the series to outlying school districts in the state. These remarkable concerts continued for twenty years without public funding, the Symphony itself paying the tab. Abravanel enjoyed young audiences and always insisted on playing great music. "And they loved it," he recalls.

Meanwhile, Donald P. Lloyd's Associated Grocers' Association (AG) agreed to subsidize a whole series of free youth concerts in the Tabernacle on Saturday mornings. The first was held in January of 1953, the last in 1971, for a total of fifty-four concerts. A lifelong Symphony backer, Lloyd was also a longtime Board member.

While the AG Foodstores' free concerts made a great contribution toward Abravanel's vision of enriching the cul-

"Big Mo" signs autographs for enthusiastic admirers. MAP.

tural life of the state's children, and "growing" Symphony audiences for the future, they couldn't serve children outside the immediate area. "After twenty years of free [school] concerts subsidized entirely by the Utah Symphony, we desperately needed statewide public or private support. In 1969," recalls Abravanel, "I sat down with Glen R. Swenson, chairman of the Utah State Institute of Fine Arts, to discuss our plight." The Institute had been a principal supporter of the Utah Symphony, which had been a division of the Institute since the early forties. While the Symphony had always received the lion's share of the Institute's state appropriation, by the late sixties the long-neglected visual arts had gained voting control.

In the early days of Governor Calvin L. Rampton's second term, Abravanel laid the problem before him: "The orchestra needs $200,000 for school concerts. What is your advice?" Governor Rampton, always one of the Symphony's most enthusiastic supporters and an astute politician, cautioned against directly requesting an appropriation for the Symphony. "It wouldn't have a ghost of a chance in the Legislature," he said. Women were picketing the state capitol daily during the legislative session with "no more taxes" and "slash the budget" placards. Abravanel's request was in greater trouble from outside than from within the capitol walls.

"There is a way, however," continued the Governor. "It could be placed appropriately in the state's multi-million-dollar education budget, which the Legislature rarely tampers with. The appropriation is definitely for 'educational' purposes and would not be questioned seriously by lawmakers." By law, Utah's governor submits the budget to the Legislature. Rampton cautioned that "it is difficult" initially to add an item to the budget, but "once it's in it is usually there to stay!" Abravanel credits Governor Rampton with "great courage" for taking the initiative and the political gamble.

Senator Haven P. Barlow, Senate President, carried the ball in the upper house. Others helped. Dr. Terrell H. Bell, who headed the state's education system at the time (and who later became U.S. Secretary of Education), sat in on a Symphony school concert in Ogden during this legislative session. "Maestro Abravanel, you certainly sold me!" he exclaimed after the concert. Bell lent official support for the appropriation as "education of the best kind."

Joining Abravanel at crucial committee hearings were

Governor Calvin L. Rampton presents the Maestro with a watch on the occasion of his twentieth anniversary as Music Director of the Utah Symphony, March 29, 1967. MAP.

Symphony Board President Wendell Ashton and Shirl Swenson, Symphony manager, who was the orchestra's lobbyist though the years. Abravanel also praises Senator Alan Mecham, who was "the most supportive of all legislators." Mecham requested a "committee of the whole" and invited Abravanel to speak. The Maestro was always persuasive when speaking about his musicians. Lawmakers expressed deep respect for Abravanel's position, but explained that their constituents had ordered them not to raise taxes.

"There were also three observers from Kennecott [Copper Corp.] in the gallery," Abravanel recalls. "Kennecott was opposed to the Symphony request, because it represented more taxes. This lobbying trio became such a nuisance that even the Republicans objected."

Nevertheless, the Legislature approved the budget early in 1970 without questioning the funding of Utah Symphony school concerts as part of the education budget. The appropriation was earmarked for school concerts—"not pop concerts, but great music of the masters," emphasizes Abravanel. Eventually the concerts took the Symphony to 75,000 students in nearly half of the state's public schools. School con-

"Professor" Abravanel rehearsing musicians in the Music Hall. MZPC.

cert budget figures reached $437,400 in the 1985–86 season and continue in the state's education budget.

In early December of 1948, Abravanel initiated a prestigious choral-orchestral series in Kingsbury Hall with Beethoven's *Missa Solemnis*, teaming the Symphony and the University of Utah's combined choruses. While the performance was a great success, this unique choral opportunity became a bitter pill for some to swallow. The dramatic change from easygoing, fun pop glee clubs to the complexities of Beethoven within a few months was wrenching. The three University choral organizations were the A Cappella Choir of 180 members, Richard P. Condie, director; the Girls' Glee Club of 100 members, William Peterson, director; and the Boys' Glee Club of 90 members, John Marlowe Nielson, director—a total of 370 young singers.

Subsequent enrollments dropped dramatically because of the stress involved in the preparation of the Beethoven work. This created a severe problem for the choral conductors, as radically reduced enrollments for the winter and spring quarters of 1948–49 made it difficult to organize the choral groups as in previous years. Condie's A Cappella Choir dropped from 180 to 40; Peterson's, the showpiece of the campus, from 100 to 40—and to 20 following his premature death in 1951. Nielson's chorus fell from 90 to 30, and the combined total was 110 compared with nearly 400 for the *Missa Solemnis*.

Abravanel required greater numbers for both Bach's *St. Matthew Passion* and Verdi's *Requiem*, scheduled in 1949 and 1950. Music department chairman Leroy Robertson authorized formation of a Collegium Musicum headed by youthful David A. Shand, even though the Collegium would be in direct competition with Condie's A Cappella Choir. Shand out-recruited Condie and fielded a singing group of around 100. Condie, already frustrated by personal and professional problems, was upset by the defection to the Collegium of some of his students. (His appointment as Tabernacle Choir conductor in 1957 was a happy solution.)

Like most choral specialists, the University's choral conductors resented rehearsing their students for the public performances under Abravanel's direction, thereby "doing all of the work and getting little credit." Torn between loyalty to Robertson and Abravanel and their own student ensembles, they watched their groups deteriorate.

Adjustments were made. In 1955 Shand was named overall conductor with Condie and Nielson assisting. The University Chorale, an evening chorus that became the basis for a "new look" in subsequent years, was added in 1958, with Nielson directing. Hoping for a more unified direction, Abravanel suggested to Robertson that Ardean Watts, University faculty member and official pianist with the Symphony, head a reorganized University of Utah Chorus from 1960 to 1962. This smaller group of 150 under one baton recorded Honegger's *King David* with the Symphony in 1961.

In 1962 Newell Weight, one of the West's leading choral conductors, joined the University faculty. One of his principal tasks was to propose a new organization to perform with the Utah Symphony in joint performances and recordings. He immediately grasped the problem of multiple daytime choruses and conductors. With John Marlowe Nielson's collaboration he used the University Chorale as the basic evening chorus and quickly molded it into a professional group of mature off-campus singers.

Abravanel was pleased. Some distance still remained between him and the choral conductors, particularly on Weight's part as tension increased with final rehearsals and performances. Weight was surprised and disappointed when his name did not appear on the 1966 album-cover credits for the Vanguard recording of Darius Milhaud's *Pacem in Terris* because of a clerical error in either the Symphony or the Vanguard offices. When this was brought to Abravanel's attention, he expressed surprise and concern and graciously invited Weight to guest-conduct a choral-orchestral performance the following season.

Through the years Abravanel upgraded the University's choral repertoire from glees to masterworks of Beethoven, Bach, Verdi, and Mahler, sharpening the focus on the great music.

GOLDEN VOICES

Frustration met Abravanel's hopes to join with the Mormon Tabernacle Choir in the first Utah performance of Beethoven's Ninth Symphony during his initial season. His invitation was rejected by the Choir's conductor–to the dismay of many Choir members. Abravanel turned to the University of Utah choruses, which performed the Beethoven in the Tabernacle on March 27, 1948. Three months later the Utah Symphony moved to the campus, where it made its home for twenty years, continuing the tradition of annual and semiannual joint performances.

Abravanel initiated further proposals for joint Tabernacle Choir–Utah Symphony performances. Leroy Robertson's *Book of Mormon* Oratorio seemed a logical opening and was Abravanel's next ploy. This 1948 invitation was rejected. Abravanel was incredulous–this was the greatest Mormon work, commissioned and composed expressly for the Tabernacle Choir by the most significant Mormon composer. Abravanel turned again to the University of Utah, whose combined choirs premiered the Robertson oratorio in 1953, after a six-year delay.

Admittedly, Tabernacle Choir officials had their priorities and scheduling difficulties. The essential assignment of this volunteer group was its weekly CBS radio and television broadcast. There are rehearsals for recordings, tours, and LDS General Conference assignments in addition to the regular Thursday and Sunday rehearsals and broadcasts. While Choir conductor J. Spencer Cornwall and Choir president Lester F. Hewlett made the group's decisions in Abravanel's early years, Richard L. Evans, an influential member of the Quorum of the Twelve Apostles, emerged as policy- and decision-maker until his death in 1971.

During his years of writing and announcing "the spoken word" for the weekly broadcast, Evans exerted unprecedented influence over the Choir's activities. He nurtured and was justifiably jealous of the Choir's invaluable association with Eugene Ormandy and the Philadelphia Orchestra. He deserves credit, with President Hewlett, for the Choir's designation in 1958 as the Philadelphia Orchestra's official recording choir for Columbia Records.

These were the Choir's "golden" recording years. Ormandy conducted the joint forces in two unprecedented "gold" albums. The first two, *Beloved Choruses* and *The Lord's Prayer*, were released in 1958. The latter featured Robertson's Lord's Prayer setting from the *Book of Mormon* Oratorio. The sleeper, added as an afterthought in this otherwise all-sacred album, was the "Battle Hymn of the Republic," winner of a Grammy award in 1959. The Choir's second gold album was Handel's *Messiah* in 1959, with soloists Eileen Farrell, Martha Lipton, Davis Cunningham, and William Warfield. Brahms' *Requiem* and Beethoven's Ninth Symphony were also critically acclaimed. A stream of other successes followed: a variety of sacred and patriotic works and several Christmas recordings.

Thus, the official reason for the Choir's not singing with the Utah Symphony through the years was "Why should we sing with the Utah Symphony when we can sing and record with 'The World's Greatest Orchestra'?" Underscoring the Choir's bonanza in its Philadelphia Orchestra connection is *Time* magazine's music page for April 25, 1969, outlining a sixty-year tug-of-war between the two recording giants, Columbia Records and RCA: "For 25 years, Eugene Ormandy and the Philadelphia recorded exclusively for Columbia Records. Last May when the orchestra's contract came up for renewal, RCA, which had recorded it from 1917 to 1943, grabbed the ensemble off by outbidding Columbia."

The Tabernacle Choir could not follow the Philadelphia to RCA for fear it might jeopardize its highest priority, the Sunday CBS broadcast, and so it was now without an official major recording orchestra. Columbia Records and CBS were keenly aware that the Tabernacle Choir was its "most valuable classical recording property" per album, and the loss of the Philadelphia Orchestra connection did not interfere with a steady succession of gold albums for the Choir.

When the Philadelphia left Columbia Records for RCA in 1968 the door was open for a possible joint performance

by the Choir and the Utah Symphony, but it did not materialize. Four Tabernacle Choir conductors later, as a result of top-level discussions between Nathan Eldon Tanner, first counselor in the LDS First Presidency, and Obert C. Tanner, chairman of the Utah Bicentennial Commission, the Utah Symphony and the Tabernacle Choir agreed to present joint concerts in the Tabernacle and throughout the state as Utah's major Bicentennial event—twenty-nine years after Abravanel's initial invitation to J. Spencer Cornwall.

Neither of Cornwall's two immediate successors, Richard P. Condie and Jay E. Welch, had sought a relationship with the Utah Symphony. Condie had been the principal conductor in preparing the Choir for recordings with Ormandy and the Philadelphia. The early gold records came during his tenure.

Welch succeeded him for six months only. It is not certain what he might have done about the Utah Symphony. Welch was musically ambidextrous—equally at home conducting orchestra or chorus—the first Tabernacle Choir conductor in his time so talented.

Welch's successor Jerold D. Ottley is also at home conducting an orchestra and has recorded several albums with Choir and orchestra. Abravanel was happy. Ottley was pleased. Ottley was significant as the first Choir conductor in twenty-nine years to endorse collaboration. But who should conduct? And how could the balance between the two major organizations be maintained?

The State Bicentennial Commission was the catalyst, commissioning a major composition as the centerpiece for Choir-Symphony concerts. Crawford Gates was commissioned to write the musical score to poems of successful Utah poet Carol Lynn Pearson. Gates guest-conducted the Tabernacle Choir and the Utah Symphony in the premiere of his Symphony No. 4, *A New Morning*. Ottley conducted the program's opening section; Abravanel followed Gates on the podium to conclude the program with Bernstein's *Chichester Psalms*. It was a happy wedding for Choir and Symphony, with Gates as best man.

CHAPTER 13

The Musicians

The musicians are the nuts and bolts of the orchestra. "We were always fortunate to have fewer nuts than bolts," sighed one veteran violinist. "I can recall only one truly difficult personnel problem during Maestro Abravanel's thirty-two years. Of course, there were the usual day-to-day problems, but the musicians were always professionals, artists, and quality people, for the most part."

Abravanel limited the total number of musicians to eighty, adding extras occasionally when called for, as in Mahler's Second and Eighth, Strauss's *Ein Heldenleben*, and Ravel's *Daphnis and Chloé Suite No. 2.*

"When Wagner wrote *The Ring*," Abravanel points out, "he enlarged the orchestra by calling for eight horns—sometimes four horns and four different-sized tubas. He also used three trumpets and four trombones plus bass trombone and tuba. Then for the first time in his life, Wagner suggested, 'If possible, sixteen first and second violins, twelve violas, twelve celli, and eight basses.'

"But, and this is important," stresses Abravanel, "Wagner didn't write for this same large orchestra in *Mastersingers*, *Tristan*, *Lohengrin*, or *Tannhäuser*. In *Parsifal*, written after *The Ring*, there is no mention of the number of strings. The extra-large string sections called for in *The Ring* were solely for that work."

Abravanel recalls that Richard Strauss always used traditional string sections (like Beethoven and Brahms) in his colorful tone poems. "But later . . . he wrote *Heldenleben* with eight horns, five trumpets, and two tubas, two harps and sixteen first violins, and so on, like Wagner." It "became a habit . . . better to have more than less. . . ."

Abravanel doggedly held to his eighty-member theory:

It's a bit silly that larger numbers has become a *status symbol*. For many, many works it's still only one flute or one oboe that plays the solo. And when sixty strings accompany one poor little flute or one little oboe, what do they do? They have to play on "one hair of the bow." Some larger orchestras become so accustomed to playing with one hair of the bow that they cannot produce a genuine *fortissimo*, because the string players have grown so accustomed to simply touching their strings with the bow and cannot really *dig in!*"

Abravanel humorously criticizes some neophyte conductors: "The first thing they do is ask for the status symbol—an orchestra of one hundred, if possible, because if you have one hundred, you are officially in the Big League! Personally," he continues, "I have fought it since my first season in Utah,

Early Utah Symphony principals pose in the Tabernacle: left to right, front row, Sally Peck, Abravanel, Audrey Bush; second row, Don Peterson, David Freed, Harold Wolf; third row, Eugene Foster, Doug Craig, Martin Zwick; back row, Louis Booth, William Sullivan, Robert Lentz, and William Johnson. MAP.

when a well-intentioned person said: 'You know, we ought to have more strings.' I have heard that again and again. My answer: First pay the musicians properly, *then* add more strings. But first pay them properly! I think that is more important."

When asked during a major interview with television station KUED in 1986 how he built this remarkable orchestra, Abravanel replied:

> I picked my musicians, not for their artistry at their first audition but for my perception of their long-range potential. You know, I have very good instincts. I was not really concerned with their technical level at the time of the audition but, rather, their commitment to music. If accepted, they would work their heads off for their love of music. That's what happened – work, work, and more work. They simply became better and better . . . and better.
>
> During the middle sixties, the Rockefeller Foundation sponsored a marvelous project involving a few select symphony orchestras to promote and premiere works of new . . . young composers. In cooperation with the University, the Utah Symphony received a grant covering orchestra salaries for one week. Michael Steinberg, feared Boston *Globe* critic, was sent by the Rockefeller Foundation as observer. He attended every daily rehearsal and concert. He was amazed at the orchestra's demeanor. "Most orchestras give sixty or seventy percent in rehearsals. Yours gives one hundred percent."

When Abravanel came to Utah, his goal was to settle in and build a professional orchestra in Utah, a symphony predominantly of Utahns. His unsuccessful predecessor Werner Janssen had insisted on importing a third of the musicians from the West Coast. In contrast, during his first season (1947–48), Abravanel reduced the imports to seven principals: concertmaster Leonard Posner; principal cellist Paolo Gruppe; first clarinet Napoleon Cerminara; first bassoon Morris Norkin; the Fuchs brothers, Allan and Norman, horns; and first trombone John Swallow.

Local artists filled the remaining major posts remarkably well: principal violist Lorna Hogenson, principal bass Audrey Bush, first flute Allen Jensen, first oboe Louis Booth, first trumpet Stewart Grow, tuba Richard Shuck, timpanist Walter Rothaar, and percussion, harps, and piano-celeste. The first and second violins, except for Posner and Camille Gruppe, Paolo's wife, were Utahns. All viola, cello, and bass sections were local musicians except for Paolo Gruppe. The same was true of woodwinds and brass, except for Cerminara, Norkin, the Fuchs brothers, and Swallow.

Personnel has since evolved gradually, more sharply at critical moments. The present-day Utah Symphony has a very different face from its 1947 progenitor. Remarkably, however, six of Abravanel's original 1947 members remain in 1989: Kenneth Kuchler, associate concertmaster; Norma Lee Madsen Belnap, assistant concertmaster; violinists Katherine Hess Petersen and Frances Johnson Darger; violist Dorothy Freed; and principal horn Don Peterson.

CONCERTMASTER

Next in importance to the music director-conductor is the concertmaster.

Leonard Posner, Abravanel's first concertmaster (1947–49) was the most musical, with consummate artistry and beauty of tone. He was a "prize catch" for Abravanel and displayed elegance and sophistication in solo passages equal to visiting artists when he soloed in Brahms and Mozart concertos. During the 1949 crisis, when it appeared that contracts would not be forthcoming for 1949–50, Posner left the orchestra at

Concertmaster Harold Wolf and Kenneth Kuchler. J. M. Heslop photograph for the *Deseret News* in MAP.

the season's end. He had no trouble finding a new position, going directly to Arturo Toscanini's NBC Symphony and from there to the University of Texas.

Tibor Zelig succeeded Posner (1949–51). He played beautifully and with warmth and premiered Robertson's Violin Concerto, commissioned for the University of Utah's Centennial in 1950. He also soloed in the Mendelssohn Concerto in a Tabernacle concert. Zelig's Hungarian ancestry was evident in his "gypsy-influenced" style, full of warmth, wide vibrato, and subtle occasional gliding from one note to another.

Jerome Kasin (1951–52) was the least favored of the five concertmasters. As one musician put it, "Kasin didn't care for Utah or Utahns; they were not good enough for him." His stay was brief.

Harold Wolf (1952–66) enjoyed the longest tenure. Abravanel felt that as a concertmaster, Wolf was his best, although others may have been better soloists. Some members of the orchestra had personal reservations, yet respected him as concertmaster. He was a solid musician and a capable conductor. Wolf resigned in 1966 to become concertmaster of the Birmingham (Alabama) Symphony.

Oscar Chausow (1966–79), according to many the leading violinist in the Chicago area in the sixties, succeeded

Wolf at the beginning of the 1966–67 season. Chausow was the last of Abravanel's concertmasters. He was co-soloist with Nina de Veritch in the Brahms Double Concerto for violin and cello, with violist Sally Peck in the Mozart *Symphonie Concertante*, and with Kenneth Kuchler in Bach's Double Violin Concerto, and soloist in Vaughan Williams' *The Lark Ascending* (recorded for Vanguard).

Chausow and his wife Leyah were high-powered, intelligent, sophisticated, and strong-willed, often creating some distance between themselves and some of the musicians. A year after Abravanel resigned in April 1979, Chausow followed suit – not with the best of feelings toward management – and returned to Chicago.

Concertmaster Oscar Chausow and the Maestro on October 12, 1966. W. Claudell Johnson *Deseret News* photograph in MAP.

Abravanel and Norma Lee Madsen. Lignell and Gill photograph in MAP.

Van Cliburn rehearses
with the Symphony in the
Music Hall, not long after
winning the Tchaikovsky
Prize in Russia in 1958.
MAP.

Two other veteran first violinists must be mentioned. *Kenneth Kuchler* (1974-present) was Abravanel's original choice as assistant concertmaster in 1947. He had also played first violin during Janssen's season (1946–47) and became associate concertmaster in 1977. He was acting concertmaster during the 1980–81 season.

Norma Lee Madsen Belnap moved up to assistant concertmaster during that same 1980-81 season. She was a pillar of the orchestra and also contributed to the University's string program as an adjunct professor. She began under Janssen and performed throughout Abravanel's thirty-two-year tenure, continuing under his successors.

PRINCIPAL SECOND VIOLIN

Bill Douglas was principal second violin in Abravanel's original 1947–48 orchestra.

Nila Stubbs (Lee) followed from 1948 to 1951. She had been concertmistress of Robertson's Brigham Young University Symphony.

LaVar Krantz (1952–65) was the first long-term principal second violinist, heading that section for thirteen years. In 1965 he entered Rochester University's Eastman School of Music and earned his doctorate. He was later appointed to the University of Hawaii Music faculty and has been a member of the Honolulu Symphony ever since.

Percy Kalt shared the first desk with Krantz for five years, through 1960. He then joined Brigham Young University's faculty, completing his doctorate in performance at the University of Michigan in 1973. He now heads the BYU violin staff and is first violin in the Deseret Quartet.

John Chatelain led the second violin section for thirteen years under Abravanel (1966–79). He is a member of the University's adjunct faculty.

Bonnie Bennett shared the first desk with Chatelain from 1966 to 1970. *Jack Ashton* succeeded her in 1970 and continued through Abravanel's resignation.

PRINCIPAL VIOLISTS

As principal violist *Sally Peck*'s name looms large. For twenty-four years (1950–74) she was Sally, a consummate artist in her teens, a force to be reckoned with. Recognizing her superior artistry, *Lorna Hogenson* (1977–80) relinquished her own first chair to Miss Peck. Peck was a "natural"–with a big tone, warmth, and technical mastery–and was often invited to perform with touring string quartets. Abravanel recalls a phone call in 1956 from William Primrose, then the world's leading violist, telling the conductor he would not be able to make a scheduled appearance with the Utah Symphony and to find a substitute. "I have one here who plays better than most touring artists," replied Abravanel. Peck received a standing ovation as Primrose's stand-in in the Bloch Suite for Violin and Orchestra. She was guest soloist with the orchestra seven times and soloed in Vanguard's recording of Vaughan Williams' *Flos Campi*, for chorus, orchestra, and viola. Only pianists Reid Nibley (11) and Gladys Rosenberg (8) soloed more times than she. In 1974 Peck opted for a new lifestyle–a music colony in North Carolina and a quieter, less hectic life in the world of chamber music.

Christopher McKellar, one of Peck's students, was named acting principal viola for the 1974–75 season and became principal violist the following year.

PRINCIPAL CELLISTS

Paolo Gruppe (1947–49) was Abravanel's first principal cellist, possessing, Abravanel recalls, a "big tone." In acquiring Paolo, Abravanel also gained a first violinist in his wife, *Camille Gruppe*. They remained through the 1949 crisis and left with the other imports.

Harold Schneier's tenure (1949–50) was brief, but he returned later. The glossiest solo cellist of all, he left to join the Dallas Symphony, then moved on to Hollywood, where he played in the film capital's more lucrative studio orchestras. When he tired of Hollywood, Schneier returned to the Symphony as principal cellist, adding his special touch from 1953 to 1956.

Joseph Wetzels, principal cellist from 1950 to 1953, was "recommended to me by Darius Milhaud," says Abravanel. "Wetzels was a member of the famed Belgian Trio–a marvelous person and a great cellist."

David Freed enjoyed the longest term as principal cellist, from 1957 to 1966. "He was a wonderful guy," recalls Abravanel. "He would offer to play for any gatherings anywhere, anytime. His 'first' was in a Mormon Sacrament Meeting." Freed always had high personal as well as musical ideals. He was a humanitarian, environmentalist, champion of the underprivileged, conservationist, and anti-nuclear spokesman, whose letters to the editor still often appear on daily editorial pages. His brother Isadore was a leading American composer. Freed's annual outdoor performances of Bach unaccompanied cello works were anticipated events. He resigned as principal in 1966 to make way for an oncoming young artist.

Nina de Veritch, young, attractive, and playing like Piatigorsky, became principal cellist for two seasons (1966–68). She teamed with Oscar Chausow in the seldom-performed Brahms Double Concerto for Violin and Cello in a Tabernacle subscription concert. In 1968 she joined the Pittsburgh Symphony under William Steinberg.

Christian Tiemeyer (1968–75) "possessed the greatest natural flair for the cello," claims Abravanel. He was a thorough musician and gifted artist, always professional. In addition to his Symphony post, he was an adjunct professor in the University's music department, where he conducted the University Symphony Orchestra. Tiemeyer guest-soloed with the Symphony in the Saint-Saëns Concerto (1969) and Bloch's *Schelomo* (1970). He left Utah in 1975 to become assistant conductor of the Dallas Symphony.

J. Ryan Selberg (1975–present) is the seventh principal cellist and a strong section leader. He soloed in Richard Strauss's *Don Quixote* during the orchestra's–and Abravanel's–final season in the Tabernacle 1978–79.

Jack Benny rehearses in the Tabernacle in the early sixties for a benefit for the musicians' fund. O. Walter Kasteler photograph for the *Deseret News* in MAP.

BASS

Audrey Bush (1947–78) headed the bass section from Abravanel's first season to his next-to-last. She was also an adjunct faculty member at the University from 1947 to 1984.

John F. Clark followed Bush as principal during Abravanel's last season.

FLUTE

Allen Jensen (1947–48) was principal flute for only one season, Abravanel's first. He caused Abravanel some concern for a time by organizing a "competing orchestra" in Utah Valley and planning to use some Utah Symphony musicians.

Sam Pratt (1948–53) was a solid musician and a good principal flutist. His wife *Louise Pratt* was the orchestra's first harpist. Sam Pratt left the Symphony in 1953, joining Lyon and Healy, makers and distributors of harps in America. He became owner of the company and retired several years ago.

Eugene Foster (1953–72) is the principal flutist most Utah Symphony subscribers will remember – a brilliant artist, rivaled by very few in major orchestras for the beauty and power of tone which seemed to proceed directly from his instrument to the Tabernacle ceiling and back to the audience. He was one of the orchestra's treasures for two decades.

Abravanel tells of Foster's visit to the Soviet Union, where he was auditioned and reportedly offered a position with the Leningrad Symphony. On his return he asked Abravanel's advice: "Okay, Gene, you can do it, but remember, you won't be able to talk back to the conductor or management, and you'll even have to be careful what you say to other musicians!" Foster remained as principal flutist until his death in 1972.

Henry Hoffman (1972–76) followed Foster – not an easy task as he lacked his predecessor's beautiful round tone and flair. He left after four seasons.

Erich Graf (1976-present) has returned the principal flute to its Foster-era status. In addition he was an organizer, with other Symphony musicians, of The Salt Lake Chamber Ensemble.

OBOE

"Is it Louie Oboe on his Booth or Louie Booth on his oboe?" was a common shibboleth among early Symphony members. One had the feeling with *Louis Booth's* omnipresence in the middle of the orchestra that he had crossed the Plains with Captain William Pitt's Band in 1847. He was always "there" from the earliest days of the WPA and Roosevelt's program to assist unemployed musicians. His cousin Reginald Beales had been conductor of the earlier WPA-funded orchestra.

Booth was established as a professional years before Abravanel arrived. Years of study at Boston's New England Conservatory, plus degrees at Brigham Young University, working closely with Leroy Robertson, qualified him for any major orchestra. When England's Sir Thomas Beecham guest-conducted the Utah State Symphony during the 1942–43 season, he had been impressed with the orchestra's youthful, balding principal oboist and invited Booth to accept a similar position with him in the Seattle Orchestra.

Booth chose to stay in Utah and was the centerpiece of the orchestra's woodwind section. He commuted from Provo to play under Werner Janssen, then moved to Salt Lake City as principal oboe for Abravanel's first season. He joined the University faculty in 1947 and developed an enviable chamber music program. At the end of the 1967–68 season he resigned from the orchestra to devote full time to his University duties.

Beecham was the greatest English conductor of this century. A millionaire-heir to the Beecham Pill organization, he was a witty raconteur. He was also the target of many jokes. Abravanel loves to tell one:

> Sir Thomas Beecham was a marvelous conductor, because he was the one man in his musical generation who was totally financially independent. All conductors I knew were dependent, except Koussevitzky and Beecham. Beecham's father and grandfather developed and manufactured the Beecham "little liver pills," and in England – please excuse me for saying so – people were often constipated. They needed the liver pills, the Beecham Pills. So, anytime a Britisher was constipated it helped the cause of music in England!

Darrell Stubbs, one of Booth's students, succeeded him as principal oboist. He was a Brigham Young University student and played under Abravanel from 1968 to 1979, resigning to return to full-time teaching at BYU.

Kay Roylance (1947–54) was the first English horn player, but *Gary Post* played English horn for the longest period, 1955 to 1974. Post resigned to devote his full time to private business. *Jerold Clark* moved into the oboe section in the autumn of 1974 and doubled on English horn. *Holly Gornik* joined the section at about the same time and doubled on English horn. In retrospect, however, *Larry Thorstenberg* dominated the English horn scene. A student of Louie Booth, he soon surpassed his teacher and joined the Boston Symphony, where he has since been principal English horn. Prior to Gary Post, *Blaine Edelfsen* played for a brief period.

CLARINET

Martin Zwick (1949–77) is remembered most among the orchestra's clarinets because it was his solo sound – and his alone – that was heard for twenty-eight years in the Tabernacle, a beautifully-honed clarinet tone, played with innate musicianship. He was a University adjunct professor and also made a rich contribution in the Granite School District, where he taught elementary school children – beautifully. One parent reflected the thought of many: "There was never nor will there ever be another teacher like Mr. Zwick!" His skill as a photographer can be seen in many of the photographs in this volume.

Two distinguished clarinetists preceded Zwick. *Napoleon Cerminara* (1947–48) and *Herbert Blayman* (1948–49). During the 1949 exodus, Cerminara moved on to the New York Philharmonic, Blayman to the Metropolitan Opera Orchestra. Both remained high in their praise of Abravanel and the orchestra.

Christie Lundquist (1977-present) almost makes one forget Zwick. She joined the orchestra in 1977 as the first woman principal in the wind sections. Lundquist had considerable and rich experience, playing under some leading conductors. She has soloed twice with the Utah Symphony, in the Copland Clarinet Concerto and Bernstein's *Prelude, Fugue and Riffs*.

Dow Young sat beside Zwick as second clarinet from 1950 until his tragic death in 1971. *Loel Hepworth*, the orchestra's third clarinetist, doubled on bass clarinet. Until his death in 1984, he was a musician and a person of quality. One of several Utah Symphony musicians to serve as president of the musicians' union, Hepworth seemed to do it with the least effort and best feeling all around. In addition to daily rehearsals and concerts and administering union affairs, the versatile Hepworth was a full-time associate professor at the University. He also doubled on saxophone when occasional French composers, Gershwin, or jazz-related scores called for a jazz sound.

BASSOONS

Principal bassoonist *Douglas Craig's* tenure (1953-present) tops all others. Abravanel tells of auditioning Craig: "It was on the West Coast. There were three bassoonists waiting to be auditioned. The agent said: 'This one has played with the Chicago Symphony; the other with the Pittsburgh. But I was interested in the third one," remembers Abravanel. "But he's had no experience!" protested the agent. "Nevertheless, I want the other one." Abravanel remembers it as if it were yesterday: "The remaining one had just returned from the Korean War, was shell-shocked. I hired him because of something I felt was there." Douglas Craig was "the third one."

He and Eugene Foster joined the orchestra the same season (1953–54). Already in place were Martin Zwick and Louis Booth. National critics sometimes criticized the Utah Symphony brass or string sections, but never the woodwind principals, who could hold their own in any metropolitan orchestra.

Craig's familiar beard came out of the sixties and hides a gentle, handsome face. From the audience it is difficult to see the real Craig; his beard seems longer than his bassoon and is purportedly one reason some patrons attend concerts. His is a magic bassoon. It screams in contemporary scores and whispers a near-inaudible caress when called for. His technique is amazing. How often have audiences sat in awe as he negotiates rapidly-moving sixteenth notes *presto* perfectly, rhythmically and musically – in what seems to be one leisurely breath! Craig is the sole survivor of the distinguished era of Foster, Booth, and Zwick.

Craig's predecessors were *Morris Norkin* (1947–49), *William Watilo* (1949–51), and *Walter Green* (1952–53). There were many second and contrabassoonists: *Grant Baker, Howard Bleak, Grant Mack, Maurice Peterson,* and later, long-standing members of the section, *Brad Steorts* (1969–87) and *Mitchell Morrison* (1966-present).

PRINCIPAL HORNS

The *Fuchs* brothers, *Allan* and *Norman*, were imported as principal horn players during the orchestra's tentative first two seasons. Following the 1949 crisis they went eastward.

What Tabernacle audiences soon learned was that *Don Peterson* and *Glen Dalby*, who had rounded out the original

Cellist David Freed in performance. MAP.

section as third and fourth horn, sounded no different, perhaps even better, than the Fuchses when they advanced to first and second horn in 1949. Peterson played beautifully in any style at any tempo and is still doing so as a charter member of the 1947 ensemble. His combined stamina and artistry is one of the miracles of Abravanel's tenure. He appears frail but is held together by bands of steel. Like most musicians of Abravanel's first twenty years, when rehearsals were at night, Peterson "daylighted" as a teacher at Olympus Junior High.

Second to Peterson was *Edward Allen*, third horn and associate principal, an orchestra member from 1965 through Abravanel's tenure. A number of other excellent musicians have played in the horn section through the years: *Maurice Tueller, Gaylen Hatton* (now a Brigham Young University professor), *Ben Winn*, and *Lynn Larsen*, Peterson's best student.

TRUMPETS

William Sullivan was principal trumpet (1952–78) and co-principal with *Edmund Cord* (1978–81). Except for Don Peterson, Sullivan's was the longest tenure among the brass principals. Three others preceded him for brief periods. *Stewart Grow*, a veteran jazz trumpeter, played one season, Abravanel's first. He fared well until the final concert's *Bolero*, when, some say, his indisposition found his trumpet improvising in an interesting but non-Ravellian manner.

Herbert Eisenberg (1948–49) was one of the crisis musicians; he left for a large salary at New York's Radio City

Music Hall. His successor, *Wesley Lindskoog* (1949–52) remained for three seasons when he, too, left for a better-paying position.

William Sullivan enjoyed almost a thirty-year run, from 1952 to 1981! A visible citizen, he entered into the life of the community, served as president of the musicians' union and was an adjunct faculty member at the University, playing in the brass ensemble there. At his best Sullivan was brilliant, and he was always a musical performer. Abravanel brought Edmund Cord in to share the principal trumpet duties, and for Sullivan's last two seasons, he and Cord were co-principals. Cord became principal in 1978, adding strength and power to the entire brass section. His tone was straight and clear; it was also big and brassy. He played as if nothing bothered him, confident of every sound he produced. Even when he played a wrong note, it sounded right.

Other prominent trumpeters include second trumpet *Sheldon Hyde* (1947–80), who was also the orchestra's personnel manager from 1951 to 1982, and *Keith Smith*, a longtime third trumpet under Abravanel.

TROMBONE

Principal trombonist *John Swallow* (1947–49) left for the Radio City Music Hall following the 1949 crisis. *Lorn Steinberger*, a veteran West Coast professional, blew a consistent, dependable trombone for twelve years (1948–60). *Ned Meredith* (1960–62) was followed as principal by Salt Laker *Marion Albiston* for one season (1962–63), after which

The Utah Symphony in the University Music Hall in the late fifties. Hal Rumel photograph in MAP.

Meredith returned (1963–64). *Dennis Smith* next headed the trombone section and remained for four years (1964–68).

With the exception of Steinberger, *Ben Ivey* (1969–81), was the trombonist best known to symphony-goers. He played first trombone during the seventies and also taught at the University. He resigned from the orchestra in 1981 and was succeeded by *Larry Zalkind* (1981-present). Important to the three-man section through the years were *Marion Albiston*, a fixture since 1959 as second trombonist, and *Harold Gottfredson*, bass trombonist since 1956. Both players are members of the orchestra's property staff.

TUBAS

One ordinarily thinks of tubas *vis-à-vis* marching bands—and rightly so. But a single tuba makes all the difference to the orchestra's brass section and to the orchestra as a whole by extending the pitch range one octave lower. An orchestra, essentially a "string thing," finds that most scores are written predominantly for the string sections. The woodwinds play roughly fifty to sixty percent of the time; the brasses perhaps twenty; and the percussion even less. Of all the instruments the tuba is written for least, for both musical and historical reasons. The tuba's sound does not lend itself to solo passages, but a few contemporary scores call for brief solos in humorous passages with a skippy-melody, *staccato.*

Utah Symphony audiences do not see or hear the tuba player except in Wagner and post-Wagner works. The Symphony's leading tuba players have been *Richard Shuck* (1947–50), *Earl Jardine* (1950–51), *Reed Walker* (1960–63), *Charles Eckenrode* (1969–78), *Gene Pokorny* (1978–83), and *Gary Ofenloch* (1983-present).

HARP

The modern harp was not used extensively in the orchestra until the time of Wagner and Berlioz. Bach, Handel, Mozart, Haydn, Brahms, Mendelssohn, Schubert, Schumann, and Beethoven wrote for the harp in rare works. Without harps there would be no Impressionists—no Debussy, Ravel, Satie, Ibert, or Respighi. When harpists are seen warming up before

Abravanel and oboist Louis Booth on October 12, 1966. W. Claudell Johnson photograph for the *Deseret News* in MAP.

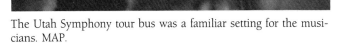

The Utah Symphony tour bus was a familiar setting for the musicians. MAP.

the concert, the audience can expect Wagner, Berlioz, the Impressionists, or some twentieth-century composers.

Utah Symphony harpists include four early ones: *Grace Webb, Adina Bradley, Louise Pratt,* and *Rebecca Wagner.* Later harpists include: *Camille Lamoreaux Guernsey, Shru DeLi Smith Ownbey,* and *Sarah Bullen,* who joined the New York Philharmonic in 1987.

TIMPANI

The timpanist was the least transient of all Symphony principals. There were only two during Abravanel's years, *Walter Rothaar* and *Robert Lentz.* Rothaar joined in 1947 and remained through 1955–56. Robert Lentz replaced him in the autumn of 1956 and stood or sat at the timpani through 1981. A flamboyant performer, he caught the audience's eye at strategic moments, which may have been a factor when he and his timpani found themselves on a lower stage level throughout the remainder of his tenure. Lentz also founded and conducted the Utah Youth Symphony.

PERCUSSION

Although actual notes written for them are few and far between, the percussion instruments are very important, particularly in contemporary scores. The orchestra has fielded a host of percussion players, beginning with *Joseph Mallory, Lowell Hicks,* and *Eugene Selick* (all from 1947), and including *William Billeter, Bill Johnson, Stan Katz, Jerry Epperson, Keith Guernsey, Jan Hyde, Craig Fineshriber,* and *Don Main.* Craig Fineshriber was designated principal percussionist in 1978–79, during Abravanel's final season.

PIANO-CELESTE

Both piano and celeste are occasional instruments, used sparingly in the orchestra. When called for, they bring some of music's most charming, impelling sounds (for instance, the celeste in Tchaikovsky's *Nutcracker* or the percussive sound of the piano in Stravinsky's *Petruchka*). Abravanel's original harpist was *Adina Bradley,* who doubled on piano and celeste. As the orchestra's repertoire and audiences grew, specialists on each instrument became essential.

Reid Nibley, brilliant young University pianist in early years, became the orchestra's pianist in 1948. He was a fixture, not only as an ensemble player, but also soloing in the

concerto literature eleven times during three successive years. Nibley was with the Symphony from 1947 until 1959. He joined the Brigham Young University faculty in 1959 and remained there as distinguished pianist and teacher until retiring. *Gladys Rosenberg,* a frequent and popular guest soloist during the Abravanel years, replaced Nibley during his sabbatical study at the Vienna Conservatory (1954–55).

Ardean Watts followed Nibley on piano and celeste and continued for twenty years (1959–79) until he resigned as associate conductor, following Abravanel's lead. Violinist *Bonnie Bennett* also doubled occasionally on piano.

ORGAN

The organ is rarely heard in strictly orchestral works. But where would the Mahler Eighth (*Thousand*) be without the opening solo organ *fortissimo* chord? Abravanel's obvious choice was Tabernacle organist *Alexander Schreiner,* who always added a special quality. He soloed in and recorded Saint-Saëns' Third (*Organ*) Symphony and appeared as soloist with Abravanel and the orchestra on seven occasions. His impeccable musicianship and his sense of humor added to the conviviality of rehearsals and performances.

When the internationally acclaimed Schreiner resigned as Tabernacle organist in 1977, he followed opera diva Lotte Lehmann's lead, retiring in his prime. Schreiner was succeeded by his gifted pupil *Robert M. Cundick,* who had been destined for the Tabernacle organist appointment since his youth. An excellent composer, Cundick has had compositions performed in Symphony Hall, but he has yet to play there, as there is no organ; the Symphony management still awaits a donor. When and if an organ is eventually in place, Cundick may be expected to be at the console.

THE NATURE OF THE BEAST

Abravanel has said much in praise of his musicians:

. . . a good orchestra musician must be able week after week after week to learn new music and to play it well. . . . A good orchestral musician is a man who must be able to control himself for an average of fifty minutes or one hour at a time before the intermission and about the same length after intermission, during which he has to concentrate every split second of the time, because in

The Maestro conducting. W. Claudell Johnson photograph for the
Deseret News in MAP.

The Utah Symphony in the Tabernacle in the late sixties or early seventies, with many beards in evidence. Utah Symphony photograph in MAP.

an orchestra, if there is only *one guy* who plays wrong, this is the musician everyone hears—not just if he plays trumpet or horn or an exposed solo. I mean even in the string section, you hear it.

    . . . He cannot cough. He cannot get up and go to the water cooler. He cannot go a little further—you know where! Even the most highly paid business executive, at the most important meeting, if he doesn't know the answer, can always cough and say, "one minute" and get up and go to the window or ask his secretary to come in.

On top of everything, a good orchestral musician must be "red hot." Otherwise the whole performance is dull. Unless *each* musician gives his most, it's dull!

So this is a good orchestral musician in my book. He deserves the best possible conditions and the best possible salary. . . . But today some musicians will complain: "Oh, Brahms again! I've played it three times!" Rubinstein played the *Emperor* Concerto five hundred times and would be as excited the next time, still love it, and still find new beauty every time. If orchestral players do not *feel* that love, they should be honest and leave the orchestra quickly and do something for which they are better fit, and there would be no hard feelings.

It is like the urologist who says: "I'm sick and tired. I would rather do a brain operation on you. Why should I always be a urologist? I've been that for thirty years." And you know very well you would say, "Thank you very much, goodbye!"

Abravanel also had very little patience with a player who, referring to a new score, "doesn't want to play that awful music. Musicians have been saying this for two hundred years. They have done it to all the masters as they emerged."

Abravanel compares his idea of a real musician to Ravel's *Bolero*:

It's not that the *Bolero* is such a great piece, although it's a pretty good one. Zubin Mehta filmed it with the Los Angeles Philharmonic. There is a moment in the film where they ask the string bass player just before they perform it: "How does it feel to play that monotonous bass part day after day? That's pretty dull isn't it?" He answered: "Don't say that. When I come here and the orchestra starts playing, it just envelops me, it engulfs me! I might have had an argument with my wife, the kids might have made me very mad at home and nervous. But the moment I hear that orchestra around me, I am transfigured. This is the life! This is beauty!" I could have kissed that man then and there!

Abravanel brings it closer to home:

I must say for the Utah Symphony that I convinced all of our players way back that no musician has the right to judge a new piece of music *unless* he first masters it. First, you play it right. After that, you play it again. After that, anything goes. *Then* you have the right and have earned the right to say "I still don't like it—I think it's bad!" Okay! But not before, or even when, he first plays the music and doesn't have the slightest idea of what it's all about.

If a musician who must live with Beethoven, Mozart, Brahms, et cetera, really becomes bored and cannot control himself to give a good performance, he should then have the honesty, the integrity to say, "I quit; I can't do it any more."

Lucy Abravanel. *Deseret News* photograph in MAP.

Miraflores

There is a building in California—not in Utah—named Abravanel Hall. The Santa Barbara *News-Press* announced on August 30, 1971: "Groundbreaking Held for New Music Hall. Maurice Abravanel, music director of the Music Academy of the West, put aside his familiar baton Saturday afternoon and took up a gold shovel to break ground for the new rehearsal hall at the academy complex."

Miraflores is about six miles south of Santa Barbara, situated on the Pacific coast in Montecito, on the former John Percival Jefferson estate. The Abravanels made their summer home there from 1955 to 1979, a refreshing respite from the Utah Symphony seasons.

In a symbolic ceremony Academy Board President Reginald Faletti handed Abravanel the shovel, saying, "During its twenty-five years of operation, the Music Academy of the West has developed a program of instruction . . . that has placed [it] in the forefront of musical training centers. That quality of training and excellence of the faculty are direct reflections of the inspiration and leadership of our music director, Maurice Abravanel." Abravanel Hall was completed the following summer.

Abravanel rehearsing the orchestra of the Music Academy of the West on September 27, 1956—performing "the annual miracle of training a complete symphony orchestra in a brief fortnight." George Newell photograph in MAP.

Seventeen years earlier Santa Barbara's *News-Press* had heralded Abravanel's appointment in a four-column headline with a large photo on November 7, 1954: "Maurice Abravanel Named New Musical Director of Academy." He succeeded Viennese-American conductor Richard Lert, director of the Academy from its founding in 1946, in an appointment effective July 1, 1955.

The Music Academy is a non-profit summer school for advanced music students. At the time of Abravanel's appointment, Mme. Lotte Lehmann headed the artist faculty. As the leading German soprano and music personality of her generation, Lehmann had created starring roles in most of Richard Strauss's operas and had sung all of Wagner's operatic roles plus those of Mozart, Beethoven, Weber, and others. She dominated German opera for decades. And, a true artist, she announced her retirement at the peak of her career, to the disappointment of the music world. Unlike some great opera stars who, ill-advised, continue after the voice is gone, Mme. Lehmann will always be remembered at her best—in her final personal appearances and recordings.

During Abravanel's inaugural summer of 1955, his picture appeared on a full page of the *News-Press* with the legendary diva at his side. Twenty years earlier he had conducted many of her stunning performances at the Met. Lehmann was honorary president of the Music Academy and director of its vocal department. She staged and supervised the Academy's annual opera productions, conducted by Abravanel.

Abravanel Hall, 1972. MAP.

Honorary President, and
Musical Director

MUSIC ACADEMY OF THE WEST

Maurice Abravanel, *Musical Director*

Tenth Summer Session, 1956
July 5 through August 30

FACULTY

Madame Lotte Lehmann, *Honorary President*
Darius Milhaud, *Honorary Musical Director*
Richard Lert, *Honorary Musical Director*

Gregor Piatigorsky, *Musical Advisor*
Jascha Veissi, *Assistant to the Musical Director*

German diva Lotte Lehmann and Abravanel in 1956, at the beginning of their long association at Miraflores. MAP.

Although she had retired as a performer, she continued to teach and direct the operas each summer until 1961, when she staged a farewell production of Beethoven's *Fidelio.*

Abravanel's second summer, 1956, saw an expansion of the Academy's faculty and programs. Darius Milhaud, distinguished member of The French Six, and Richard Lert were listed as honorary music directors.

Gregor Piatigorsky, one of the world's great cellists, was named musical adviser at this time. Other artist faculty included Sascha Jacobsen, violin; Sally Peck, viola; Gabor Rejto, cello; Emmanuel Bay, piano and chamber music; Gyorgy Sandor, piano; as well as leading wind, brass, and percussion artists, mostly from the Los Angeles area.

Sally Peck was hand-picked by Abravanel, having been his principal violist in the Utah Symphony since 1950. She was among the first of a gradually expanding Utah contingent that went to Santa Barbara each summer. Most were talented students who qualified for scholarships on Abravanel's recommendation. By 1961, Abravanel's sixth year, twenty-seven young Utah student artists were playing under his baton in the Academy Symphony Orchestra and studying privately with the artist faculty.

During Abravanel's first summer, Lotte Lehmann directed Richard Strauss's *Ariadne auf Naxos.* Patterson Greene, music critic of the Los Angeles *Examiner,* wrote:

> General stage direction has been taken over by Lotte Lehmann, who knows Strauss's intentions from having sung often under his direction. . . . The performance is enriched by her knowledge, enkindled by her imagination. . . . Maurice Abravanel, a major figure among conductors, gives pulsating life to the musical score, with its prismatic yet transparent orchestration, played admirably by the student orchestra.

The cast, stage director Lehmann, and music director Abravanel take their bows for *Ariadne auf Naxos* at the Music Academy of the West on August 26, 1956. Eldon Tatsch photograph in MAP.

Ariadne auf Naxos was staged during Abravanel's first summer in Santa Barbara. Eldon Tatsch photograph in MAP.

Santa Barbara's proximity to metropolitan Los Angeles attracted its major critics to many Academy presentations. Albert Goldberg, then senior critic for the *Los Angeles Times*, reviewed the Academy's *Magic Flute* on August 25, 1959, with this reference to Abravanel: "To Maurice Abravanel goes the credit for the solid musical assurance of the production. Everyone knew what to do and how. Mr Abravanel's authoritative conducting kept the student orchestra in line, with playing strict in rhythm and admirably nuanced, and it guided the singers over the rough spots so well that one was hardly aware that difficulties existed. . . . "

Miraflores' location – on the blue Pacific – was ideal. The estate mansion, a building of considerable proportions, lent itself naturally to the informal conservatory approach. Before the construction of Abravanel Hall, the mansion had served for orchestra and opera rehearsals as well as individual practice. In common with most music education facilities, it lacked sufficient practice rooms and concert halls.

An unusually high percentage of the Academy's students were Utahns, ranking second in numbers only to Californians. Nearly all the students eventually became Utah Symphony members, so that by the mid-sixties the Music Academy of the West had become a principal training ground for Utah Symphony members.

The *Salt Lake Tribune* for August 18, 1963, noted that:

For years now, Maurice has flown to Santa Barbara directly from the University of Utah Summer Festival. The past three years have seen him turn the Summer Festival baton over to Ardean Watts immediately after the opening night of the Broadway musical to permit him to assume Santa Barbara duties a few days earlier. . . .

If the roll call of the past nine years at the academy were called, nearly fifty percent of the Utah Symphony's personnel would have summered at the academy at one time or another. . . . LaVar Krantz . . . longtime Utah Symphony principal second violinist, is Abravanel's concertmaster this summer. . . . The following youthful Utah Symphony members are playing under Abravanel's familiar baton: Linda Brown, John Loutensock, Ronald Horton and Jack Ashton, violins; Mary Lindblom, cello, and Richard Fletcher, horn.

During his Santa Barbara years, Abravanel was often invited to conduct the Los Angeles Philharmonic at the Hollywood Bowl. Albert Goldberg of the *Los Angeles Times* reviewed a concert conducted there by Abravanel on August 6, 1964:

> Mr. Abravanel . . . treated Tchaikovsky with the conscience of a true musician, which is a luxury the Russian master is not often permitted to enjoy. He did not maul the music, tear passion to tatters or push it around to show how original or how different he could be. He was content to abide by the letter of the score and by and large, it was a relief and a pleasure to hear the music unadorned by willful distortions and personal idiosyncrasies.

Of Tchaikovsky's *Italian Caprice*, Goldberg wrote that Abravanel's

> careful tempo changes made it sound like a much better piece than usual; the niceties of orchestration could be clearly heard and savored and the orchestral tone was solid and agreeable.
>
> It was much the same with the Fourth Symphony. . . . This time one heard exactly what the composer intended. The points were made without heavy underlining or unnecessary italics, and it was hard to see that anything suffered by the restraint.

Patterson Greene of the Los Angeles *Herald-Examiner*, an ardent supporter, always made favorable mention of Abravanel's Utah Symphony connection. Reviewing the same Tchaikovsky Hollywood Bowl program, Greene wrote: "Abravanel, who has devoted many years to raising the Salt Lake Symphony from obscurity to nationwide recognition, particularly by virtue of its exceptional recordings, showed an easy and unconventional mastery of the Russian composer's *Italian Caprice* and Fourth Symphony."

Abravanel's student orchestras at Santa Barbara were near-professional. His programs were the same as those of large professional orchestras. An August 2, 1961, review from the Santa Barbara *News-Press* is typical. "A crisp performance of the overture to Weber's *Oberon* opened the concert." The "exuberance of the youthful players" was noted:

> Mr. Abravanel captured the romantic mood of Samuel Barber's haunting *Adagio for Strings*. The orchestra responded magnificently.
>
> Always a *tour de force*, Stravinsky's *Firebird* Suite concluded the first half of the program. . . . The youthful musicians emphatically provided assurance of their musical achievement. All the excitement and color of Stravinsky's score were there. . . .

That concert concluded with Gyorgy Sandor joining the youngsters in the Brahms B-flat Piano Concerto. "The orchestra played with authority. . . ."

Abravanel's astute programming was noted by reviewer Donald Pond: "The first number in Maurice Abravanel's brilliantly constructed program told us of the miracle that awaited us. The *Adagietto* from Mahler's Fifth Symphony's performance answered what is likely to be one's first question about an orchestra: How good is the intonation of the strings? The question was answered affirmatively. . . ."

Pond then praised Debussy's *Nuages* and *Fêtes* for their virtuosity of performance. Rimsky-Korsakov's *Capriccio Espagnol* concluded this program: "The skill and élan with which . . . the orchestra handled the instrumental and rhythmic pyrotechnics of this vivid score were without reproach. . . . "

A three-week West Coast tour in June of 1968 brought Abravanel and his Utah Symphony to Santa Barbara. Californians who knew him as conductor of the Academy student orchestra and opera now saw him on the podium of his own major symphony orchestra, whose internationally acclaimed Mahler recordings, particularly, had made him a considerable figure.

It was a homecoming not only for Abravanel but for many Symphony members who had spent a summer or more at Miraflores since 1955. The Symphony's concert in

A performance of the Mozart *Requiem* in Santa Barbara on September 27, 1956. The soloist second from the right is young Grace Bumbry. MAP.

Santa Barbara was sponsored by the Academy and presented in the 1,400-seat Granada Theatre. The program included Mahler's Fourth Symphony, with Jean Preston, soprano; Prokofiev's Third Piano Concerto, with Grant Johannesen, soloist; and Ravel's *Daphnis and Chloé Suite No. 2.*

At no time did Abravanel program "down" to his young musicians or their audiences. In the summer of 1971, Abravanel's student orchestra played Stravinsky's three major ballet scores on one program: *The Firebird, Petruchka,* and *The Rite of Spring.* The performance was remarkable. One critic termed it "unbelievable." Few professional orchestras have programmed all three ballets on the same program; two perhaps, but not three. Abravanel made an exception,

however, leading the Utah Symphony in all three on October 23, 1971, in the Salt Lake Tabernacle. He was well prepared after having rehearsed and performed them two months earlier in Santa Barbara.

Professionally-produced and -performed opera continued to highlight each summer. In 1971, when Weber's *Der Freischütz* was presented, Martial Singher had succeeded Lotte Lehmann as opera director. *Los Angeles Times* critic Albert Goldberg's review was restrained. He felt that the opera itself, while still popular in Germany, "is a work that seldom transplants satisfactorily. . . . It does not take kindly to foreign soil. . . . Only the eminently authoritative conducting of Maurice Abravanel and the playing of his excellent orchestra managed to capture whatever durable qualities have kept [it] alive for a century and a half." Goldberg was critical of Singher's staging, but Lotte Lehmann was assuredly a difficult act to follow.

By 1975, Abravanel's twentieth year at the Academy, the faculty had changed significantly. Mme. Lehmann's name no longer appeared as honorary president, but Gregor Piatigorsky was still honorary musical adviser. Zvi Zeitlin, who subsequently soloed with the Utah Symphony three times, headed the violin area. Utah Symphony concertmaster Oscar Chausow continued on the faculty, and pianist Jerome Lowenthal had been added. He, too, is well known in Utah, having premiered Leroy Robertson's Piano Concerto during the 1966–67 season and appeared as guest soloist on three other concerts.

The Bicentennial summer produced one of the greatest days in Abravanel's life. A full page in the Santa Barbara *News-Press* on Sunday, July 18, 1976, announced in huge headlines: "MUSIC ACADEMY WEEK, HIGHLIGHTED BY A PERSONAL APPEARANCE BY VAN CLIBURN IN ABRAVANEL CELEBRATION DAY." Celebrity friends of the Abravanels had gathered for the occasion: "See the special presentation by Dorothy Kirsten of Metropolitan Opera fame. . . . See Dorothy McGuire, Nancy Hanks, Frederick Loewe of Lerner and Loewe, Gregor Piatigorsky, and others [who have] come to pay tribute to the distinguished Director of the Music Academy," concluded the front page of the entertainment section.

The Abravanel Festival program included concerts of all types. Cynosure of the week's events was pianist Van Cliburn in an outdoor performance in the Santa Barbara County Bowl.

Jascha Heifetz, Abravanel, and Gregor Piatigorsky at Miraflores. MAP.

He joined Abravanel and the orchestra in an "Academy Spectacular" on July 21, playing the Grieg Piano Concerto. The orchestra performed Ravel's *Daphnis and Chloé Suite No. 2* and Stravinsky's *Firebird*, with Berlioz' *Roman Carnival* Overture as an opener. During the intermission, Dorothy Kirsten made a special presentation to Abravanel; she had sung under Abravanel in Chicago thirty years earlier. There were many printed tributes in both concert program and press, plus a king-sized plaque to remind him of the event and the love and appreciation it represented.

One reviewer termed Abravanel's 1977 work with the Academy orchestra "the annual miracle of training a complete symphony orchestra in a brief fortnight." Not one to rest on his laurels, according to the *News-Press*, "Last week he flew to New York to make his debut with the Mostly Mozart Festival in Avery Fisher Hall in Lincoln Center, conducting a program of Mozart and Haydn symphonies. On July 30 Abravanel will again conduct the Academy Festival Orchestra in a concert at the Lobero Theatre."

The latter concert opened with the Adagietto of Mahler's Fifth Symphony. "Maestro Abravanel is regarded as one of the world's foremost interpreters of Mahler, having recorded all nine Mahler symphonies, plus the *Adagio* of the unfinished Tenth with the Utah Symphony." The remainder of the program consisted of Brahms' Second Symphony and Schumann's *Spring* Symphony.

Reviewer Kenneth A. Brown reminded readers that the young musicians were hand-picked and carefully screened, the resulting personnel bordering on professional:

> Even so, the professional competence of the academy's orchestra is always a source of delight.
>
> The very youth of the musicians gives to their playing a quality of freshness and excitement which even the finest professional orchestras do not always provide. These young people never lapse into what is merely routine. They give everything they have. One senses, moreover, a close and friendly rapport between the conductor and his players. The young musicians are well disciplined, as they must be, but clearly they are not browbeaten.

The demanding summer of 1977 followed the most difficult Utah Symphony season Abravanel had faced. The shock

Abravanel with Lotte Lehmann. MAP.

of open-heart surgery in November of 1976, followed by a return to the podium a mere two months later and performances of both Mahler's Second (*Resurrection*) and Eighth (*Thousand*) symphonies combined to make the subscription season extremely difficult. Plus there were four tension-filled post-season "specials"—one with Beverly Sills, a "Salute to the Tabernacle," and two historic performances with the Mormon Tabernacle Choir of Leroy Robertson's *Book of Mormon Oratorio*.

In April and May, Abravanel led tours of Northern California, Washington, Oregon, Montana, and Wyoming. Then summer again in Santa Barbara—a two months' "oasis in the desert." After an incredibly stressful year, Abravanel still led his musicians on a thirty-day, nineteen-concert tour to Greece, Austria, West Germany, and Spain. The year 1977 made demands on Abravanel that would lead inevitably to his resignation.

Abravanel and Associate Conductor Ardean Watts. Photograph courtesy of Elna Watts.

CHAPTER 15

Right Arm

"Should I work on a doctor's degree?"

Ardean Watts posed this question in the late summer of 1968. "Not if you plan to be a conductor. Ph.D.'s are not for performers, conductors, or composers. Can you conduct?" Ardean nodded. He already knew that, but there was more on his mind: "Abravanel has asked me to be his associate conductor—associate, not assistant!" he emphasized. "Take it!" I said. He already had. Abravanel had revealed two weeks earlier that he was about to make this important appointment because of his increasing work load. He had already reduced the possibilities to two: Watts and Crawford Gates. Gates was in his third year as music director of orchestras in Beloit, Wisconsin, and Rockford, Illinois. Watts was Abravanel's choice.

Watts had enrolled in the graduate program at the University in 1956, after graduating from BYU. He was assigned to the opera workshop as a teaching assistant and became the Symphony's official pianist in 1958. He earned his master's degree and was appointed to the University of Utah faculty in 1960.

In the autumn of 1957, the University opera workshop was experiencing difficulties. Carl Fuerstner, an excellent musician who had held similar positions at the Eastman School of Music and BYU had been dismissed because he lacked organizational and human relations skills.

Standing at the counter of the music department office one day, Watts was asked, "What do you know about opera? Do you think you could fill in as acting director of the opera workshop for the rest of the year?" In his matter-of-fact way, graduate student Watts indicated that he would "give it a shot." The program went well, and in 1965 he proposed an enlarged University opera company with the complete Utah Symphony in the pit. From 1965 to 1978—thirteen years—Watts was in turn founder, Executive, and Artistic Director of the University of Utah Opera Company in a total of eighteen productions with the Utah Symphony, six of them staged by him. Among his board members were Sterling M. McMurrin, Keith M. Engar, J. Boyer Jarvis, and the author.

The opera productions included *Madame Butterfly*, *The Flying Dutchman*, *Don Giovanni*, *The Magic Flute*, *La Traviata*, and *The Crucible*. The performances were in Kingsbury Hall, with some cooperation in staging from the Pioneer Memorial Theatre when that facility was built. "In my mind," recalls Watts, "the most significant single performance I have ever done was Bernstein's *Mass* in the new University Special Events Center on April 19 and 20, 1974, under the auspices of the Symphony and the Associated Students of the University—only three years after its premiere at the dedication of the Kennedy Center."

Artistically, the productions also went well, delighting both adult and student opera-lovers. Annual deficits, partially underwritten by the University, were troublesome, however. In 1978 a top-level University administrative committee determined that it was not financially feasible for the state university to continue to underwrite a professional opera company as part of its music program.

Coincidentally, at about this time Glade Peterson, Utah's sole international opera figure since Emma Lucy Gates Bowen, returned to his Salt Lake City home from Europe. A leading tenor of the Zurich Opera Company for fifteen years and guest artist in Europe's major opera houses, as well as New York's Metropolitan Opera, he returned with a dream. With a high-powered organizational team that included Governor Calvin Rampton and Obert C. Tanner, Peterson spearheaded the formation of the Utah Opera Company near the opening date for the renovated Capitol Theatre of the Salt Palace complex. The Utah Opera Company, which celebrated its tenth anniversary in 1988, has taken its place alongside the Utah Symphony and Ballet West as one of the state's three major performing arts groups.

Watts's thirteen years of University of Utah Opera productions provided a solid foundation for the Utah Opera Company. Watts was a triple-threat: Associate Conductor of the Utah Symphony, Musical Director of Ballet West, and Artistic Director of the University of Utah Opera Company simultaneously. He conducted the Utah Symphony in all three assignments, as it was the pit orchestra for both opera and ballet.

According to a December 16, 1979, *Salt Lake Tribune* feature, Watts's association with Willam Christensen began with the annual *Nutcracker* in 1957, when he was the Symphony's pianist and celeste player and soloed in the "Dance of the Sugar Plum Fairy." He "also played the ratchet and the gong when the Mouse King is killed," he recalled.

Watts first conducted for Ballet West in 1966 and was soon conducting its out-of-town appearances, including tours of Europe (1971) and the United States. His titles with Ballet West included guest conductor, resident conductor, principal conductor, and finally music director (except for the period from 1975 to 1979, when Ronald Horton held that position). Watts left the company in June of 1983.

But his heart lay with the Utah Symphony, which is where Watts made his most significant contributions during that amazingly productive period. He was Abravanel's "right arm" as his associate conductor from 1968 to 1979, but he was the right arm long before the official designation Associate Conductor was conferred.

When Watts joined the Utah Symphony in 1958, he had been ready and waiting since 1956. Two other capable pianists had arrived ahead of him—Reid Nibley and Robert Cundick. Nibley was the Utah Symphony's first official pianist, and Cundick was Abravanel's assistant and rehearsal accompanist for University Summer Festivals and joint choral-orchestral performances. During those waiting years, Watts taught in the Salt Lake public schools and was the busiest jazz band leader in the state, conducting big bands and shows at the Saltair and Lagoon resorts and the Rainbow Randevu ballroom (later the Terrace). He also concertized as soloist and accompanist throughout the western states.

Watts recalls his first meeting with Abravanel: "It was in 1956 in the old World War II barracks, Building No. 440 at Fort Douglas, which housed the offices of the Music Department and College of Fine Arts." Abravanel was auditioning a singer. Watts was accompanying her:

> She was singing the "Liebestod" from Wagner's *Tristan and Isolde*, and I had never seen the music before. I had twenty-four hours' notice and practiced all night. I really didn't know much about reading music. As a jazzman I improvised, and I knew the jazz-chord symbols. Apparently it came off all right, for I remember distinctly that at the conclusion of the audition Abravanel turned to someone and whispered: "Who is the pianist?"

Later that year Abravanel phoned Watts and asked him to play Mendelssohn's *Italian* Symphony at the keyboard the next day for a ballet rehearsal. It was Summer Festival time, and in addition to the opera and musical, there was to be a night of ballet. Watts was given only an hour's notice and was greeted by Willam Christensen and Abravanel on his arrival. Abravanel "conducted" Watts at the piano to set the correct tempos while the ballet rehearsal went ahead under Christensen's direction. Watts's second contact with Abravanel was also successful.

A few months later Watts asked Abravanel if he could audition as Symphony pianist. The answer was "No, not at this time." Abravanel was still committed to Reid Nibley, who had been the official pianist for over a decade.

The third Watts-Abravanel "connection" came in the spring of 1957. Abravanel had selected Richard Strauss's *Salome*, with Oscar Wilde's scandalous libretto, for the Uni-

Ardean Watts. MAP.

versity Summer Festival opera. He gave Watts twenty-four hours' notice for a rehearsal at the Abravanel home on east Seventh South Street. Again it went well.

A few months later lightning struck! It was January of 1958 and Reid Nibley was ill. Abravanel asked Watts to substitute in the piano part of Shostakovich's Fifth Symphony at a Granite High School concert. "The rehearsal went perfectly, but I muffed the performance," admits Watts. "But

Abravanel didn't say a word, which was typical of him during our entire relationship." Two months later, Watts was asked to rehearse the Mozart Double Piano Concerto with Nibley and the orchestra preparatory to the Tabernacle appearance of the international piano-duo Luboschutz and Nemenoff.

Nibley joined the Brigham Young University faculty in 1958 and relinquished his Utah Symphony position. Finally, after two years of assisting Abravanel, Watts was named to

Warming up at the University. Steve Parker photograph for the *Deseret News*, courtesy of Elna Watts.

succeed Nibley as official pianist of the orchestra. He performed at the piano and celeste keyboards from 1958 to 1979, continuing even after his appointment as the orchestra's associate conductor.

Long before his conducting position was official, Watts had conducted many school and out-of-town concerts—"as many as sixty in the middle sixties," he guesses. In the seventies he conducted all the orchestra's school concerts and most of the Intermountain and in-state tours.

During his early years as associate conductor, Watts faced opposition and hazing—a game widely played by orchestra musicians, particularly with guest, assistant, and associate conductors. The game gets rough at times, and it was no exception with Watts. Abravanel did not intercede. He could easily have done so at any time and dispelled the tension, but he let Watts fight it out.

After the first few years things seemed to go better. Then some musicians complained about Watts in a letter to executive director Huck Gregory. Watts recalls talking with Gregory, reading the letter, and then calling an immediate after-rehearsal meeting with the orchestra in the Tabernacle, where he had a verbal exchange with the complainers. Again Abravanel let Watts "go it alone," privately assuring him of his support.

One complaint difficult to overcome concerned programming, over which Watts had no control. The repertoire at school concerts was nearly always the same and no longer challenging for the highly sophisticated players. Its lack of variety was distressing to sensitive musicians. There were other complaints that were "managerial—scheduling, booking, etc." Many were simply highly-charged personality gripes.

One of Watts's most unforgettable experiences in his role as associate conductor came with the guest appearance of the Soviet Union's highly acclaimed piano virtuoso, Lazar Berman, who played Rachmaninov's Third Piano Concerto with the orchestra on Thursday, April 7, 1978, in Ogden, Utah, and in the Tabernacle the following evening. He gave awesome performances of what some experts consider the repertoire's most difficult piano concerto.

But that is not the story. Abravanel's open-heart surgery was only four months behind him. He had made a successful recovery and returned to the Tabernacle podium after missing only four subscription concerts. Two of these had

featured guest conductors Crawford Gates and Watts, and both had immediately preceded Berman's appearance, affording Abravanel a respite of several weeks.

Watts remembers vividly the Tabernacle rehearsal for Berman's Thursday night concert: "Berman took a lot of exaggerated rubatos and other unusual solistic freedoms. The rehearsal didn't go well at all! I had been informed by the Symphony management some time before to 'Be ready to go on for Maurice at any time.' " So Watts always had all the scores in his head and was ready to appear in white-tie and tails on a moment's notice:

> In Ogden, Shirl [Swenson, the orchestra's manager] told me "You're on! Maurice is ill!" I entered Maurice's dressing room, and he was wearing his overcoat. "I can't go on tonight, Ardean. I'm going home to Salt Lake." So I went into the adjoining dressing room to change clothes.
>
> Then I heard Berman enter Maurice's room. Their conversation was heated—Maurice trying to explain his illness, Berman loudly intoning "Nyet! Nyet!" He spoke minimal English, which was part of the problem. When I came out in tails with scores in hand, Berman made

Departing on the fourth international tour in September 1977, Ardean Watts stows baggage while Shirl Swenson, behind Abravanel, appears concerned about the travel arrangements. Wendell Ashton is seated across the aisle. MAP.

one more attempt to dissuade Maurice. At this point a frustrated Maurice threw his overcoat on the floor, picked up his baton and headed toward the door. Berman, finally realizing that Maurice was very ill, said "No, Maestro! No, Maestro!"

Berman took Watts's arm, and together they joined the orchestra on stage. "The performance went off smoothly," says Watts, who also conducted the Tabernacle performance the next night. Rumors and misunderstandings about the Berman affair circulated widely, suggesting that it was simply a battle of artistic temperaments. "Not so," says Watts. "Maurice was unwell."

In addition to his three major assignments, Watts became co-conductor of the University of Utah Summer Festivals. When Abravanel relinquished the podium for the Broadway musicals, Watts took over. He also conducted the last two summer operas, except for the opening nights, which Abravanel conducted before flying to his summer appointment in Santa Barbara.

Watts's dynamic musical direction of eight productions for the University of Utah Theatre from 1958 to 1967 is less well known. He also prepared the University chorus for joint Tabernacle appearances and recordings with the Symphony from 1960 to 1962. Among those recordings were Scarlatti's *St. Cecelia Mass*, Milhaud's *Pacem in Terris* and, more importantly, Honegger's *King David*, which in 1962 received the orchestra's first Grammy nomination. Watts taught part-time on the University's music faculty throughout his Utah Symphony career, and he conducted the University Symphony from 1970 to 1972. The ubiquitous Watts also served as interim department chair from 1977 to 1979 and headed the ambitious University–Snowbird Summer Music Programs.

Watts's letter of resignation from the Utah Symphony followed Abravanel's by about one month. Its effective date was the same, August 1, 1979. During that month he offered to continue temporarily as interim music director until reorganization could take place. Board President Wendell J. Ashton declined the offer.

Watts returned to his full-time teaching position at the University the following month, enthusiastically resuming academic life. Within a year he was tapped as acting chairman of the ballet department. The following year the "acting"

The Abravanels on April 20, 1961. *Deseret News* photograph in MAP.

designation was deleted. His singular achievement, highly publicized and deservedly so, was a plan to integrate the community's three major ballet forces: Ballet West, Willam Christensen's Junior Academy, and the University's own student ballet corps. "Mr. C" returned to the campus out of retirement, Ballet West's Bruce Marks agreed to the association, and the University ballet department became Ballet West's official training school.

Watts was designated University Professor, one of the school's most prestigious distinctions, for the academic year

The Maestro radiating a genuine warmth in his smile. MZPC.

of 1984–85. Working with synthesizers now tops his priorities.

Watts has probably known Abravanel better than anyone but Lucy, playing under him for twenty-one years, working closely as his associate conductor for eleven and, perhaps as importantly, chauffeuring him to and from rehearsals and other appointments for twenty-one years. He offers some impressions:

I was always impressed with Maurice's prodigious memory and his genuine – not surface, but genuine – concern for people. Following one of our Tabernacle concerts, a middle-aged woman approached him: "You don't know me, do you? You wouldn't remember me?" I was amazed when Maurice's face lit up: "Of course, I remember you. You sang in the chorus when we performed and recorded *Israel in Egypt*." And then Maurice repeated her name!

Maurice always treated the musicians and visiting artists in a gracious manner, no matter how things were going. There were never any "scenes" with the orchestra.

Maurice was a true Renaissance man, well-versed on every conceivable subject. He was not simply a musician and conductor of considerable stature, he was well read. He knew, or knew of, nearly everyone of importance in most fields.

He was single-minded. Everything he did or said was done solely for its effect on the Utah Symphony. It was his admittedly tough, unyielding attitude on principle that saw the Utah Symphony through its roughest problems and strengthened its sinews. Opposition and some feelings may have followed, but Abravanel's singleness of purpose moved the orchestra forward.

"He was fun to be with," Watts continues. "He had a marvelous sense of humor and delighted in unusual things." Few people ever saw Abravanel drive a car. Lucy was always his chauffeur. Watts insists, nevertheless, that Abravanel drove at times during the early Utah years but ceased because he "was too creative a driver."

Maurice wanted to be personally involved with his musicians. He knew the names of their children and husbands and wives and was genuinely interested in them as people, who also just happened to be musicians.

He was absolutely devoted to his wife Lucy. Maurice wouldn't have been the easiest person to live with, but Lucy always seemed to be on top of every situation, able to anticipate his moods and serve as a calming, leveling influence. A Parisian, she was a gourmet cook, a marvelous mother for her sons Pierre and Roger, and a loving grandmother to five grandchildren. She attended every subscription concert, traveled on all five of the orchestra's overseas tours, and toured during many western states tours. She attended all the meetings of the Utah Symphony Guild, where her advice was always sought, and

Watts conducting the "Star-Spangled Banner" at the University of Utah Commencement exercises in June 1980. Paul Barker photograph for the University of Utah in MAP.

she was involved in a variety of Symphony-related civic and social activities. Lucy was the conductor's wife.

Abravanel was obviously very fond of Watts, who at times must have felt like the Abravanels' third son, so constantly was he at the conductor's side.

Watts's resignation in the spring of 1979 had been preceded by continuing abuse from some members of the orchestra who were determined that he would not be Abravanel's successor. This tension had surfaced and became increasingly bitter with the influx of a number of new out-of-state musicians in the middle and late seventies—some excellent principals, all very concerned with the orchestra's two-tiered A and B contracts, retirement program, salary scale, scheduling, and touring. Some obviously disliked Watts to the point of being unnecessarily unkind.

To this vocal group, Watts had become "part of the problem." As in the earlier conflicts, Abravanel did not intervene. By this time, personal considerations and his impending resignation commanded his entire energy. But he was adamant then, and has been in the years since, concerning his respect for Watts as a musician and his devotion to him as a person. Asked about Watts's ill treatment during his final years with the orchestra, Abravanel mutters, "I'll never forgive those guys! I'll never forgive those guys!"

Abravanel praised Watts verbally on numerous occasions. He also went on record in a series of lectures on the University of Utah campus during the winter quarter of 1980, soon after his resignation and after working with Watts daily for twenty-one years. Speaking of the training of young conductors, he referred to the various methods of four well-known local conductors—Varujan Kojian, then recently appointed as Abravanel's successor; Robert Henderson, Kojian's assistant conductor; Chris Tiemeyer, assistant conductor at Dallas and former Utah Symphony principal cellist; and Watts:

> You have a conductor here—Ardean Watts—who conducted the University orchestra, whom I engaged and who did marvelously with the Utah Symphony. His beautiful work was praised by our top guest soloists who played under his direction—people like the USSR's piano virtuoso Lazar Berman, the Metropolitan Opera's Judy Blegen, and others. All praised Ardean to the skies, and for many years he had great joy conducting the Utah Symphony and doing a wonderful job. He was praised to the skies by Bill Christensen and Ballet West and also conducted many good operatic performances.

When Abravanel gave the University's Commencement address that June, with Watts conducting the Utah Symphony, he praised him in more glowing terms: "Ardean Watts is that magnificent musician who is the pride of your music department and the man thanks to whom I could carry on as music director of the Utah Symphony long after my health would have dictated many times to give up during the past five years."

DAVID AUSTIN SHAND

Although Watts was Abravanel's only associate conductor, there was one longtime assistant conductor. David A. Shand joined the Utah Symphony in Abravanel's first year. He brought excellent credentials: a bachelor's degree from the University of Utah, a master's from Harvard, and a doctorate in musicology from Boston University.

The reorganization of the Utah Symphony under Abravanel and of the University of Utah music department under Leroy Robertson brought Shand and his family home to Utah. He was appointed assistant professor at the University, and Abravanel hired him as assistant conductor—a position he held for seventeen years, until 1965. During this period, however, there were minimal opportunities for conducting.

Robertson later assigned Shand to conduct the University Symphony. After several years he gave it up for health reasons. His final campus years were difficult, but he continued to teach his classes. He passed away in the summer of 1982 after a lingering illness.

CHAPTER 16

The House That Maurice Built

"My Board has betrayed me! My Board has betrayed me!" Maurice Abravanel was beside himself at the action just taken by the Utah Symphony Board of Directors. "The vote was eight in favor, one opposed, and two abstentions!" he half shouted.

The vote, sent by letter to the Salt Lake County Commission, agreed to the elimination of the concert hall from the proposed Salt Lake County Civic Auditorium Complex: "The Utah Symphony Board on Friday, November 25, 1966, approved this statement of its position in relation to the proposal that the concert hall be eliminated from the first phase of construction."

The Board reminded the Commission, however, that: "There is ample evidence that when the citizens of Salt Lake County voted to approve a bond issue of $17,000,000 on November 3, 1964, that it was the understanding that a concert hall would be included in the complex."

At a September 13, 1963, meeting of the Salt Lake County Commissioners, the chairman of the County Civic Auditorium Committee had submitted estimates which included "an arena, an exhibit hall, ten meeting rooms and related facilities and a concert hall."

Abravanel conducts the chorus from *Elijah* for the Commencement at Westminster College of Salt Lake City. *Salt Lake Tribune* photograph in MAP.

The Symphony Board's lengthy statement made a case for the concert hall while recognizing a greater immediate need for a convention center. Between estimated costs in 1963 and actual costs in 1966, the building industry had fought a losing battle with inflation and all available funds were spent on the arena and exhibit hall. There was simply no money for the concert hall.

In a series of articles, "The Saga of Symphony Hall," in the Utah Symphony's 1975–76 concert programs, Huck Gregory outlined the entire story from 1963 to the hall's official dedication in September of 1979: "In the fall of 1966, as bids . . . for the new civic center were opened, it was found that actual bids exceeded the architects' estimates by about $4 million." That triggered the tug-of-war between Symphony fans lobbying for the concert hall and the Symphony Board, all prominent businessmen, prodded by downtown promoters to support a convention center and temporarily postpone the concert hall.

Obert C. Tanner, Utah Symphony Board member and one of the orchestra's most generous supporters, recalls: "As a member of the Utah Symphony Board, I reluctantly [felt] that, in view of the facts, we [should] forego the symphony hall, reserving our plans to use the location north of the Salt Palace when funds might be available.

"As the years went by," Tanner continues, "there was no apparent opportunity to obtain the amount of $8 or $10 million necessary to build a new symphony hall." The oppor-

Rehearsing in the Tabernacle with soloist Rudolf Serkin. Serkin autographed one photograph: "To Maurice in remembrance of our *first* music-making together, with admiration. April 13/14, 1973." Martin Zwick photograph in MAP.

tunity *was* to arise six years later, however, and Obert Tanner would play a key role.

Abravanel's disappointment and frustration at his Board's action is understandable. After all, he had striven for a concert hall for nearly two decades. He had lived with the idea day in and day out. He had lobbied, delivered speeches, and buttonholed key politicians and businessmen. For the Board it was essentially a political-business decision arrived at objectively. For the Maestro it was personal and emotional – his heart and soul. Time blunted the disappointment and healed much of the hurt. In the meantime he controlled his feelings, knowing he must lose this battle to win the war.

A *Salt Lake Tribune* editorial headed: "$4 Million Architect's Error" sought to pacify Symphony devotees. This headline became a bitter byword among music lovers during construction of the Salt Palace, while the concert hall site became a parking lot.

The decision of the Board was crucial, and it occurred during Wendell Ashton's first weeks as president. The Symphony was riding the crest of its most successful year in history. The triumphant European tour was behind it, an unforgettable achievement. The Ford Foundation's matching endowment had been approved, and the Big Machine was gearing up to raise matching funds.

Old friends Abravanel and Yehudi Menuhin. MZPC.

Although it was a bitter pill for Abravanel and his followers to swallow, in retrospect the Board's decision was justified. The November 1966 letter to Salt Lake County officials identified the fundamental problem and attached some strings.

> We also believe that the business sector of our community, which will benefit most from revenues from a convention center, owes a moral obligation to support our orchestra's drive, commencing soon, for a million dollars in matching funds for a Ford Foundation grant. The achieving of this million dollar goal is a necessity for maintaining the quality of our orchestra which has done so much to bring national and international recognition to this community and state.

Ashton and the Board had foreseen how impractical it was to involve the business community in two major fund-raising drives at the same time – the Symphony's Ford matching endowment and the civic center. *High Fidelity–Musical America's* November 1968 issue editorialized:

> It may seem difficult on the face of it to understand what prompted the Utah Symphony board to vote unanimously [*sic*] to condone the scuttling of the concert hall, without a token protest. Yet, financial figures tell something of the story: the orchestra would have had to pay rental for the new facilities; and it would have had to play pairs of subscription concerts instead of the current single one. . . . Even more urgent was the very real problem of raising $1 million dollars to match the

Symphony's Ford grant. A "deal" was apparently made within the community power structure wherein the board agreed to forego the concert hall "temporarily," until the fund drive was over.

"Thank God for the Mormon Church is the sentiment of Greek-born, Jewish Maurice Abravanel," reads the opening sentence of an article in the November 1968 issue of *High Fidelity–Musical America* magazine. Entitled "The Tabernacle Tenants Stay On," the story deals with the "temporary" loss of the Utah Symphony's long-anticipated new home. "Abravanel now has renewed reason to ponder his indebtedness to Salt Lake City's founding fathers–in effect, his landlords ever since the Utah Symphony began presenting its subscription concerts in the Mormon Tabernacle in 1946."

Abravanel was expressing gratitude for the long-term "loan" of the Tabernacle to the Utah Symphony by the LDS First Presidency, and he hoped for a continuation during the concert hall's postponement.

The generosity had become a problem, however, because the Church's use of the Tabernacle had steadily increased with the years. And the Symphony was lengthening its season. It became necessary to schedule one or two concerts in April that conflicted with the Church's semiannual conference. The Tabernacle was therefore unavailable for some dress rehearsals, and as a result the orchestra's annual recording sessions were postponed from April to May, which found Temple Square jammed with the crowds of nearly two million tourists now visiting annually. This combination of problems demanded high-level resolution.

Ashton recalls that as early as 1972, "[LDS Church] President Harold B. Lee . . . advised Huck Gregory and me that while the Church had provided the . . . Tabernacle as the . . . Symphony's home for twenty years, the time had come . . . to provide a home for the Symphony. He felt the Tabernacle's use should be confined more to expanding Church uses."

But this was not just a graceful way to dump the Symphony. Gregory recalls, "The First Presidency gave every assurance that the LDS Church intended to continue providing a home for the Utah Symphony as long as there was no other suitable facility."

President Lee died and was succeeded by Spencer W. Kimball. In mid-1975, the new First Presidency met with

Abravanel had a warm relationship with LDS President Spencer W. Kimball and was always vocal in his appreciation for the Symphony's use of the Tabernacle. MAP.

Ashton and Gregory to discuss proposed changes in policy once again. In a letter to Governor Rampton dated June 4, 1975, the First Presidency expressed "pride and satisfaction in . . . our longstanding relationship." The letter recalled the Church's original gift of the tract of land for the proposed concert hall and concluded, "We are pleased, therefore, that plans are being considered to construct the concert hall and center for the arts. Our state has long needed such a facility."

This endorsement of construction actually had resulted from a chance meeting three years earlier between Rampton and Obert C. Tanner, as recorded in Tanner's volume, *Bicentennial Center for the Arts*:

One day in April, 1972, I ran into Governor Calvin Rampton and we paused to exchange greetings. He asked me if I had any free time, and I quickly replied in the negative, fearful that he might have some big assignment. A state governor always has many projects under consideration, and there is always need for volunteers to carry them out.

Abravanel rehearsing with violin prodigy Lilit Gimpel during the 1973–74 season. MZPC.

"I thought you might be willing to help get a symphony hall," he explained.

"That's different," I answered. . . . I instantly gave him an affirmative answer. . . . Governor Rampton . . . sensed my second thoughts and added, "It wouldn't take over about four hours a week."

Tanner loved the assignment, for he loved good music. "This was to be an assignment, a public service, that I esteemed above all others: the beauty of a new symphony hall and, far more important, the beauty of the world's best music." Tanner willingly took on the assignment despite having just retired as professor of philosophy from the University of Utah, with hopes to commence work on two or three books and a projected "considerable expansion of the O. C. Tanner Company."

Abravanel and Vladimir Ashkenazy rehearsing during the 1973–74 season. MZPC.

At a meeting in Governor Rampton's office later in April, Tanner explains, "It was Governor Rampton's plan that the best way for Utah to celebrate the two hundredth anniversary of our American democracy would be with a beautiful new symphony hall. [He] explained that he wanted me to be chairman of Utah's Bicentennial Commission, and in that capacity, I could work for a new symphony hall."

On July 7, Tanner invited leading citizens to a luncheon at the Alta Club to solicit their advice and cooperation. It was a distinguished group: Governor Rampton; Nathan Eldon Tanner, First Counselor in the LDS First Presidency; U.S. Senator Frank E. Moss; U.S. Congressmen Sherman P. Lloyd and Gunn McKay; LDS Presiding Bishop Victor L. Brown; representatives of the federal government and State Senate and House; and Milton L. Weilenmann, director of Utah's Development Services.

"While the luncheon was about the bicentennial observance, from the paper that I gave to all those present, one will note the high priority given to a future symphony hall," writes Tanner. While Chairman Tanner outlined the roles to be played throughout the state during the Bicentennial, he made the concert hall the centerpiece:

> [O]ur emphasis will be: A center for the performing arts on the north half of the Salt Palace square. One reason for such a center is that Utah is the place where visitors from America and abroad, especially in summer, stop to rest. People who stop here are not just weary of long travel in the desert and mountains. They are hungry for that which restores them in spirit—music, lectures, all things beautiful. So we need this center for the arts for them, as well as for ourselves. It will be a priceless asset for generations to come.

This speech sounded the note Tanner would repeat for several years.

The U.S. government's initial Bicentennial plans envisioned an appropriation of $1.25 billion from Congress to be divided equally among the fifty states to use as they chose. Utah's share was to be $25 million. Tanner suggested names to Rampton for an interim commission to develop preliminary plans: Wendell J. Ashton, vice-chairman; Oakley S. Evans, retired J. C. Penney executive; LDS Presiding Bishop Victor L. Brown; Stephanie D. Churchill, director of the Utah Her-

itage Foundation; Edward I. Hashimoto; and McCown E. Hunt. Evans "gave his full time for six months, a period when he was free before he took over the presidency of ZCMI." (He continued to serve as a member of the Commission after he became ZCMI president.)

"The balloon burst," continues Tanner's account, "when Congress, in 1973, suddenly decided the bicentennial celebration would be entirely local . . . each state . . . to pay for its own celebration." Instead of the hoped-for $25 million, a paltry $45,000 was allocated, to be matched with state funds.

"To say that things looked pretty dark for a time would be an understatement. No money, no concert hall. For those few weeks in 1973 . . . we were pretty silent," admits Tan-

Rehearsal with Artur Rubinstein, now eighty-nine, on November 20, 1975. MZPC.

ner. Discouragement gave way to hope later that year, when Rampton appointed a twenty-five member Bicentennial Commission for Utah, "composed of outstanding citizens from every walk of life, with the widest possible representation of the state's minority and majority groups." It was an impressive list, headed by Obert C. Tanner and Wendell J. Ashton as chairman and vice-chairman. Obviously neither the Governor nor Tanner was discouraged, although naturally disappointed, by the lack of federal funding.

Second and even more important, Tanner explains, was "another idea of Governor Rampton's, a very workable idea: the possibility that some of an existing state treasury surplus could be used for a concert hall. A generous legislature

agreed . . . and appropriated $8 million to the Bicentennial Commission, $6.5 million . . . to be used for a concert hall, with the stipulation that it be matched by other than state money. We were now back in business again!"

In 1974 the concert hall project was nearly scuttled again. "Because Salt Lake County was planning to hold a bond election seeking to raise nearly $50 million for recreation . . . it was decided that the Bicentennial Arts Center proposal be voted on in the same election," Huck Gregory writes. The combined totals were $43 million for recreation and $6.5 million for the arts center, a total of $49.5 million. It was very bad planning, and voters of Salt Lake County defeated this proposal two-to-one on August 13, 1974. The over-

Abravanel rehearsing with the young violinist Daniel Heifetz. MZPC.

whelmingly negative vote was labeled a repudiation of "the center for toe-dancing" by its opponents, but backers of the concert hall knew their day would come.

The defeat of the bond election was felt on Capitol Hill and "left the whole idea of the Bicentennial's plans for art centers in serious doubt." However, the 1975 Legislature reconsidered its original Bicentennial appropriation. "After lively debate," recalls Gregory, "[the Legislature] decided to let the appropriation stand but with an expiration date of December 31, 1975, if by that time matching funds were not forthcoming." It also clarified the previous bill by letting interest on the $6.5 million accrue through the Bicentennial Commission to the art center fund. This legislative action, with its new expiration deadline, granted the art center appropriation a nine-month reprieve. At the same time, the interest provision would add another $1 million when the funds were eventually needed.

On the heels of the Legislature's action, Rampton moved quickly and appointed a "blue-ribbon" committee "to do whatever was needed . . . to carry out the Legislature's mandate for building the art center," recalls Gregory. Ashton defined the committee's challenge as to "enlist the support of the business people, the media and others in a Salt Lake County bond issue to provide the approximately $10 million needed to complete the funding for the Symphony Hall."

Tanner pondered who would be the right chairman for the new committee. "I held a number of meetings with Milton Weilenmann, Wendell Ashton, and others." At a meeting in June, Ashton suggested John W. (Jack) Gallivan, publisher of the *Salt Lake Tribune* and civic leader. Tanner instantly agreed. "With Gallivan as chairman," Ashton wrote, " . . . we should have an excellent opportunity to get support of not only both of Salt Lake City's daily newspapers but of all three television stations . . . and the business community." Tanner agreed; Rampton was enthusiastic; and at a breakfast meeting Gallivan accepted.

A second requirement was a full-time executive director to "pull all the needed elements together, day by day." Tanner found this key man in youthful Richard Eyre, whom he had met in February in Washington, D.C., at a national Bicentennial convention. There Eyre had consulted with Elder L. Tom Perry, Utah's commission member. Perry recommended Eyre, a graduate of Utah State and Harvard Universities, then with a Washington consulting firm specializing primarily in political campaigns. Earlier he had headed Senator Jake Garn's successful campaign for the U.S. Senate. Eyre agreed to join Tanner's Utah Bicentennial team. His assignment: to deliver a successful bond election on December 16, 1975 – only fifteen days before the Legislature's deadline!

Obert Tanner credits Eyre with:

first conceiving the idea of remodeling the Capitol Theatre building. I had sent him . . . on tours of concert halls throughout the United States. . . . [H]e learned of a remodeled theatre in St. Louis that was a considerable success. . . . [H]e tells of glancing at the Capitol Theatre as he drove down Second South, and at that moment the idea was born! He parked his car, explored the theatre, and within an hour . . . was in my office full of enthusiasm. Soon all the pieces fell together favorably: consent of artists and conductor, the great value of historical preservation, and our feeling of broad public support. We anticipated, with some hopeful calculation, that remodeling that beautiful old theatre would get a lot of votes.

Huck Gregory and Eyre attended the annual meeting of the American Symphony Orchestra League in San Diego in June. Cyril Harris, an acoustical expert with an international reputation, was a featured speaker. On Abravanel's advice, Eyre conferred with him about plans for the Bicentennial Center for the Arts in Salt Lake City. Gregory says, "When he told Harris that we would be building a multi-purpose hall, to Cyril's eternal credit he told Eyre, 'I am flattered that you would like me to help, but I am not interested in a multi-purpose hall. They never have worked and they never will.'"

Harris's unequivocal position no doubt helped to inspire Eyre's subsequent interest in the Capitol Theatre. The rest is history: separate "homes" for Utah Symphony, Salt Lake Art Center, and Ballet West–Utah Opera Company, with Cyril Harris's acoustics "second to none" in the Symphony Hall.

Gallivan had moved swiftly to implement his assignment, appointing subcommittees for design, administration, budget, parking, and publicity. It was at the first committee meeting that the LDS First Presidency let it be known "that they fully supported the project and would assist in every appropriate way to assure its successful completion," Gregory recalls. Parenthetically, he notes that "on October 29 they underscored their support by announcing that they would make two additional acres available at a token payment of $1 per year for 50 years to assure . . . there would be adequate parking for the center."

Obert Tanner identified as "one additional factor of success," Nathan Eldon Tanner, First Counselor in the LDS First Presidency and "one of the greatest men I have known." (Despite the name they are not closely related.) "His concern for the public interest, his sense of life's finest values . . . his desire to help generously, these are just some of his great qualities. If I were to name the one whose help meant most to me when I needed the help as chairman of the Utah Bicentennial Commission, it would be Nathan Eldon

The Maestro with LDS Church leaders N. Eldon Tanner, Spencer W. Kimball, and Marion G. Romney. MAP.

Tanner." Chairman Tanner is also quick to designate Governor Calvin L. Rampton as "outstanding."

Eyre and his well-organized forces, including the Utah Symphony office staff, mounted an impressive campaign. The media played the bond election to the hilt. For apprehensive concert-goers, a Symphony program article issued a last-ditch appeal for volunteers to telephone and go door-to-door. On December 5 a two-page editorial in the program with a bold headline, DECEMBER 16, reminded symphony-goers of the crucial bond election's life-or-death aspect.

Election day "was a dramatic date for so many of us," writes Obert Tanner. "It was all-or-nothing. Had the bond election of $8.75 million failed, . . . the $6.5 million appropriated by the legislature would have reverted to the state general fund. All would then be lost, and probably lost for a long time to come. Winning meant $22 million worth of buildings for the arts."

The victory celebration in the Capitol Theatre was one of great joy and relief. The vote was 32,932 for, 25,716 against! The twelve-year battle for funding was over. Many Symphony and ballet artists were present. Joining in the revelry were Maestro Abravanel, Willam Christensen, Huck Gregory, Jack Gallivan, Wendell Ashton, their wives, and many artists and friends of the arts.

Abravanel recalls in his 1986 KUED interview that one of his most important conversations took place in this noisy, exuberant atmosphere:

> The bond election to approve funds for the new hall was successful. Jack Gallivan, publisher of the *Salt Lake Tribune*, was chairman of the building committee and a wonderful concerned citizen. I said, "Okay, Jack. Let's make a deal. I'll stay out of your way if you call this man and put him in charge." I gave him Cyril Harris's phone number at Columbia University. Jack Gallivan invited Harris to Salt Lake. He came, and Lucy cooked some wonderful meals for the State Building Board, and they hired Harris.
>
> My contribution to the new Symphony Hall was a simple one. I had met Cyril Harris, known particularly for correcting the acoustical disaster in Lincoln Center's Philharmonic Hall. He had also designed acoustically-excellent halls in other American cities.

Satisfaction, as the hard work begins to show results. MAP.

He was an architect *and* acoustician. The Symphony Hall is the only one in the world where, instead of first hiring an architect and telling him to consult an acoustician, it was the other way around—a concert hall must first be "good for the ear, then for the eyes!" So, in this case, Utah has the distinction of first hiring an acoustician and putting him in charge. He passed on the architects . . . who knew they could not get away with a single brick unless it was the best possible, acoustically. This is why the Boston Symphony and all other visiting orchestras say "This is the best modern hall we have ever played in!"

There are those who say I built the new Symphony Hall. I didn't build it! My musicians did. . . .

Aerial view of the long-awaited combined performance of the Utah Symphony and the Mormon Tabernacle Choir in the O. C. Tanner Amphitheater on the edge of Zion National Park, May 1976. MAP.

Interior of the splendid new Symphony Hall in Salt Lake City.
MAP.

Rampton and the county commissioners quickly appointed Gallivan as chairman of a six-member committee "to advise them," according to Tanner, "as a design and construction committee." Other members were Thayne Acord, Frank Nelson, George Nicolatus, Glen Swenson, and Tanner. This Bicentennial Arts Center Planning and Construction Committee "met, usually once a week, to plan and supervise the construction of the new building," recalls Ashton. The committee's charge, in addition to the concert hall, was to construct an adjacent art center and renovate the Capitol Theatre as a home for Ballet West and the Utah Opera Company and other stage attractions.

The committee "retained Georgius Y. Cannon, retired, one of Utah's ablest architects, to advise. . . . Robert Fowler

and Associates won our approval as the architectural firm to design the new buildings. Stephen Baird was selected as the architect for remodeling the Capitol Theatre," writes Tanner of the committee's early decisions.

It was January 1976, and the bond election victory was a month old. Tanner felt that "the big victory had been won. We had obtained the money, and now the specialists could and would do their excellent work." With four years of planning behind him and the key advisers and planners in place, Obert Tanner resigned from the Planning and Construction Committee. Rampton appointed Ashton in his place.

Tanner felt impelled to devote the bulk of his time to his assignment as chairman of the Utah Bicentennial Commission, which was sponsoring and fostering projects throughout the state. The 1976 Bicentennial year now confronted him with urgent tasks, and one of the most significant was a goal he had long shared with Abravanel: bringing the Tabernacle Choir and Utah Symphony together for the first time in history as the centerpiece of Utah's Bicentennial celebration. The dream was realized the last week in May. The first and final concerts were in the Tabernacle with six others in communities throughout the state.

The Bicentennial Arts Center was built under the direction of Gallivan's Planning and Construction Committee, with groundbreaking ceremonies on March 10, 1977. Governor Rampton presided, and the dignitaries in attendance included recently elected Governor and Mrs. Scott M. Matheson, Mayor and Mrs. Conrad B. Harrison, members of the Utah Bicentennial Commission, Salt Palace board members, Mr. and Mrs. Wendell J. Ashton, John Gallivan and members of the Planning and Construction Committee, architectural and construction representatives, and others. Obert Tanner was the principal speaker.

Eight months later, in October 1977, the cornerstone was laid. Maestro Abravanel led the orchestra outdoors in works of Handel, Mozart, Sibelius, Copland, Weinberger, and Gould. Distinguished guests were again present, Mayor Ted Wilson having succeeded Harrison. The participants reviewed the progress to date and implied possible completion of the project within a year. Utah Bicentennial Chairman Obert Tanner again acknowledged all who had cooperated in making the three-facility Bicentennial project a reality.

The completion date projected that day would have seen the Utah Symphony and Maestro Abravanel inaugurating the hall during the 1978–79 season, but there was a year's construction delay. The orchestra had to request a year's extension of their use of the Tabernacle.

Ironically, that year's delay meant that Abravanel, after a thirteen-year wait, would never conduct in Symphony Hall. His resignation preceded the hall's opening by five months. He was coaxed, cajoled, and begged to guest-conduct during the gala inaugural season. He declined. The request was repeated for the all-Beethoven season finale in April of 1980. He demurred. University of Utah President David P. Gardner invited the Utah Symphony to share the University's 1980 Commencement with Abravanel as speaker-conductor and recipient of its Distinguished Professor Award. Abravanel gave the address but tapped his longtime associate conductor and University professor Ardean Watts to conduct. Finally, as plans were formulated to celebrate Abravanel's eightieth birthday on January 3, 1983, the invitation was repeated. Again he refused. He had closed the door on conducting forever.

The Utah Symphony Board, at its quarterly meeting at the Hotel Utah on November 29, 1978, voted unanimously to recommend that the new concert hall be named Symphony Hall. Huck Gregory, as executive director, was asked to convey this recommendation to the Salt Lake County Commission.

No one in attendance at that meeting was aware that Abravanel would resign as music director and conductor the next April, but there was already sentiment for naming the hall in his honor. Letters to the editor appeared. Abravanel's most ardent supporters lobbied.

It is most common for wealthy donors to have halls that bear their names: Louise Davies, San Francisco; Dorothy Chandler, Chandler Pavilion, Los Angeles; New York's Avery Fisher Hall (formerly Philharmonic Hall) at Lincoln Center; and of course Carnegie Hall. Utah Symphony Hall, shortened later to Symphony Hall, followed the pattern of the Boston and Chicago Symphony halls and Berlin's Philharmonic Hall.

Even though few halls are named for conductors, there is one in Santa Barbara named Maurice Abravanel Hall.

Regardless of its name, however, Symphony Hall will always be "the house that Maurice built." The Alvin Gittins portrait of the Maestro—the only art work hanging in the sumptuous foyer—looms impressively as a reminder. "The song is over, but the melody lingers on . . . "

CHAPTER 17

Abravadämmerung

"I just can't do it any more, Ardean."

It was early Wednesday morning, April 4, 1979. Ardean Watts recalls that when he made his regular stop at the Abravanel driveway, as he had done for years, it was a fatigued Abravanel who came slowly down the steps in dressing gown and pajamas, carrying an armful of orchestral scores.

"Good luck, Ardean," Abravanel said quietly, handing the scores to his colleague who, stunned, drove off for the day's rehearsals alone. The formal resignation came two days later. Abravanel told a press conference:

> While I am generally in reasonably good physical condition, considering what I have gone through lately, including heart surgery, I have had days of immense fatigue that made conducting absolutely impossible. On the advice of my doctor, I am compelled to step down at the end of this season, which I infinitely regret. The worst thing a man in my position can do is stay too long. I have been a "full-blast" music director. I don't believe in half measures. It's not my character.

He also resigned as director of Santa Barbara's Music Academy of the West, which he had guided from 1955.

Alvin Gittins portrait of Maestro Abravanel that hangs in Symphony Hall in Salt Lake City. Courtesy of the Alvin Gittins Family Trust.

Abravanel's resignation was not precipitous. There had been earlier warnings. The *Salt Lake Tribune* for November 25, 1976, had carried a brief notice that "Ardean Watts will conduct the Symphony" and that "Maurice Abravanel . . . is taking a rest on the advice of his physicians. He will return to conduct the Utah Symphony–Utah Chorale concert December 4"; the paper also reported that from November 25 to 28 he would be "undergoing tests" in a local hospital.

On Sunday, November 28, the *Tribune* announced that "Maurice Abravanel will conduct Ernest Bloch's *Sacred Service*, 'Prelude' and 'Love-Death' from Wagner's *Tristan and Isolde*, and Strauss's *Death and Transfiguration* December 4 in the Tabernacle." Abravanel had been in the hospital for three days when that story appeared, however, and underwent open-heart surgery the next day. It is of more than passing interest that all three of the selections he had programmed dealt with death, transfiguration, and things metaphysical.

Three days after surgery, concerned that Abravanel's convalescence might slow the orchestra's momentum in mid-season, Utah Symphony President Wendell Ashton, in a diversionary move, told the media: "The Symphony plans a fall European tour." He expressed confidence that "Abravanel will be able to make the tour. Should he not," continued Ashton, "my feeling is that Ardean Watts would lead the orchestra on this tour."

One week later, Abravanel's physicians predicted full recovery "within six weeks to two and one-half months."

Ashton expressed confidence in Ardean Watts's "ability to continue to function as acting music director and conductor. We're hopeful that Mr. Abravanel will be back in February, but that's a hope–not a statement of fact."

Watts filled in for Abravanel through January and half of February. Guido Ajmone-Marsan guest-conducted the January 12 concert. Abravanel's long-anticipated Mahler Cycle–three complete evenings–was a casualty, reduced to a single symphony.

True to his physicians' predictions, Abravanel returned to the podium in mid-February and completed the season. More important, he guided his musicians through the taxing European tour from September 16 to October 15, "unquestionably the most triumphant of the orchestra's four international tours." Greece, Austria, Germany, and Spain seemed to revitalize Abravanel with the month-long break in the normal routine.

But in retrospect, the final concerts of the 1976–77 season may have drained his energies. Abravanel had not been well enough to conduct at Soviet pianist Lazar Berman's appearances on April 7 and 8.

Bach's *B Minor Mass* on April 16 was taxing, and a post-season Beverly Sills "Special" on May 24, while affording a pleasurable personal reunion, made additional demands. Nearly a quarter of a century earlier, long before her rise to stardom, Abravanel had unveiled a little-known, slim Miss Sills to the University of Utah outdoor Summer Festival audience as Violetta in *Traviata* (1953) and Aida (1954), for an incredible fee of $500!

Abravanel had also conducted a tiring tour of Northern California, Oregon, Washington, Montana, and Wyoming in April and May–less than six months after his surgery.

He had seriously considered resigning during the stressful spring of 1977. After his resignation two years later, he referred to it: "Without the overwhelming affection and love of the community I could not have resumed my duties over two years ago when I first offered my resignation."

Encouraged by the "lift" and success of the fall 1977 European tour, he sailed into the 1977–78 season, programming the two most demanding Mahler symphonies: the Second (*Resurrection*) in December and the Eighth (*Symphony of a Thousand*) as the season finale for April 15.

Lucy and Maurice with Beverly Sills in May 1977 at a party celebrating Abravanel's thirtieth anniversary as Music Director of the Utah Symphony. MAP.

Grant Johannesen, Conrad Harrison, and Abravanel–old friends and true. MAP.

Acknowledging the audience applause. MZPC.

The Eighth, the recording of which had catapulted Abravanel and the Utah Symphony to the top of the recording world fourteen years earlier, makes superhuman demands of the conductor. During the intermission of the Eighth's performance, Abravanel was seated in his dressing room, soaking wet, bare-chested, drying himself with a towel. (He lost from six to eight pounds each concert and always changed wet dress shirts for dry ones during intermission.)

"I just can't do these big works any more – 800 performers and requiring so much energy!" He was exhausted. Yet fifteen minutes later he seemed completely revived as he ran the obstacle course to the podium for the Mahler's second half. The performance was inspired. Abravanel was exhausted.

He plunged ahead regardless into post-season "Specials," topped by historic, long-overdue performances of Leroy Robertson's *Book of Mormon* Oratorio with the Tabernacle

Danny Kaye, known to have anonymously called Abravanel and sung the March from Tchaikovsky's Pathétique Symphony over the phone, gives a dignified press conference with his old friend and mentor. MAP.

The conductor making a point in an interview. MAP.

Choir on May 25 and 26. Sadly, the "greatest Mormon composer" had been dead for seven years. Abravanel had single-handedly kept this important work alive despite apathy and opposition, conducting it statewide more than a dozen times with University of Utah choruses before 1978.

Abravanel followed with the orchestra's popular "Tribute to the Tabernacle" on June 10, 1978, joined by pianist Grant Johannesen, Metropolitan Opera baritone Robert Merrill, and Utah's Osmond Brothers. The concert was a gesture of appreciation to the LDS Church for its generosity in making the Tabernacle available as the orchestra's official concert hall from 1946 to 1979.

So ended the 1977–78 season. Then came word of a six-month, and then a year's, delay in the completion of the new concert hall. Abravanel would finish his thirty-two-year tenure where he began it—in the Tabernacle.

Abravanel's final season included an unprecedented four guest conductors. Never had he relinquished his baton so often during a Symphony subscription series. But now he programmed guest conductors in six concerts: Peter Eros, Robert LaMarchina, Sara Caldwell, and Ardean Watts, who

conducted three Tabernacle subscription concerts. Abravanel was obviously pacing himself. When he handed the scores to Watts on the morning of April 4, he was turning the podium over to him for Metropolitan soprano Judith Blegen's concert, one he would never willingly have missed conducting himself.

Only the season finale on April 21—the Verdi Requiem—remained. Emotions ran high. Abravanel acceded to urgings that he mount the Tabernacle podium one last time.

Watts recalls picking him up and driving him to the first rehearsal since his resignation on April 6, the first rehearsal of the Verdi Requiem: "He seemed as normal as any other day as we rode to the hall. He loved to talk about anything from the weather to politics . . . sometimes even music! I'm sure he had thought about what he would say to the orchestra, but he didn't seem preoccupied. There was considerable anxiety in the hall when we arrived."

Abravanel glanced over the orchestra and then began speaking with emotion. Watts jotted down what he could, and this is his paraphrased version:

For the last fifty-five years I've been looking for a way to get out of this crazy business. On the other hand I have often wondered, "Who am I to have the special privilege of making beautiful music?" Since my operation I have felt emotional stress much more keenly. I used to be able to deal with the stresses with relative ease, if not some exhilaration, but now the same stress sometimes leaves me completely immobilized.

Already, on the night of the first concert of the season I thought of calling Ardean because I didn't feel strong enough to go through with it. Somehow I managed. Then again later, with the Andre Watts concert in Ogden, the same feelings returned.

It was like an umbrella of poison completely overshadowing me. I was unable to eat or sleep. So I had to ask Ardean to take over for me the next night in Salt Lake. The doctors who saw me through my operation advised me to avoid emotional stress. I thought I could either avoid it or handle it, but they were right. There are times when I cannot handle it.

I know it is good for the orchestra that I step down. It is a big headache right now. I thank you for putting up with me for thirty-two years. We've had some disagreements like those expected between husband and wife. Despite the disagreements you have never let me down.

Dissatisfied with his written version of Abravanel's remarks, Watts added: "As I read this over it doesn't sound like it was. There is something about the Abravanel delivery that transforms ordinary words into a testament sealed by passion and fire and love—and that is what the real memory is like."

The *Tribune*'s Paul Wetzel wrote poignantly of Abravanel's farewell performance on April 21:

> As the echoes of the final, chantlike strains of the Verdi *Requiem* died away, applause began to ripple through the Salt Lake Tabernacle.
>
> It was subdued and respectful at first. . . . Conductor Maurice Abravanel directed the attention of the audience to the four soloists, then to the Utah Chorale.
>
> The conductor next motioned for the musicians of the Utah Symphony to rise. They did not. Instead they

kept their seats and warmly applauded the man who for thirty-two years guided the destiny of the orchestra.

The 76-year-old maestro turned to face the audience and, grasping the steel railing which surrounds the podium, began his final bows as music director of the orchestra he has built from a semi-professional ensemble into one of the nation's twenty or so major symphonic instruments.

The applause swelled in a great crescendo as the audience poured out its appreciation and affection. Some cheered, some stomped.

The ovation continued for nearly ten minutes as soloists, Utah Chorale music director Newell Weight and Mr. Abravanel took several curtain calls. Rhythmic clapping called the maestro back to the podium twice for solo bows. He shook the hand of each principal player

The continent-hopping Abravanels. MAP.

in the orchestra's string section. He took the Verdi score from his conductor's desk and raised it over his head with both hands. He threw kisses to the musicians and to the audience.

Then it was over. The house lights came up, signaling the end of a musical era in Salt Lake City. The capacity crowd, a few with vision clouded by a tear or two, passed into the warm Saturday night air.

CHAPTER 18

Transition

When I picked up the phone on April 7, I heard Wendell Ashton's voice. "Will you serve on a search committee for Abravanel's successor?" Abravanel had announced his resignation only the day before and Ashton was moving swiftly to assure minimal slow-down.

On Sunday, April 8, the *Salt Lake Tribune* announced the committee headed by University of Utah vice president R. J. Snow. Members included Barbara Tanner and Guild president Blanche Freed, both longtime Symphony supporters; Christie Lundquist, the orchestra's principal clarinetist; Thomas J. Moore, president of the Ogden Symphony Guild; M. Walker Wallace, Board member and treasurer; and the author.

Ashton announced that the committee would begin its work immediately and that "the final decision on hiring a new music director will be left to the 12-member executive committee of the Symphony Board." He estimated that the search would take between six and twelve months and that "the orchestra will seek a superior musician who is young, a good manager of people, and a 'decent citizen' who also will be able to relate to the business community."

Snow ran an efficient and extensive search, convening the first committee meeting April fourteenth. At that meeting the committee was informed that one applicant for the vacancy would make a brief stopover at the Salt Lake International Airport on April 26, shortly after Abravanel conducted Verdi's *Requiem*, his final concert. Thomas Moore,

Blanche Freed, Barbara Tanner, and Huck Gregory visited with youthful Varujan Kojian, the only applicant of 107 who expressed interest in the Utah Symphony position in person. The candidates included several Utahns. Ardean Watts withdrew his name. Crawford Gates, after consideration in early stages, withdrew because of his commitments in the Midwest. Others were Brigham Young University's Ralph Laycock and former Utah Symphony timpanist Robert Lentz.

The Symphony management had previously signed five guest conductors for the 1979–80 season; Stanislaw Skrowaczewski of the Minnesota Symphony for Symphony Hall's inaugural concert, Maurice Peress (Kansas City Symphony), Kenneth Schermerhorn (Milwaukee Symphony), Christopher Keene (Syracuse Symphony), and Uri Segal (freelance).

By August 20 the search committee had reduced its list to ten finalists, recommending that each of the finalists appear as guest conductor for a pair of concerts during the season. Huck Gregory scheduled accordingly.

Skrowaczewski was not a candidate. Peress appeared on September 24 and 25 with minimal reaction from musicians or press. Schermerhorn was next, on October 7 and 8. He had resigned from the Milwaukee orchestra and seemed drained physically and emotionally. However, his performance of Mahler's First Symphony was exciting.

Kojian was next on October 26 and 27, in Beethoven's Fourth and Shostakovich's Fifth Symphony. He had thor-

Autographed photograph of cellist Mstislav Rostopovitch to his "dear friend" Maurice Abravanel. MAP.

oughly prepared these two scores, and his rehearsals of the Shostakovich brought spontaneous enthusiasm from the orchestra. This feeling steamrollered from musicians to Symphony staff, to Board, to the Board's executive committee, to the press, and to the audiences. By Monday morning there was a consensus for the youthful Armenian.

The committee expressed unanimous sentiment for Kojian at its next meeting, on November 2, although Walker Wallace felt that the remaining guest appearances should take place before the announcement was made. But Ashton was anxious to proceed, and Symphony Board members approved of Kojian overwhelmingly in a joint meeting of Board and search committee. Wallace again demurred but went along.

Daniel Lewis (Pasadena Symphony and University of Southern California) and James DePreist withdrew; Lewis in protest over the committee's screening method, DePreist because he had accepted the music directorship of the Oregon Symphony. The others made their scheduled guest appearances. Only Uri Segal proved to be serious competition to Kojian. A formal announcement was withheld pending the

working out of details. Kojian agreed to three weeks' silence and proceeded with guest conducting assignments elsewhere.

On November 13, Wendell Ashton hosted a Hotel Utah dinner meeting with Kojian, Snow, and the author to finalize the offer. After dinner, around 10 p.m., Ashton suggested walking one block west to Symphony Hall to finish the discussion. By midnight Ashton and Kojian had reached an agreement — after a lively bidding war on salary — with Kojian offering to make no other commitments before checking with Ashton.

Ashton had already sent Huck Gregory for Abravanel, who had been alerted at his home. Fifteen minutes later Abravanel walked in saying, "Please take good care of my little girl!" and gave Kojian a bear hug. Then Ashton, the advertising veteran, waved newspaper photographers into the board room for late-night public relations photographs.

The salary agreement was subject to the Board's approval. The contract was to reach Kojian in Louisville, where he was guest-conducting and recording. On Monday, November 19, Kojian phoned Ashton from Louisville. They had offered him more money to become their own music director. Ashton convinced Kojian to sign with the Utah Symphony and arranged to meet him at the Washington, D.C., airport at 1 p.m. Wednesday, November 21, where Kojian would be en route to conducting engagements in Sweden. Ashton hastily called a Board meeting for Tuesday, November 20, 1979, at 7:30 p.m. in Symphony Hall's Abravanel Room. The Board voted unanimously to sign Kojian.

Early the next morning, Ashton flew to Washington, signed Kojian to a three-year contract, and bade him farewell until April 4, 1980, when he would return to conduct Beethoven's Ninth Symphony.

END OF THE HONEYMOON

The musicians' contract expired August 31, 1980, and they voted to work without a contract for thirty days while negotiations continued. They also threatened a strike if an agreement was not reached or substantial progress made by then. According to a *Tribune* headline of September 25, "The Symphony Board Makes 'Final' Offer." Progress or lack of progress appeared daily in the press and on television for the next two weeks. Finally, October 7, 1980, a headline announced "Musicians Ratify Contract with Symphony

Officials"–just in time for the orchestra's opening concerts on October 11, 12, and 13.

The negotiation issues were: (1) Who has final control over hirings and firings? In the final contract, the music director retained final control but was obliged to seek the advice of committees appointed by the musicians. (2) All Symphony members should be "A" level; the Symphony management agreed to phase out all "B" or part-time musicians, raising all to full-time status. Symphony officials said this would require six years.

The following spring the orchestra made its fifth overseas tour from May 17 to June 3, l981, this time to Scandinavia and Germany. Kojian shared conducting duties on the tour with his assistant conductor, Robert Henderson, and with Polish conductor Witold Rowicki, who had been hired for the tour prior to Kojian's signing with the Utah Symphony. Kojian conducted the concerts in Denmark, Norway, and Holland, flying back to the United States between concerts to guest-conduct a pair of concerts with the New York Philharmonic. A tour highlight was "Utah Day" in Bergen, Norway, with Governor Scott Matheson and other dignitaries in attendance. It was in Bergen that rumors of Kojian's "lifestyle" surfaced. More specifically, it was his alleged misconduct with a woman musician.

After the tour Wendell Ashton convened the Board's executive committee June 24 to air the matter. Kojian dismissed the incident as a friendly glass of champagne with two orchestra members. There was a thorough discussion . . . and the Salt Lake *Tribune* for June 25, 1981, printed the complete text of a statement from Ashton: "There have been rumors and comments regarding activities of our Utah Symphony music director. Our Symphony board executive committee has explored the situation in depth. There have been some misunderstandings. Varujan Kojian continues as our music director. He has the support of our executive committee. There is no further comment."

While there were no further comments, there was considerable gossip, behind-the-scenes activity, and a serious breach between Kojian and Ashton. The judgment that Kojian's lifestyle was "unacceptable to the community" persisted in certain quarters. But this was not all. Within eighteen months the orchestra itself had shifted their initial support for Kojian 180 degrees.

The author, left, with Wendell J. Ashton, Varujan Kojian, and R. J. Snow. MAP.

It was amazing–unbelievable–to observe. Kojian received a spontaneous, unanimous welcome from the orchestra during his first showcase concerts in Symphony Hall in October 1979. Yet in April 1982, Ashton would call for his resignation. The Board agreed with a few exceptions, and the musicians to a member were after his scalp.

During the closing days of the debate, the author bumped into John Chatelain, veteran orchestra member and principal second violinist. "John," I asked, "what happened between the original unanimous vote for Kojian and the present unanimous opposition? Did Kojian fool all of you during his showcase appearances in 1979?"

"Yes," Chatelain said flatly. "He fooled us with a fantastically prepared program of Beethoven's Fourth and Shostakovich's Fifth. He had prepared thoroughly for the audition and knew every note. As time went on, we gradually discovered that his knowledge of the broader repertoire and rehearsal techniques didn't measure up to everyone's expectations."

Kojian had supporters–a handful on the Board, some on the staff, but very few orchestra members. Huck Gregory put it this way: "Abravanel would have been a hard act for anyone to follow—thirty-two years with the orchestra and a cherished member of the community."

Before Abravanel came to Utah he had conducted for eleven years in Germany and France, two in Australia, two at the Metropolitan Opera, and more than seven on Broadway. During those twenty-two years he made his debut at the Berlin State Opera, the Paris Opera, and the Metropolitan Opera. "Kojian was bound to have problems of youth, age 35, no experience as a permanent conductor, although [he was] associate conductor at Seattle briefly and [had done] some conducting at the Swedish Royal Opera," Gregory explained. Inexperience gradually eroded his credibility with the musicians. His alleged misconduct with women members of the orchestra only fanned the flames. He was a gentle, likeable person and a promising, gifted conductor who fared well with the media. He was no politician, however, and he may not have related to the Board as he might or to management and the business community.

Who knows the real reasons his contract was not renewed? Whatever they were, the president of the Board, musicians, and conductor could no longer work together.

Kojian had signed a three-year contract. With the completion of his second year on June 30, Ashton appointed a review committee to examine the situation in depth. In April of 1982 Kem Gardner, chairman of the management committee of the Symphony Board, was appointed to chair an ad hoc committee to review Kojian's performance and to recommend whether his contract should be renewed beyond June 30, 1983. The committee members were all Board members: Burtis Evans, Don Stringham, R. J. Snow, Walker Wallace, Barbara Tanner, and W. Boyd Christensen, who had been appointed executive vice president and chief operating officer of the Symphony on November 5, 1981, and served as committee secretary.

The committee heard twenty hours of testimony from Board members, Ashton, Kojian, Abravanel, several orchestra members, University of Utah composer Ramiro Cortés, and the author. After lengthy discussions committee feelings were mixed. Two Board members favored termination of Kojian's contract. Gardner proposed that his remaining year be probationary, and the committee accepted that compromise.

Vice President Boyd Christensen soon made it known that President Ashton was "apprehensive about the committee recommendation." Gardner invited him to meet with the committee on June 17 to discuss the problem. According to Gardner, the committee was surprised to hear that "Ashton held strong views . . . and could not live with the committee's recommendation." Ashton asked the committee to choose between himself and Kojian. A revised proposal that the president and executive vice president make the decision about renewing Kojian's contract found the committee deadlocked three to three. Chairman Gardner then cast the deciding vote, placing Kojian in Ashton's and Christensen's hands: "He [Ashton] deserves a music director he feels good about raising money for," said Gardner.

On July 7, the Board announced that it would not renew Kojian's contract, giving as the principal reason his "lack of leadership with the orchestra's musicians." Many predicted that Kojian would resign immediately and leave angrily, taking his coming season's salary with him. He didn't. "How can you conduct musicians who helped unseat you and who do not respect you?" he was asked. His reply: "We'll make music together, because we are all professionals." Kojian delivered an exciting 1982–83 season anchored to two masterworks: Ravel's *Daphnis and Chloé Suite No. 2* with Ravel's original scoring with chorus in December and Mahler's Second (*Resurrection*) Symphony climaxing the final concert in April.

Kojian retained his condominium overlooking Temple Square in Salt Lake City for several years, but he lives in Santa Barbara. He brought his elderly parents to Salt Lake and bought them a home in 1980 and visited them frequently. He was appointed music director of Chautauqua, the summer home of the New York Philharmonic, on Zubin Mehta's recommendation in 1980 and was music director of Ballet West from 1983 to 1987. In 1985 he was appointed director of the Santa Barbara Symphony. He guest-conducts frequently, including the Chicago, St. Louis, Baltimore, Indianapolis, and San Francisco Symphonies, and he was conductor-in-residence of the Symphony of Western Australia in Perth for several months in 1987.

With the Kojian matter settled, Ashton lost no time in appointing a search committee for a new music director. Named chair was Donald P. Lloyd, veteran Board member

Joseph Silverstein. Utah Symphony Collection in Special Collections, University of Utah Marriott Library.

and sponsor of the AG Foodstores' Saturday Youth Concerts in the Tabernacle during the fifties and sixties. His search committee included Georgia White of Ogden, Barbara Scowcroft, Allan F. Frank, Ross E. Thorsen, Richard G. Allen of Provo, and Bonnie Bennett, a member of the orchestra's violin section. Abravanel, Grant Johannesen, and the author were advisers. The press announced the committee's formation on August tenth.

The search committee held its first meeting on September 2, 1982. More than a hundred names were considered, but Joseph Silverstein, renowned concertmaster and assistant conductor of the Boston Symphony since 1971, did not appear on the list of candidates until just before the committee was to select the final candidates. In an unexpected move, Don Lloyd circulated copies of a beautifully handwritten four-page letter from Silverstein, expressing serious interest in the position. It was impressive. Silverstein was one of the country's most respected musicians – a concert

violinist of the first rank, and a concertmaster par excellence in addition to his assistant conducting duties. He had also guest-conducted more than twenty major American orchestras, including the Los Angeles, Washington, D.C., Houston, St. Louis, Rochester, and San Francisco ensembles; had been principal guest conductor of the Baltimore Symphony since 1981; and had been interim music director of the Toledo Symphony and music director of the Worcester (Massachusetts) Symphony. He was also on Boston University's faculty, where he had conducted the orchestra for more than ten years. "Silverstein" was suddenly very much on the committee's lips when only the day before his name had not even appeared on the initial long list of applicants.

After recounting his professional experience, Silverstein expressed personal feelings of the kind never circulated by agents or managers on behalf of their clients. "I am fifty years old, am in very good health, run almost every day, and play a reasonable if somewhat erratic game of golf." He was obviously a genuine human being with a sense of humor. "A marriage of almost 29 years . . . a great source of happiness and inspiration. . . . We have three children, two girls and a boy ranging in age from twenty-five to sixteen."

Silverstein mentioned honorary doctorates from Tufts University (1971) and Boston College (1981) and that he had served on adjunct faculties at Yale and Boston universities. He extolled Abravanel: "Your orchestra under the guidance of dear Maurice Abravanel has embodied the statement and importance of the musical experience as it affects the human spirit in a most extraordinary manner."

After the lengthy list of impressive professional assignments and distinguished references, he concluded with a touching revelation of his feelings for the Boston Symphony: "My availability could be September 1983 in a strictly legal sense, but my concern for the continuity of the Boston situation would force me to qualify that by saying at least ten weeks in 1983–84, possibly 'more' but the 'more' is directly related to my complicated relationship with this remarkable and venerable institution." He closed with looking forward to "the very exciting possibility of my future involvement with your orchestra."

By mid-October the list of candidates had been reduced to three, according to the *Tribune*'s Paul Wetzel. They included Silverstein, Gerard Schwarz, music director of the Los Angeles Chamber Orchestra; and Lawrence Smith, music director of the San Antonio Symphony. The consensus favored Silverstein.

The search committee's choice by late October was so obvious that three representatives were sent to observe Silverstein as he guest-conducted the Baltimore Symphony at Baltimore and at the Kennedy Center on October 28 and 29, respectively. The observers were chairman Don Lloyd, Bonnie Bennett, and the author, who traveled, attended concerts, and interviewed the candidate separately, one on one. On returning to Salt Lake, all enthusiastically favored Silverstein.

Search committees are advisory groups, with final selection made by the Board. After the committee's consensus was forwarded to the Board, there was a delay of nearly three months before the final selection was announced. In mid-December Silverstein and Gerard Schwarz were invited to meet with the orchestra and management. A few members of the Board and management were apparently wary of

Silverstein's appearing to be the sole finalist, feeling that the "appearance" of more competition in the final round would look better. Schwarz spoke to the orchestra but did not conduct. He was not interested in the position because of his permanent appointments with the New York and Los Angeles Chamber Orchestras. Symphony officials were busy preparing a gala eightieth-birthday tribute to Abravanel, set for January tenth. Silverstein's appointment came the following week on January 19, 1983.

The delay in announcing his appointment had compelled Silverstein to renew his contract with the Boston Symphony for 1983–84 to meet their deadlines. As a result, the Utah Symphony Board named him Artistic Director temporarily and Music Director later with a three-year contract retroactive to September 1983.

Abravanel's influence on Silverstein's appointment was not direct. They had known each other for some time and were colleagues at Tanglewood. While some felt that Abravanel might have encouraged Silverstein's effective handwritten letter, he says "No."

Silverstein brought confidence based on solid musicianship and thirty years' experience as an orchestral musician—essentially what the musicians felt the younger Kojian lacked. Silverstein had played every piece in the repertoire "umpteen" times. He knew the literature. He knew rehearsal techniques. He knew the orchestra. He also brought something new and unique in his dual roles as violin soloist and conductor.

Silverstein's programming has been solid and well balanced. Chamber music is a first love, and he expanded the Chamber Orchestra series, opening a new world to many. He has sought out lesser works of the masters, including many unfamiliar Haydn symphonies, and has introduced seldom-heard works of contemporary composers. One of Silverstein's most significant contributions has been his enriched servings of baroque music. Many works of Bach and Handel never before performed locally have transformed the chamber concerts into delightful and popular events. Silverstein has led the way as soloist and conductor in the early eighteenth century's most ingratiating sounds.

During the post-Abravanel years, significant changes in the administration and management of the Symphony were initiated by Wendell Ashton. W. Boyd Christensen was named executive vice president and chief operating officer on November 5, 1981, serving with Huck Gregory and Shirl H. Swenson, who continued as executive director and manager, respectively. Christensen had impressive credentials from the world of business and education and was also general manager of the Utah Associated Municipal Power Systems. Ten months later, in September 1982, he resigned due to the "difficulty in working two jobs" but continued as a Board member.

Ashton moved quickly to name youthful Stephen W. Swaner executive vice president and chief operating officer in late September. A native Utahn, Swaner had held executive positions in California for sixteen years. He took over during Kojian's "lame-duck" year and the transition to Silverstein.

A surprise story in the April 4, 1985, *Tribune* read: "Wendell J. Ashton Retires, Accepts Call to LDS Mission Presidency in London. . . . Will retire as publisher of the *Deseret News* . . . and also step down before July 1 as President of the Utah Symphony, a position he has held since 1966." Although not entirely unexpected, the announcement shook Symphony Hall. Ashton had also served as president of the Salt Lake Chamber of Commerce Board of Governors, as organizer of an enlarged public relations wing of the LDS Church, and as an LDS Regional Representative. His Chamber of Commerce assignment involved him directly in the move to Salt Lake City of the Utah Jazz of the National Basketball Association.

Ashton was widely acknowledged by the business community as "one of the most powerful men in Utah." Indefatigable and able to master many diverse major assignments, he lost no battles and was resilient in times of stress. The Utah Symphony presidency was not his principal professional assignment, yet he gave it thirty hours a week for twenty years. Ashton was the Symphony's unchallenged fundraiser. His record is unparalleled even among major big-city orchestras over a continuous twenty-year period.

"Where can we find someone who can raise $1.5 million annually over two decades?" was the rock-bottom question in Symphony Hall following Ashton's resignation. "That's 30 million dollars!"

Two weeks after his resignation, Ashton tapped Salt Lake businessman Jon M. Huntsman as his successor with the unanimous approval of the thirty-two Board members who were present at the April 16 meeting. This action was ratified at a meeting of the full Board on May 20, when Huntsman was formally elected chairman and chief executive officer of the Symphony Board. DeeDee Corradini, local business executive and longtime Board member, became its first vice chairwoman. Stephen Swaner advanced to the rank of president and chief operating officer, effective July 1, 1985. He resigned three months later, however, to return to the private sector.

Huntsman thus became the first "chairman" of the Board. President Ashton had thought of moving up to Board chairman on several occasions, but none of the No. 2 candidates for the presidency had met his qualifications.

Huntsman named the following Board Executive Committee: Rodney H. Brady, Spencer F. Eccles, Burtis R. Evans, John R. Evans, C. Dean Larsen, David K. Richards, David E. Salisbury, Barbara L. Tanner, M. Walker Wallace, Alonzo W. Watson, Jr., and Gloris P. Goff, Symphony Guild President. Also confirmed or reelected were sixty Board members, eighteen special advisers, a national Advisory Board of thirty members, and an office staff of twenty.

On June 13, 1988, Huntsman resigned as chairman after completing a three-year term. He was succeeded by DeeDee Corradini, who was approved unanimously as the first chairwoman of the Board. Corradini is president of Bonneville Associates, Inc., and serves on the boards of Utah Power and Light and Intermountain Health Care, and has served on the boards of the Greater Salt Lake Area Chamber of Commerce, Ballet West, and the Snowbird Institute. M. Garfield Cook, president of IRECO, a manufacturer of explosives, was named vice chairman.

"It's been a deep honor to represent as chairman what I consider a world-class orchestra. . . . I've learned more than I've given," Huntsman said. "I would do it all over again." A Board resolution saluted Huntsman for his outstanding leadership and service, and his company, Huntsman Chemical Corporation, donated $250,000 as a challenge grant to match gifts to the orchestra.

Abravanel standing in front of his portrait in Symphony Hall. MAP.

CHAPTER 19

"The melody lingers . . ."

Although Abravanel resigned on April 6, 1979, as music director and conductor of the Utah Symphony, his pace never slackened in the larger world of music.

He had been appointed to the National Council for the Arts by President Nixon in 1970 for a six-year term, and he continues as an adviser to the Council, which advises the National Endowment for the Arts (NEA) on all appropriations. Abravanel traveled throughout the country evaluating orchestras for the Endowment, and few afternoons passed in his basement studio without phone calls from Washington. Members of the Council during Abravanel's initial term included Gregory Peck, Marian Anderson, Rudolf Serkin, Charlton Heston, Clint Eastwood, Beverly Sills, Robert Merrill, and Gunther Schuller.

He was vice chairman of the American Symphony Orchestra League (ASOL) and received the League's prestigious Gold Baton award in 1981. Recipients of the award include Leonard Bernstein, Eugene Ormandy, and Arthur Fiedler. He remained a permanent adviser to the League, participated in its conductors' workshops, and was a frequent judge at major music competitions.

Abravanel was designated Music Director Laureate of the Utah Symphony following his resignation, but he sought to maintain very low visibility until Kojian's appointment in November 1979. He was determined to leave his successor a clear field. He had also resigned as director of the Music Academy of the West. He was persuaded, however, to spend his usual July and August in Santa Barbara as an adviser, where he and Lucy were greeted by an outpouring of love and affection from faculty, students, and the public.

During the autumn of 1980, the Abravanels went abroad, spending considerable time in Paris, Lucy's birthplace. Although she adopted Salt Lake City as her home during her husband's years with the Utah Symphony, Lucy's first love was always the French capital. The summer stay in Santa Barbara, coupled with the European trip, afforded Abravanel the necessary time and space to unwind. Following Kojian's appointment, the Abravanels were usually seen in their Symphony Hall seats next to the President's Box.

In January 1980 Abravanel appeared on the University of Utah campus before a distinguished audience of townspeople, faculty, and students in a series of eight lectures on subjects of his own choosing. The weekly lectures, "Conversations with Abravanel," lasted through January, February, and early March. Brilliant, perceptive, and entertaining, they were taped and subsequently released over KUER, the University's public radio station. Some thought was given to publishing them. Sterling M. McMurrin, in particular, encouraged publication, and Betty Durham transcribed the tapes for preliminary editing. Abravanel himself felt that they did not lend themselves to publication; however, he authorized their use in this volume.

In his opening lecture, on Tuesday afternoon, January 15, Abravanel spoke of his feelings since his resignation:

I am asked, isn't it tough? Sure it is tough! It is very tough! Thirty-two years nurturing an organization and working with human beings, caring for everything that goes through their minds—otherwise, in my book, you can't make really good music. Any music that is dependent entirely on a baton is missing something. Having devoted myself to music for fifty-five years, how can one simply give it up without being entirely dead? Which I am not—for sure.

But I don't miss it as much as most people thought I would for one very simple reason which I did not realize. I thought I was very passionate about *conducting*. Wrong! I discovered I was very passionate about *music*—and there is a big difference.

Since resigning, I am asked "What are you doing now?" My reply, "I am studying music." Isn't that beautiful? At last, I have time to study music, because if you are performing the way I have been doing the past fifty years, you simply don't have time.

President David P. Gardner invited Abravanel to deliver the University's 111th June Commencement address three months later and to guest-conduct the Utah Symphony on that occasion. Abravanel agreed to speak but suggested that Ardean Watts conduct. His improvised address to the graduates was wise and witty.

For fifteen years you have pursued an education, dealing mostly with the verbal language. That is the only means of knowing facts and certainty. We are grateful to our philosophers, scientists, and mathematicians who provide us with those certainties. Yet we do not function on the intellectual level alone. We live all day long on another level which I used to call a deeper level until I read Rainer Maria Rilke, and (I paraphrase): "Where words leave off, music begins."

In World War II our troops aboard ships had a record library—mostly entertainment recordings. As they sailed further from home a strange thing happened. They huddled together to listen to a few classical recordings. Beethoven's Fifth was there, Mozart's *Eine Kleine Nachtmusik*, and Tchaikovsky's *Nutcracker* and *Pathétique*. They needed this. They needed this music, something more than music that was skin deep. Enter-tainment is fine. We all need it. But if we really need food for our souls, my kind of music comes in.

President Gardner surprised Maestro Abravanel by honoring him that day with the designation Distinguished Professor Emeritus of Music, a rare and enviable distinction.

In the summer of 1981, Abravanel taught conducting at Tanglewood, summer home of the Boston Symphony and the Berkshire Music Festival. The following year Seiji Ozawa, the Boston Symphony's music director, invited him to serve as acting director of the Berkshire Festival in the absence of Gunther Schuller, who was on leave. Schuller returned in 1983. Abravanel nevertheless was invited back as artist in residence through the summer of 1985, and at a dinner in 1986 he was designated artist in residence for life.

President David P. Gardner and Distinguished Professor Abravanel in June 1980. Howard C. Moore photograph for the *Deseret News* in MAP.

Abravanel and President David P. Gardner at the podium from which the Maestro delighted his huge audience at the University of Utah Commencement exercises in June 1980. MAP.

Abravanel with Seiji Ozawa at Tanglewood. Walter H. Scott photograph in MAP.

LUCY

The Utah music world was saddened when Abravanel's companion, Lucy, passed away on May 27, 1985, at eighty-two after a three-month illness. Few realized her significant role in the Utah Symphony's successes. Maurice Abravanel knew:

> Nobody realizes how much Lucy worked for the Symphony and the arts in this community while keeping strictly in the background. She was fiercely independent, and nobody on this planet could make her do anything that she did not believe in or could stop her from doing anything she thought she needed to do or say.
>
> In particular, our entire recording program was collapsing for purely technical reasons, and where I myself had given up the idea of continuing, it was she, with her blessed stubbornness, who forced me to find a way to continue. It is no exaggeration to say that without her the recording program would have stopped before we completed the hundred-odd recordings for which music lovers all over the world hold this orchestra in particular affection.
>
> She was a most loving wife, totally loyal, and gave me total support every minute of the way, but also because the Utah Symphony was my life, she subdued any personal ideas to the interest of the Symphony. That she did for thirty-two years.

Lucy had married Abravanel in September of 1947 in Richmond, Virginia, one month before they came to Utah. In addition to Abravanel, Lucy is survived by two sons, Pierre Carasso of Santa Monica, California, and Roger Carasso of Westwood, California, five grandchildren, and a sister, Blanche Menasse, of Paris.

Lucy accompanied Abravanel to Tanglewood for three summers. In February of 1985 they had planned a three-week holiday – two in New York, one in Santa Barbara. Their plans also included a return to Tanglewood.

They flew from Salt Lake City to New York on February eighteenth. Four days later, while they were attending a concert with a granddaughter, Abravanel stepped into the lobby at intermission. When he returned Lucy was in great distress, obviously quite ill. Abravanel's secretary, Carleen Landes, recalls that Lucy had suffered a similar attack preceding the Utah Symphony Ball on January 25, a month earlier. Three days later Abravanel took Lucy to a doctor, who sent her directly to a hospital. She had a massive blood infection and related problems. Still in New York, she subsequently underwent open-heart surgery and was placed in intensive care, where she remained for over a month.

A celebration with Lucy and members of the Utah Symphony Guild, whose support has been so vital to the building of the orchestra. MAP.

On April 30, Abravanel brought Lucy home. She was taken to Holy Cross Hospital, where she remained until her death in late May. She had hoped to accompany Abravanel to Tanglewood in June. He kept that assignment alone.

LAUREATE

Abravanel is highly regarded by students and faculty at Tanglewood for building the Utah Symphony to major status and for the quality of the orchestra's recordings. The respect of Tanglewood's music community "borders on a quiet reverence," said the late Donald P. Lloyd, longtime Symphony Board member, who visited Tanglewood during the summer of 1982. "Tanglewood is a rewarding continuation of Abravanel's post-resignation career."

He has been a much sought-after judge in major competitions during these later years and was visible on the nationwide telecast of the finals of the 1981 Van Cliburn Piano Competition. Several panels of Exxon's Affiliate Artist Program benefited from his expertise. He also judged the Rockefeller Foundation Carnegie Hall Competition, the General Motors Competition for Violinists in Los Angeles, the New York Philharmonic Young Artists competition, and the National Federation of Music Clubs contests.

Many academic institutions have honored him. All of Utah's institutions of higher learning have conferred honorary doctorates on the Maestro through the years. Weber State College was the latest, with an honorary Doctor of Humanities in 1980. Abravanel delivered the 1982 Commencement address at the Cleveland Institute of Music, where Grant Johannesen was director.

On the effective date of his resignation in 1979, Abravanel was appointed to the Utah State Fine Arts Board by Governor Scott Matheson. There he was a dominant voice in the allocation of appropriations for the state's arts projects. He was reappointed for a second four-year term through 1988.

Carleen Landes recalls that in 1983 the Arts Council complied with the Governor's request that budget requests be limited to minimal increases. After the budget was submitted to the Governor, Abravanel met with him privately to say that he felt the budget figure submitted by the Arts Council was "all wrong." After a half-hour conversation, according to Landes, Governor Matheson thanked Abravanel for his advice and increased the appropriation by $150,000.

When David Stockman proposed slashing funds for the National Endowment for the Arts during the first Reagan budget hearings, Abravanel was selected by the NEA to rebut Stockman's proposals. A *Salt Lake Tribune* headline of March 27, 1981, with a Washington, D.C., dateline read: "Abravanel Testifies. Maestro Critical of Budget Cuts." He criticized Stockman's proposed $88 million budget cut as being counterproductive. He called for "belt tightening–but not tightening up on art and culture."

Senator Orrin Hatch, a hearings committee member, praised Abravanel: "The maestro is conducting his lobbying like he did the Symphony: 'with class.' " However, Abravanel's protestations came to naught. Reaganomics held sway and the NEA, along with other government-funded agencies, suffered serious budget cuts.

Two months after his resignation, President Ashton and the Symphony Board designated Abravanel Music Director Laureate and named the Board room the Abravanel Room. A heroic-sized portrait of Abravanel by Alvin L. Gittins was unveiled in Symphony Hall's impressive foyer about the same time. In white-tie and tails, Abravanel is proud, but not haughty.

Many attempts were made to persuade Abravanel to conduct after his resignation. He steadfastly refused all invitations. When he resigned, he resigned. Abravanel's eightieth birthday was January 3, 1983. A gala Ashton fund-raising affair paid lavish homage to the octogenarian Maestro with a Symphony concert, music, food, reception, and much media coverage. Metropolitan Opera soprano Leontyne Price, who had sung under Abravanel several times, was the glittering guest artist. Officials remained certain that Abravanel could be persuaded to conduct at least an overture. They were wrong.

Abravanel married Carolyn Cheney Firmage at Tanglewood on July 2, 1986, during his sixth summer in residence. It was that summer that he was named artist in residence for life. Carolyn had been invited for dinner at the home of Dr. and Mrs. Maxwell M. Wintrobe, where she met Maurice for the first time. The Wintrobes had been Abravanel's close friends since his arrival in Utah. A longtime member of the University of Utah's faculty as Distinguished Professor of Medicine, Max Wintrobe was a world authority in hematology, and he had been a member of the Symphony Board

during the sixties. Becky Wintrobe had played a prominent role in the Symphony Guild's fund-raising.

Soon afterward, Carolyn attended a Symphony concert with Abravanel, "reluctant at first," she admits, but enjoying a "marvelous time." A friend who has known her since grade school says that Carolyn's "outlook is cheerful and positive. . . . Kindness and compassion characterize her. . . . She is an excellent listener, an entertaining conversationalist . . . a most lovely companion."

Maurice and Carolyn Abravanel in May 1989. Sandria Miller photograph courtesy of Carolyn Abravanel.

IN RETROSPECT . . .

Abravanel's 1986 KUED interview was an opportunity for the Maestro to reflect upon his Utah years and his artistic life.

Abravanel was a dedicated citizen and patriot. He filed for citizenship shortly after his arrival in New York from Australia in 1936. One night in 1943, while he was conducting the Broadway run of Weill's *One Touch of Venus*, the entire cast greeted him onstage before the curtain went up, singing *The Star-Spangled Banner* and waving tiny American flags. Abravanel had received his U.S. citizenship papers earlier that day.

I first came to America in 1936 with a three-year contract to conduct at the Metropolitan Opera. The Metropolitan then was not American. You spoke no English. You spoke German, Italian, French–but no English. I wanted to go back to Europe right after the end of the first season. I really did not taste America until I left the Met and conducted . . . on Broadway. During those years I knew I was a European wanting to be a loyal citizen. I had already conducted all over Europe and Australia.

Then after the Met and Broadway I returned to Australia in 1946. There were no planes over the Pacific; so I had to go to London by ship and then [fly] on to Australia. . . . There was an abundance of foodstuffs at Shannon, Ireland–food from America which had been in short supply for years, because we felt it our duty to send it to the Allies. . . .

Australia was saved by MacArthur and American troops. . . . Australians were singing songs about the G.I.'s who had the money and cigarettes and, therefore, the girls. In Switzerland, where I spent my youth, I heard all kinds of jokes about the Americans with the dollar as their God and yet the Americans were still rationed. At that time I became a Yankee chauvinist. All of a sudden I felt like an American, and I came back from Australia to the USA in '46 feeling exactly like an American and no more like a European. A year later, when I came to Utah, it was even more so. I mean, all the beauty you people don't realize. . . . I love the mountains. They remind me of Switzerland, especially in Utah. I found more kindness here.

Abravanel was an ecumenical man. More than any other he was able to bring the diverse forces of the community together, with music the glue. He continually expressed gratitude to the LDS Church for making the Tabernacle available for dress rehearsals and concerts. He enjoyed warm personal relationships with five LDS Presidents but faced some problems with their second and third echelons.

David O. McKay? He was marvelous. He would phone me to say he could not come to the concert because Emma, his wife, had a cold or whatever. He was marvelous, but even he was influenced by a few in the hierarchy. Many give him credit for giving us the Tabernacle "rent free" in 1950. But it was President George Albert Smith in 1946, one year before I came here. . . .

In 1949 I think some of the brethren decided not to help the Utah Symphony any more because of its 1949 financial crisis. I understand it was President McKay who reversed that decision by President J. Reuben Clark, Jr., that we could not use the Tabernacle any more. President McKay reversed that decision, and we were permitted to play there until the new Symphony Hall was completed in 1979.

President Spencer W. Kimball was marvelous during the building of Symphony Hall. Most of the Church hierarchy were marvelous. Some underlings were not so.

I am asked "did you have the basic support of the Church in your endeavors?" Yes and no. Yes and no. After the state deficit appropriation was voted almost unanimously by the Senate and the House, [Governor J. Bracken] Lee vetoed it, urged on by Orval W. Adams, a leading Church banker. This is not gossip but was told me by a Republican member of the State Senate thirty years later, who said that President J. Reuben Clark, Jr., sent Adams to the state capitol to urge the Lee veto.

Because music's major masterworks are for combined chorus and orchestra, Abravanel's initial efforts in 1947 included an invitation to the Tabernacle Choir to join in Beethoven's Ninth Symphony. Twenty-nine years later, their first joint appearance highlighted the Bicentennial.

Through the years many have asked why the Tabernacle Choir refused to sing with the Utah Symphony

Abravanel in a contemplative mood. MAP.

for nearly thirty years. I believe it was because the Tabernacle Choir had always been the only internationally and nationally known institution in Utah, and some people were afraid that if the Symphony were successful, it would take away from the luster of the Tabernacle Choir. There was probably also something personal, because my first visit after my arrival in Utah was with the head of the Tabernacle Choir.

It was very funny. The Symphony manager arranged for an interview. We went to his studio and knocked at the door. "Come in." The man [J. Spencer Cornwall] got up and stayed up, never asked us to sit down, although the Symphony manager was a lady. So we stood, and I said, "I came to pay my respects, and I assume that Beethoven's Ninth has never been performed in Utah . . . wouldn't it be wonderful to join forces?"

He said "no!" And I said, "but why?" "It would kill their voices," he said. I replied, "I have never killed voices. Believe me, I am known to be very understanding of voices." "No!" Finally he said, "Well, you are the state, we are the Church – the two don't mix."

Abravanel was determined from the outset to make the Salt Lake City–based Symphony a "Utah" Symphony, and he prided himself on taking concerts to small communities throughout the state and to school audiences.

Governor Lee's veto of the deficit appropriation during our 1949 financial crisis influenced legislators negatively for many years. When we were unable to secure state funds we decided to underwrite the orchestra's expenses in concerts in smaller communities. Walter L. Roche, finance chairman of the Board, objected: This is a sucker's deal. We have to stop that nonsense." I answered: "We are not going to stop! We are going to tour all over the state, and someday we will be morally entitled to a state subsidy."

Nearly two decades after coming to Utah, Abravanel led the orchestra on its first international tour: These tours were a prime factor in the Symphony's rise to major-orchestra status.

Overseas tours, international tours have great significance. Like citizens in remote places, Australia, for example, Utahns have a two-fold attitude about home-grown products – the Utah Symphony, for example: One, we are no good and, two, we are better than anybody. No matter what we did, they would say, "How could Salt Lake City and Utah have such a good symphony orchestra?"

Early on, our recording program attracted the attention of the national press. by the mid-sixties, with the Vanguard recordings of Mahler's Second and Eighth symphonies, we were hailed as a leading interpreter of Mahler, both at home and in Europe. Then along came Gina Bachauer, who insisted that we tour Europe and secured an invitation to the Athens Festival as guest orchestra with performances in Athens and Salonika.

As a result, a British agent who knew me from my early years in Germany as guest conductor of the Berlin Philharmonic, plus my years in German opera houses climaxed by guest conducting at Berlin's State Opera, phoned me in Salt Lake City: "Is that Maurice de Abravanel? Can I book you a tour throughout Europe, after Greece?" We were subsequently invited to the Berlin Festival, the greatest in Europe. Sixteen concerts! And it all began with Gina Bachauer!

Abravanel is a philosopher as well as an artist, often expressing penetrating thoughts:

> I need art. Bracken Lee did not. The majority do not. We all need food. Many need athletics, TV, rock music, travel, religion. But we are all proud of what art has brought to America. What does art do? Many believe in evolution, many in creation, I think we are all a combination of both.
> Through art we are brought "a little closer to the angels" and "a little further from the apes." In 1969 I was questioned by Larry Pressler, congressman from South Dakota, at a congressional hearing on funding for the National Endowment for the Arts: "Can you tell me in fifteen seconds why I should support the arts as a representative of South Dakota? We don't have any arts there."
> I said: *For the same reason that your farmers also plant flowers!*

Abravanel spent his entire professional life in Utah working to build an orchestra and a permanent "home" for his musicians. Circumstances brought about his resignation a few months before the Symphony Hall's completion. He never conducted in it.

> I am told I will be remembered as one who was influential in the building of Symphony Hall. No, it was the musicians . . . the musicians. I would like to be remembered as one who tried to be useful to the community. I made a lot of speeches after we went bankrupt in 1949 when Bracken Lee was the barbarian! I made a lot of speeches and never failed to mention the need for a public library and a desperate need for an art gallery.

> I believe in the total picture, just as I've supported the Utah Opera and Ballet West. I brought Bill Christensen from San Francisco to Salt Lake (I say "brought" because it was for the University of Utah Summer Festival). Later I conducted all *Nutcracker* performances free of charge except for a few principals, and my musicians played at minimum scale. I'd love to be remembered as a backer of the University Museum of Fine Arts and Frank Sanguinetti. I would like to be remembered as a good citizen first, as musician second.

The Maestro making an impassioned point at an interview. MZPC.

Six months after the KUED interview the first of more honors originated locally: "Abravanel Receives First Bass Award, $5,000 Fellowship," stated a *Salt Lake Tribune* story on May 1, 1987. "Maurice Abravanel . . . became the first recipient of the annual Richard D. Bass Achievement Award at a Thursday ceremony in Symphony Hall." The award was presented to Abravanel by its donor, Richard D. Bass, and the Snowbird Institute for the Arts and Humanities "in recognition of his work with the Utah Symphony, exemplary leadership, great accomplishment and contribution to the state of the arts and quality of life in Utah."

The Maestro and a less animated counterpart at Abravanel Hall in Santa Barbara. MAP.

Nearly twelve years after his 1976 coronary bypass, Abravanel faced another health crisis—in his eighty-fifth year. The month following the Bass Award he was stricken in Kansas City. "The other main artery was blocked." Physicians decided it was "too dangerous to intervene," but "found they were able to work on the small circumflex artery," clearing enough of the obstruction that Abravanel is able to function quite well. He says they cleared the small artery "to sixty-five percent obstruction" and guesses that he has "thirty-five percent use of it." Carolyn was at Abravanel's side during his Kansas City illness.

Abravanel was honored on the occasion of his eighty-fifth birthday at the Symphony concert on January 8, 1988. Prior to the concert, Symphony Board Vice Chairman DeeDee Corradini read letters of praise from President Ronald Reagan, Senators Jake Garn and Orrin Hatch, Governor Norm Bangerter, Mayor Palmer DePaulis, and the First Presidency of the LDS Church. The audience rose to applaud Abravanel and joined in singing "Happy Birthday."

A few weeks later, Abravanel was the featured speaker in a commemoration of Lotte Lehmann's one-hundredth birthday at the Music Academy of the West on March sixth. She would have been one hundred years old on February 27, 1988. Abravanel and Lehmann had worked together for years at Santa Barbara's Music Academy, she as honorary president and director of the vocal department, and he as music director. They collaborated on operatic productions each summer. Abravanel had conducted many of her performances during his years at the Metropolitan Opera, when the legendary Lehmann had been the leading German soprano and music personality of her generation.

A national symposium honoring Mme. Lehmann was held on May 27–29, 1988, on the campus of the University of California at Santa Barbara, which houses her personal library and files. The *Los Angeles Times*'s Martin Bernheimer wrote:

> After the inaugural ceremonies Friday, Maurice Abravanel, retired music director of the Utah Symphony, took the podium. Now 85, he offered vivid recollections of his collaboration with Lehmann, as conductor and as administrator of the Music Academy of the West. He spoke with extraordinary warmth of her impetuosity

and her flexibility. He invoked the poetic excitement of her creations and confirmed the prosaic insignificance of her miscalculations. He was the first of many speakers to stress the singer's concern for the word and its telling inflection. "With Lehmann," he said, "expression was everything."

"Utah Symphony conductor Emeritus Maurice Abravanel has been designated recipient of the ninth annual Distinguished Service to the Arts Award by the National Governors Association," reported the *Salt Lake Tribune* during the summer of 1988. The award was established in 1976 "to provide annual recognition for distinguished service to state government." Abravanel was nominated by Utah Governor Norman Bangerter, who called the Maestro "Utah's most significant artistic figure. The Utah Symphony under his baton has whetted a Utah appetite for artistic excellence that has spawned more excellence."

Abravanel was a member of the panel of judges who selected the five distinguished American performing artists for the 1988 Kennedy Center Honors, a major annual event in the artistic world.

In early 1989 the newly founded Corporate Council of the Utah Symphony established the Maurice Abravanel Leadership Award "to recognize outstanding service and leadership by a member of the Utah corporate community on behalf of the Utah Symphony." On April 17 the group presented its first award to Obert C. Tanner, who has championed the Symphony since its beginnings. Tanner's Bicentennial work was well known in Utah, and in 1985 he had been appointed by President Reagan to the federal committee responsible for the celebration of the Bicentennial of the U.S. Constitution. More recently he had been awarded a 1988 National Medal of Arts, the first Utahn ever to be so honored. Utah Symphony favorites Rudolf Serkin and composer Virgil Thomson were among the illustrious recipients in the White House ceremony.

As "one of the most significant figures in Utah's recent history," Abravanel was honored at the Utah State Historical Society's annual meeting on July 14, 1989. The Society's theme for the year was "Utah and the Arts," which also commemorated the ninetieth anniversary of the Utah Arts Council.

"ONE OF THE GREATEST . . . "

Abravanel waited twenty-nine years to conduct Utah's two internationally-known music organizations together. In his KUED interview he relishes the memory.

To complete the Tabernacle Choir picture, I must say that in 1976, during the nation's Bicentennial, I was allowed to conduct the Choir, and, believe me, it was one of the greatest moments in my life when I was introduced to them. As we worked together there was absolutely universal love. It was one of my greatest experiences.

I also conducted them with the orchestra in Robertson's *Book of Mormon* Oratorio, including a CBS recording, and again it was a marvelous, marvelous experience. But there were some negative powers . . . through the years . . . which at times were more influential than the positive ones. About the Church—President Kimball and the highest hierarchy were for us. Jerold Ottley and his staff were for us. The rank and file were passionately for us, passionately. Through the years there were a few people in between who saw it from a very different angle and were definitely against us.

One of Abravanel's most cherished legacies to those who would follow was the continuation of the Symphony's relationship with the Tabernacle Choir. This hope permeated

his thirty-two-year stewardship. Collaborations continued on the heels of Abravanel's resignation, with Jerold Ottley conducting the Choir and the "Columbia" Symphony, comprising members of the Utah Symphony. Ottley "conducted nineteen albums during 1980–81, ten with members of the Utah Symphony," he recalls.

In 1983, future Tabernacle Choir–Utah Symphony joint performances in the Tabernacle were assured when the Obert C. and Grace A. Tanner Gift of Music Trust was established with the expressed goal of offering *free of charge* every two years "an unparalleled degree of excellence in music performance." Threefold provisions of the Trust include: (1) the Tabernacle Choir, (2) the Utah Symphony, and (3) the Tabernacle itself as the performance site. Symphony Board President Wendell J. Ashton, who worked closely with Tanner from the inception of the idea to its fruition, indicated that the Trust will cover all expenses, including those for guest conductors and soloists, and will continue indefinitely into the future.

In 1976 Obert Tanner had joined with President Nathan Eldon Tanner of the LDS Church's First Presidency to bring about the long-awaited first joint performance of Choir and Symphony during the Bicentennial. The two Tanners loosed the ties that had bound this reunion for twenty-nine years and paved the way for Leroy Robertson's *Book of Mormon Oratorio* to be performed and recorded for CBS Records.

In 1985, while conducting a workshop at Kansas State University, Ottley suggested to guest-conductor Aaron Copland that his unrecorded *Old American Songs* be recorded by Choir and Symphony. Two years later Copland agreed and recommended that Michael Tilson Thomas conduct. The label lists Tabernacle Choir and Utah Symphony, and the 1987 recording is on the new CBS Records label.

In 1988 the Utah Symphony and Tabernacle Choir again joined forces to tape Crawford Gates's revised *Hill Cumorah* score for the annual summer productions of that LDS pageant in New York State. The composer conducted. During the post-Abravanel years, Jerold Ottley has been the effective "glue" that has held together this mutually advantageous and pleasant collaboration.

Abravanel is in love with music, not merely with conducting. "Music reflects what goes on in our minds and bodies . . . and this is true everywhere around the world. Music's underlying principle is: tension versus relaxation, breathing in and breathing out, the calm after the storm, and so on. This is what music is. It is universal and is the principle in all aspects of life. And this is why people around the world spend millions and millions of dollars annually for music of all kinds."

Abravanel the philosopher concludes KUED's interview with a quiet but stirring benediction on the past and optimism about the future.

I am asked "Have the years been long or short?" Very short. It's a beautiful life. It's a beautiful state. Whether we are Mormons or not, we are all inheritors of those pioneers who settled here for spiritual reasons and not material ones. Even if many of their descendants have forgotten it, we are all the beneficiaries.

It is a great state, and let me tell you in closing how I see things. There is a very large majority here who are happy to intermingle. There is a small minority of bigots, both Mormon and anti-Mormon, who are very vocal and will see a "Mormon" under every rug. But they are a small minority. The beauty of this state is that the Church, as we call it, has the wisdom to accept, with open arms, people who come here and contribute something of worth.

The entire medical school faculty at the University, which is marvelous, is an example. This is the beauty of Utah. The way I have been treated, by and large, has been beautiful. I have had a lot of hard knocks, but still—by and large—I have been treated marvelously. You talk about what I have done for the state. Let me tell you what the state has done for me. And that's a lot.

And that's my way of looking at it.

Although he had occasional critics and personnel problems, Abravanel was respected and honored and, in some quarters, revered. "Abravanel's name is more commonly known in this region than any except the President of the Mormon Church," says one Abravanel devotee. He traversed the length and breadth of the Intermountain region many times during his thirty-two years, performing in many small rural communities. Media coverage stamped his name and face indelibly in the collective mind.

There are always the chronic complainers: "He plays too much contemporary music" and, conversely, "He plays too little contemporary music." "He plays too much Mahler." "Why doesn't he play more Mahler?" "He plays too many 'war-horses' from the standard repertoire." "He doesn't play enough standards." "He performs too many works with chorus." "The choral-orchestral concerts are among his best." "The orchestra's tours exhaust the musicians for Tabernacle concerts." "The orchestra's size should be increased to one

hundred." "Eighty musicians is adequate and what we can afford."

Detractors have questioned his ranking among his peers: "If Abravanel is so good, why did he remain with the Utah Symphony for thirty-two years?" "If he is so great, why didn't he move up to a better, larger orchestra?"

Abravanel rejected an offer to move "up" to Houston as music director and conductor in 1949, remaining in Utah to battle Governor J. Bracken Lee and other powerful anti-Symphony forces. He and Lucy repeatedly held that one reason they remained in the Salt Lake Valley was its surrounding mountains, reminiscent of Abravanel's boyhood home in Lausanne, Switzerland.

Abravanel was quick to admit that his "ear was not always what it should be, intonation-wise, but I compensated with an uncanny knack for rhythm and timing."

Abravanel knew instinctively where music's Big Moments were and how to arrive there dramatically. Concert audiences came to expect the virtually inevitable magical moments in each evening.

Eugene Ormandy and Abravanel were almost the last conductors to remain with major orchestras: Ormandy for forty years, Abravanel for thirty-two. George Szell stayed with the Cleveland Orchestra for fifteen years, transforming it into one of the great ensembles, and Herbert von Karajan recently retired from the splendid Berlin Philharmonic after thirty-four years.

But the present-day jet-set conductor flies back and forth over the country and from continent to continent, living like royalty and guest-conducting the world's great virtuoso orchestras. All are charismatic media personalities, and they may even have permanent orchestras—but permanent means short-term. The best are admittedly great: Leonard Bernstein, Zubin Mehta, Seiji Ozawa, Sir Georg Solti, etc. They conduct and guest-conduct only the world's best orchestral musicians. They do not have to teach or train these musicians, who are musically their equals. These virtuosos strive for the subtle, sophisticated nuances achievable only in the large metropolitan orchestras.

None of the "name" conductors of today would or could take over a struggling community orchestra in the American hinterland and patiently but surely build it into one of the

MZPC.

nation's twelve to fifteen recognized major orchestras over a thirty-two-year period. Even Ormandy's legacy was the result of the marvelous ensemble bequeathed him by Leopold Stokowski. No need to build, just maintain.

Abravanel was always a builder rather than a fine-tuner, a solid citizen rather than a remote artist, an active participant in the community, a healer of factional bruises, a citizen first and an artist second. Which is why he stayed for thirty-two years and became a legend "somewhere west of Denver."

Abravanel is the only conductor to have recorded all the Mahler symphonies with the
same orchestra. The Maestro and the Utah Symphony received the Mahler Society
award for the best Mahler recording of 1975 for the Fifth Symphony. MAP.

Discography

Utah Symphony Recordings, 1952–1979
Maurice Abravanel, Conducting

Composer: Title(s)	Label
Americana: Bernstein: Overture to *Candide*; Siegmeister: *Western Suite*; Gould: *American Salute*; Robertson: *Punch and Judy Overture*; Nelhybel: *Etude Symphonique*	Vox
Anderson: *Fiddle Faddle* and 14 Other Favorites	Vanguard
Bach-Schönberg: *St. Ann Prelude and Fugue*; 2 Choral Preludes	Vanguard
Bach-Stravinsky: *Canonic Variations on "Von Himmel Hoch"*	Vanguard
Bach–von Webern: *Ricercare from "The Musical Offering"*	Vanguard
Beethoven: *Incidental Music from "Egmont"*	Vanguard
Beethoven: *The Creatures of Prometheus*	Vanguard
Berlioz: *Requiem* (2 discs)	Vanguard
Bernstein: Overture to *Candide* (Americana album)	Vox
Brahms: Four Symphonies; *Haydn Variations*; Overtures (4 discs)	Vanguard
Copland: *Billy the Kid*; *Rodeo*	Westminster
Copland: *Rodeo*; *Billy the Kid*; *El Salón Mexico*	Westminster
Copland: *A Lincoln Portrait*; *Outdoor Overture*; *"Our Town" Suite*; *"Quiet City" Suite*	Vanguard
Copland: *Billy the Kid*; Waltz from *Billy the Kid*; *Rodeo*	Westminster
Copland: *El Salón Mexico*; Gershwin: *"Porgy and Bess" Suite*	Westminster

Composer: Title(s)	Label
Franck: Symphony in D Minor	Westminster
Gershwin: *Rhapsody in Blue*; *An American in Paris*; Concerto in F	Vanguard
Gershwin: *"Porgy and Bess" Suite*	Westminster
Gershwin: *Rhapsody in Blue*; Piano Concerto in F	Westminster
Gershwin: Piano Concerto in F	Westminster
Glière: *Russian Sailors' Dance*; Rimsky-Korsakov: *Antar Symphonic Suite*; Ippolitov-Ivanov: *Caucasian Sketches*	Vanguard
Goldmark: *Rustic Wedding*	Vanguard
Gottschalk: *Night in the Tropics*; *Grand Tarantelle* (Reid Nibley); Gould: *Latin American Symphonette*	Vanguard
Gould: *Latin American Symphonette*; Gottschalk: *Night in the Tropics*; *Grand Tarantelle* (Reid Nibley)	Vanguard
Gould: *American Salute* (Americana album)	Vox
Greig: Piano Concerto (Grant Johannesen); *Norwegian Dances*; *Wedding Day at Troldhaugen*	Vox
Grieg: Works for Orchestra (3 discs)	Vox
Grieg: *Peer Gynt Suites 1 and 2*; Piano Concerto in A Minor	Westminster
Grofé: *Grand Canyon Suite*; Gershwin: *"Porgy and Bess" Suite*	Westminster
Grofé: *Grand Canyon Suite*	Westminster
Handel: *Samson* Oratorio (three discs)	Vanguard
Handel: *Judas Maccabaeus* (three discs)	Westminster

207

Composer: Title(s)	Label	Composer: Title(s)	Label
Handel: *Israel in Egypt* (two discs)	Westminster	Rimsky-Korsakov: *Antar Symphonic Suite*; Glière: *Russian Sailors' Dance*; Ippolitov-Ivanov: *Caucasian Sketches*	Vanguard
Harris: *Folk Song Symphony*	Angel		
Honegger: *Le Roi David*; Milhaud: *Le Création du Monde* (2 discs)	Vanguard	Saint-Saëns: Symphony No. 3 (*Organ Symphony*) (Alexander Schreiner)	Westminster
Honegger: *Pacific 231*; Milhaud: *L'homme et son désir*; Varèse: *Ameriques*	Vanguard	Satie: Homage to Erik Satie (complete orchestral works) (2 discs)	Vanguard
Ippolitov-Ivanov: *Caucasian Sketches*; Glière: *Russian Sailors' Dance*; Rimsky-Korsakov: *Antar Symphonic Suite*	Vanguard	Satie: Complete Ballet	Vanguard
		Scarlatti: *Mass of St. Cecelia*	Vanguard
Mahler: Symphony No. 1	Vanguard	Schubert: *Rosamunde* Music (complete)	Vanguard
Mahler: Symphony No. 2 (*Resurrection*) (Beverly Sills) (2 discs)	Vanguard	Sibelius: Seven Symphonies (4 discs)	Vanguard
		Siegmeister: *Western Suite* (Americana album)	Vox
Mahler: Symphony No. 3 (2 discs)	Vanguard	Stravinsky: Violin Concerto; Robertson: Violin Concerto	Vanguard
Mahler: Symphony No. 4	Vanguard	Tchaikovsky: *1812 Overture*; *Romeo and Juliet*	Vox
Mahler: Symphony No. 5; Symphony No. 10 (*Adagio*) (2 discs)	Vanguard	Tchaikovsky: *Manfred* Symphony	Vox
Mahler: Symphony No. 6 (2 discs)	Vanguard	Tchaikovsky: *Nutcracker* (complete ballet music) (2 discs)	Vanguard
Mahler: Symphony No. 7 (*Song of the Night*) (2 discs)	Vanguard	Tchaikovsky: *Swan Lake* (complete ballet music) (2 discs)	Vanguard
Mahler: Symphony No. 8 (*Symphony of a Thousand*) (2 discs)	Vanguard	Tchaikovsky: Vol. I: Symphonies 1, 3, 5 (3 discs)	Vox
Mahler: Symphony No. 9 (2 discs)	Vanguard	Tchaikovsky: Vol. II: Symphonies 2, 4, 6; *Marche Slav* (3 discs)	Vox
Mahler: Symphony No. 10 (*Adagio*)	Vanguard	Tchaikovsky: Vol. III: *Manfred* Symphony; *Francesca da Rimini*; *1812 Overture*; *Romeo and Juliet*; *Hamlet* (3 discs)	Vox
Milhaud: *Le Création du Monde*; Honegger: *Le Roi David* (2 discs)	Vanguard		
Milhaud: *L'homme et son désir*; Varèse: *Ameriques*; Honegger: *Pacific 231*	Vanguard	Varèse: *Ameriques*; Honegger: *Pacific 231*; Milhaud: *L'homme et son désir*	Vanguard
Milhaud: *Pacem in Terris*	Vanguard	Varèse: *Nocturnal*	Vanguard
Nelhybel: *Etude Symphonique* (Americana album)	Vox	Vaughan Williams: *Fantasia on a Theme by Thomas Tallis*; *Five Variants of "Dives and Lazarus"*; *Fantasia on "Greensleeves"*; *Flos Campi*	Vanguard
Prokofiev: Symphony No. 3; *Le Pas d'acier*	Vanguard		
Rachmaninoff: Symphony No. 3; *Chanson Georgienne*	Vanguard	Vaughan Williams: *Dona Nobis Pacem*	Vanguard
Robertson: *Oratorio from the Book of Mormon*	Vanguard	Vaughan Williams: Symphony No. 6; *Five Variants of "Dives and Lazarus"*	Vanguard
Robertson: *Punch and Judy* Overture (Americana album)	Vox		
Robertson: Violin Concerto; Stravinsky: Violin Concerto	Vanguard		

—————————— APPENDIX II ——————————

Utah Symphony Guild Presidents

1953–55 Becky Almond
1955–57 Margaret (Mrs. Harold K.) Beecher
1957–59 Judy (Mrs. Charles A.) Boynton, Jr.
1959–61 Helen (Mrs. Donald P.) Lloyd

1961–63 Katherine (Mrs. Folke A.) Myrin
1963–65 Mary (Mrs. Edward W.) Muir
1965–66 Yvonne (Mrs. R. H.) Willey
1966–67 Blanche (Mrs. David L.) Freed

1967–68	Oma (Mrs. W. Stanford) Wagstaff
1968–70	Janice (Mrs. Robert H.) Hinckley, Jr.
1970–72	Helen (Mrs. George A.) Stahlke
1972–74	Nellie (Mrs. Glen M.) Hatch
1974–76	Dorothy (Mrs. Wilford M.) Burton
1976–78	Barbara (Mrs. Norman C.) Tanner
1978–80	Barbara (Mrs. John Major) Scowcroft
1980–81	Jean (Mrs. Thomas C.) Moseley
1981–82	Josephine (Mrs. Melvin R.) Davis
1982–83	Dorotha Sharp (Mrs. Charles R.) Smart
1983–84	Carol H. (Mrs. William L.) Nixon
1984–85	Beverly C. (Mrs. Dale G.) Johnson
1985–86	Gloris P. (Mrs. Charles) Goff
1986–87	Joyce (Mrs. Robert) DeForest
1987–88	Joann B. Svikhart
1988–89	Linda M. (Mrs. Fred) Babcock

================ APPENDIX III ================

Tables

Salt Lake Tabernacle Subscription Concerts
Abravanel Years 1947–1979

I. Composers Most Performed

Name	Number of Performances	Number of Works Performed
1. Beethoven	121	27
2. Mozart	89	39
3. Brahms	77	12
4. Tchaikovsky	57	21
5. Wagner	45	18
6. Ravel	43	14
7. Strauss, R.	34	12
8. Bach, J. S.	31	16
9. Prokofiev	29	15
10. Robertson	28	13
11. Mahler	27	11
12. Debussy	25	7
13. Stravinsky	25	9
14. Handel	24	14
15. Haydn	24	13
16. Berlioz	23	9
17. Copland	23	11
18. Rachmaninov	21	7
19. Shostakovitch	17	6
20. Mendelssohn	17	8
21. Schubert	16	6
22. Dvořák	16	7
23. Sibelius	16	5
24. Gershwin	16	5
25. Weber	16	7
26. Bartók	15	8
27. Barber	13	9

*Plus 161 other composers; a total of 1,163 performances of 677 works by 188 composers.

II. Works Most Performed

Work	Composer	Number of Performances
1. Symphony No. 3 (*Eroica*)	Beethoven	11
2. Symphony No. 7	Beethoven	11
3. Symphony No. 1	Brahms	10
4. Piano Concerto No. 2	Brahms	10
5. Suite from *The Firebird*	Stravinsky	9
6. Piano Concerto No. 5 (*Emperor*)	Beethoven	9
7. Piano Concerto No. 4	Beethoven	9
8. Violin Concerto	Beethoven	9
9. Symphony No. 4	Brahms	9
10. Symphony No. 2	Brahms	9
11. Prelude to *Die Meistersinger*	Wagner	9

II. Works Most Performed (continued)

Work	Composer	Number of Performances
12. Symphony No. 5	Beethoven	8
13. Symphony No. 6 (Pastorale)	Beethoven	8
14. *Leonore* Overture No. 3	Beethoven	8
15. *Academic Festival* Overture	Brahms	8
16. *Death and Transfiguration*	R. Strauss	8
17. Symphony No. 6 (Pathetique)	Tchaikovsky	8
18. *Daphnis et Chloé* Suite No. 2	Ravel	8
19. Piano Concerto No. 1	Brahms	7
20. Overture to *The Marriage of Figaro*	Mozart	7
21. *Egmont* Overture	Beethoven	7
22. Prelude to *The Afternoon of a Faun*	Debussy	7
23. Overture to *Oberon*	Weber	7
24. *American Salute*	Gould	7
25. Symphony No. 5	Shostakovitch	7
26. Piano Concerto No. 1	Tchaikovsky	7
27. *La Valse*	Ravel	7
28. Piano Concerto in G Major	Ravel	7
29. Piano Concerto No. 3	Rachmaninov	7
30. *Roman Carnival* Overture	Berlioz	7

III. Contemporary Composers Most Performed

Name	Number of Performances	Number of Works
1. Sergei Prokoviev	29	15
2. Leroy Robertson	28	13
3. Igor Stravinsky	25	9
4. Aaron Copland	23	11
5. Dmitri Shostakovich	17	6
6. George Gershwin	16	5
7. Béla Bartók	15	8
8. Samuel Barber	13	9
9. Ernest Bloch	12	7
10. Crawford Gates	11	8
11. Ralph Vaughan Williams	11	9
12. Darius Milhaud	10	7

IV. Contemporary Works Most Performed

Name	Composer	Number of Performances
1. Suite from *The Firebird*	Stravinsky	9
2. Symphony No. 5	Shostakovich	7
3. *American Salute*	Gould	7
4. Concerto for Orchestra	Bartók	6
5. *Punch and Judy* Overture	Robertson	6
6. *Book of Mormon* Oratorio	Robertson	5
7. Overture to *Candide*	Bernstein	5
8. *Schelomo*	Bloch	5
9. *El Salon Mexico*	Copland	5
10. Suite from *Petruchka*	Stravinsky	5
11. *An American in Paris*	Gershwin	5
12. *Rhapsody in Blue*	Gershwin	4
13. *A Lincoln Portrait*	Copland	4
14. *Mathis der Maler*	Hindemith	4
15. *Symphonic Metamorphosis*	Hindemith	4
16. *Adagio for Strings*	Barber	4
17. Adagio from Symphony No. 2	R. Thompson	4
18. Third Symphony	Harris	3
19. *King David*	Honegger	3
20. *Interlude* from *Promised Valley*	Gates	3
21. *Porgy and Bess Scenario*	Gershwin	3
22. *Appalachian Spring*	Copland	3

V. Performances by Guest Pianists*

Name	Number of Performances
1. Grant Johannesen	16
2. Van Cliburn	11
3. Reid Nibley	11
4. Gladys Gladstone (Rosenberg)	8
5. Gina Bachauer	7
6. Artur Rubinstein	6
7. Jose Iturbi	4
8. Gary Graffman	4
9. Claudio Arrau	4
10. Andre Watts	3

*There were 42 others for a total of 135 performances by 52 pianists.

VI. Performances by Guest Violinists*

Name	Number of Performances
1. Isaac Stern	6
2. Harold Wolf	5
3. Nathan Milstein	4
4. Tossy Spivakovsky	4
5. Jascha Heifetz	3
6. Beryl Senofsky	3
7. Oscar Chausow	3
8. Yehudi Menuhin	2
9. Itzhak Perlman	2
10. Zvi Zeitlin	2
11. Lilit Gampel	2
12. Tibor Zelig	2
13. Leonard Posner	2

*Plus 17 artists in single performances, making a total of 62 performances by 30 artists.

VII. Performances by Cellists

Name	Number of Performances
1. Zara Nelsova	5
2. Gregor Piatigorsky	3
3. Harold Schneier	2
4. Christian Tiemeyer	2
5. David Freed	2
6. Mstislav Rostropovich	1
7. Gaspar Cassado	1
8. Paolo Gruppe	1
9. Dorothy Eustis	1
10. Nina DeVeritch	1

VIII. Performances by Vocal Artists*

Name	Number of Performances
1. Eileen Farrell	4
2. Roberta Peters	2
3. Jan Peerce	2
4. Joan Sutherland	2
5. Helen Traubel	2
6. Rise Stevens	1
7. William Cochran	2
8. Nadine Conner	1
9. Netania Davrath	1
10. Beverly Sills	1

*There were also 11 others in single appearances, a total of 29 performances.

IX. Miscellaneous Solo Performances

Artist	Instrument	Number of Performances
1. Alexander Schreiner	organ	7
2. Eugene Foster	flute	3
3. Druke and Shaw	duo-pianists	1
4. Gold and Fizdale	duo-pianists	1
5. Luboschutz and Nemenoff	duo-pianists	1
6. Dorothy McGuire	narrator	1
7. Louis Booth	oboe	1
8. Robert Cundick	organ	1
9. Ned Meredith	trombone	1
10. Steve Mori	accordian	1
11. Angel Romero	guitar	1
12. Thomas Stevens	trumpet	1
13. Barry Tuckwell	French horn	1
14. Martin Zwick	clarinet	1

X. Appearances by Guest Conductors

Name	Number of Appearances
1. Ardean Watts	8
2. Aaron Copland	3
3. Crawford Gates	3
4. Gunther Schuller	3
5. Henri Lazarof	2
6. Joseph Rosenstock	1
7. James DePreist	3
8. David A. Shand	2
9. Ralph Laycock	1
10. Ramiro Cortés	1
11. Arthur Fiedler	1
12. Paul Whiteman	1
13. Guido Ajmone-Marsan	1
14. Richard Bonynge	1
15. Newell Weight	1
16. Lukas Foss	1

XI. Festival of Contemporary Music, 1959–1979 with University of Utah*

Number of Performances	Composer
16	Stravinsky
10	Prokoviev
8	Copland
8	Ives
6	Lazarof
5	Bartok, Rorem
4	Barber, Berg, Bernstein, Gates, Milhaud, Walton
3	Haieff, Robertson, Schonberg, Schuller, Webern

*Plus 114 one (or two) performances of works by 113 composers, a total of 164 performances.

XII. Joint Performances of Choral-Orchestral Masterworks with University of Utah Choruses and Utah Chorale

Composer	Work	Number of Performances
Beethoven	Ninth (Choral) Symphony	6
Robertson	Oratorio from the Book of Mormon	5
Verdi	Manzoni Requiem	5
Mahler	Symphony No. 2 (Resurrection)	5
Bach	St. Matthew Passion	3
Honneger	King David	3
Bach	B Minor Mass	2
Beethoven	Missa Solemnis	2
Berlioz	Requiem	2
Berlioz	L'Enfance du Christ	2
Bernstein	Chichester Psalms	2
Bloch	Sacred Service (Grammy nomination)	2
Brahms	German Requiem	2
Haydn	The Creation	2
Mahler	Eighth (Symphony of a Thousand)	2
Mendelssohn	Elijah	2
		47

The following were performed once:

Honneger	Joan of Arc at the Stake	
Handel	Israel in Egypt	
Handel	Judas Maccabaeus	
Debussy	Blessed Damozel	
Handel	Samson	
Honneger	Judith	
Milhaud	Pacem in Terris	
Vaughan Williams	Dona Nobis Pacem	
Bruckner	Te Deum	
Walton	Belshazzar's Feast	
Randall Thompson	Testament of Freedom	
Stravinsky	Symphony of Psalms (Grammy nomination)	
Vaughan Williams	A Sea Symphony	
Scarlatti	Mass of St. Cecilia	
Harris	Folk Song Symphony	15
Total: 62 performances of 29 works		62

Index

Abravanel, Carolyn Cheney Firmage, 197, 201
Abravanel, Friedel, 9, 25, 27
Abravanel, Lucy, 35, 36, 75–77, 94, 159, 193, 195–96, 204. *See also* Carasso, Lucy Menasse
Abravanel, Maurice: ancestry and birthplace, 3; in Australia, 15–19, 29; awards and honors, 67, 194, 196, 201–2; on Broadway, 23–29, 31, 34; committed to build symphony with Utahns, 36; construction of Salt Palace, 163–75; conversations on radio station KUER, 193; death of Lucy, 195; dedication to contemporary music, 63–67, 73; Distinguished Professor Award, 175, 194; divorce from Friedel, 27; eightieth birthday tribute, 190, 197; European tours, 103–111; final recording, 88; finished tenure in Tabernacle, 180–82; first conducting appearances, 8–11; first interest in Utah Symphony, 1, 33; Ford Foundation grant, 97–98, 101; formal resignation, 177; free school concerts, 123–26; friend of Milhauds, 86; in Greece, 103–07; home in Miraflores, 147–51; influence of Weill, 5–6, 8–11, 13, 21; international recognition, 79; joint performance of Mormon Tabernacle Choir and Utah Symphony, 126–27; conducting Mahler, 73–75, 79–90; Mahler Award, 79, 87; marriage to Carolyn Cheney Firmage, 197; marriage to Friedel Schacko, 9; marriage to Lucy Menasse Carasso, 35; at Metropolitan Opera, 19, 21–23, 29; move to Salt Lake City, 36; at Music Academy of the West, 94, 145–51; musical career, beginning of, 3–4; in New York City, 21–29, 31; in Paris, 11–13; in Germany, 5–11; pre-med student, 5; receives Gold Baton Award, 193; recordings, 82–88, Appendix 1; resignation, 175, 193; in South America, 111–113; surgery, 177; at Tanglewood, 194, 196; television interview 199–204; touring Western states, 117; University connection with Utah Symphony, 45–48, 51, 63, 67; unveiled orchestra in Tabernacle, 36; with Weill on Broadway, 23–24; wins support for orchestra, 56, 58; working with Bruno Walter, 11; at Zwickau, 9. *See also* de Abravanel entries.
Abravanel Hall, 145, 147, 175
Almond, Becky, 75, 77
Anderson, Maxwell: *Knickerbocker Holiday*, 23–24, 31
Angel Records, 88
Ansermet, Ernest, 3
Antoniou, Theodor, 65
Ashton, Raymond J., 72–73
Ashton, Wendell J., 91–98, 101, 111–113, 115–117, 124, 158, 164–66, 168–71, 174–75, 177–78, 185–87, 190

Bach, Johann Sebastian, 6, 18, 66, 69, 87; *B Minor Mass*, 48, 178; Brandenburg Concertos, 63; *St. Matthew Passion*, 48, 69, 125; Suite in D, 116
Bachauer, Gina, 93–94, 97, 101, 103, 105–7, 111–12, 115, 199–200
Balanchine, George, 12, 23, 29
Ballet West, 51, 170, 174, 200
Barber, Samuel: *Adagio for Strings*, 39, 63, 106, 116, 148

Bartók, Béla, 11, 31, 65; *Music for Strings, Percussion and Celeste*, 64; Second Piano Concerto, 73
Beethoven, Ludwig Van: *Eroica*, 30, 36; Fifth Symphony, 30; *Missa Solemnis*, 46–48, 60, 69, 125; Ninth (Choral) Symphony, 30, 45, 48, 126; Seventh Symphony, 60, 105, 116; Third Piano Concerto, 38
Bennett, Frances G., 58
Bennett, Wallace, 59, 103, 104
Berg, Alban, 65; *Wozzeck*, 64–65
Berlin, 5–6, 108–110
Berlioz, Louis Hector: *Childhood of Christ*, 48, 112; *Requiem*, 48; *Roman Carnival* Overture, 151; *Symphonie Fantastique*, 75
Bernstein, Leonard, 65–66, 82, 193, 204; *Candide* Overture, 106, 108; *Chichester Psalms*, 127; *Mass*, 153
Bicentennial Arts Center (Symphony Hall), 163–175
Bizet, Georges: *Pearl Fishers*, 16
Blegen, Judith, 180
Bloch, Ernest: *Sacred Service*, 48, 88; *Schelomo*, 56, 60
Borodin, Alexander: *Prince Igor*, 19
Bowen, Emma Lucy Gates, 56, 154
Brahms, Johannes: *Academic Festival Overture*, 48, 87; First Symphony, 112; Fourth Symphony, 106; *Haydn Variations*, 30, 87; Second Piano Concerto, 37–38; Second Symphony, 151; *Tragic* Overture, 87
Brecht, Bertolt, 10, 13
Brigham Young University (BYU), 43, 70, 115; A Cappella Choir, 48

Book design by Richard A. Firmage

Composition by Type Center

Printing by Publishers Press

Binding by Mountain States Bindery